**Elementary**

Student's Book

# New Headway
## English Course

Liz and John Soars

OXFORD
UNIVERSITY PRESS

# CONTENTS

| Unit | Grammar | Vocabulary |
|---|---|---|
| **1 Hello everybody!** p6 | **Verb** *to be*<br>    *am/is/are*<br>    *I'm from Germany.*<br>    *He's a doctor.* p6, p9<br>**Possessive adjectives**<br>    *my, your, his, her* p6, p7 | Countries<br>    *Mexico, Japan* p7, p8<br>Using a bilingual dictionary p10<br>Everyday objects<br>    *a key, a newspaper* p10<br>Plural nouns<br>    *bags, apples* p10 |
| **2 Meeting people** p12 | **Verb** *to be*<br>**Questions and negatives**<br>    *What's her first name?* p12<br>    *She isn't married.* p13<br>**Negatives and short answers**<br>    *No, she isn't.* p12<br>**Possessive** *'s*<br>    *Patrick's daughter* p14 | The family<br>    *mother, uncle* p14–15<br>Opposite adjectives<br>    *old – young* p16<br>Food and drink<br>    *hamburger and chips*<br>    *tea, coffee* p18 |
| **3 The world of work** p20 | **Present Simple** 1<br>    *he/she/it* p20<br>    *He works 16 hours a day.* p20<br>**Questions and negatives**<br>    *Does he speak French? No, he doesn't.* p22 | Verbs<br>    *help, make, serve* p24<br>Jobs<br>    *A pilot flies planes.* p26 |
| **4 Take it easy!** p28 | **Present Simple** 2<br>    *I/you/we/they*<br>    *I go to the gym.*<br>    *We don't go out on Friday evenings.*<br>    *Why do you like your job?* p29 | Verbs<br>    *relax, eat out, start* p29<br>Leisure activities<br>    *dancing, skiing* p34 |

**Stop and check 1    Teacher's Book    p138**

| Unit | Grammar | Vocabulary |
|---|---|---|
| **5 Where do you live?** p36 | *There is/are*<br>    *There's a book on the table.* p36<br>*How many … ?*<br>    *How many books are there?* p36<br>**Prepositions of place**<br>    *in front of the fire* p36<br>*some* **and** *any*<br>    *There are some cups.*<br>    *There aren't any plates.* p38<br>*this, that, these, those*<br>    *This is the kitchen.*<br>    *What's in these cupboards?* p38 | Rooms<br>    *living room, kitchen* p36<br>Household goods<br>    *armchair, lamp*<br>    *cupboard, washing machine* p36<br>What's in your bag?<br>    *letter, bus ticket, mobile phone* p39<br>Parts of a plane<br>    *cockpit, steps* p40<br>Places<br>    *cinema, pub* p43 |
| **6 Can you speak English?** p44 | *can/can't*<br>    *I can ski really well.*<br>    *She can't speak Japanese.* p44<br>*was/were*<br>    *Where were you last night?* p46<br>*could*<br>    *I could swim when I was five.* p46<br>*was born*<br>    *He was born in London.* p47 | Countries and languages<br>    *Italy, Italian* p44<br>Verbs<br>    *translate, check, laugh* p45<br>Words that sound the same<br>    *I, eye; no, know* p50 |
| **7 Then and now** p52 | **Past Simple** (1)<br>**Regular verbs**<br>    *She started work when she was eight.* p52<br>**Irregular verbs**<br>    *He left school in 1994.* p54<br>**Time expressions**<br>    *last night*<br>    *yesterday morning* p55 | Verbs<br>    *earn, marry, die* p53<br>Verbs<br>    *begin, leave, become* p54<br>Spelling and silent letters<br>    *bomb, listen* p58 |

| Skills work | Everyday English | Writing (in the Workbook) |
|---|---|---|
| **Reading and writing**<br>Introducing yourself p9<br>**Listening and speaking**<br>The alphabet song p10 | Hello and goodbye<br>*Telephone numbers* p11<br>*How are you?*<br>*See you this evening!* p11 | |
| **Reading and listening**<br>A letter from America p16 | In a café<br>*Prices* p18<br>*Can I have …?*<br>*How much is it?* p19 | |
| **Reading**<br>Seumas McSporran – the man with thirteen jobs p24<br>**Listening and speaking**<br>Seumas's day p25 | What time is it?<br>*It's quarter past five.*<br>*It's about six o'clock.* p27 | Personal pronouns and possessive adjectives<br>*I, me, my* WB p20<br>Rewriting a text WB p20 |
| **Speaking**<br>A questionnaire – how do you live? p30<br>**Reading and listening**<br>Three people talk about their favourite season p32<br>**Speaking**<br>What's your favourite season? p33<br>Leisure activities p34 | Social expressions<br>*I'm sorry.*<br>*Excuse me?*<br>*Pardon?* p35 | An informal letter<br>A letter to a penfriend WB p25 |
| **Speaking and listening**<br>What are the differences between the two pictures? p37<br>**Reading and speaking**<br>At home on a plane p40<br>**Listening and speaking**<br>Homes around the world p42 | Directions 1<br>*Is there a post office near here?*<br>*Yes, it's over there.* p43 | Linking words<br>*and, so, but, because* WB p31<br>Describing where you live WB p31 |
| **Speaking**<br>Questionnaire - what can you do? p45<br>**Reading and speaking**<br>Super Kids p48 | On the phone<br>Directory Enquiries p50<br>*Can I speak to Jo, please?*<br>*I'll just get her.* p51 | Formal letters 1<br>A letter of application for a job WB p36 |
| **Speaking**<br>What did you do at the end of the 20th century? p54<br>When did it happen? p55<br>**Reading and speaking**<br>Two famous firsts:<br>George Washington and Margaret Thatcher p56 | Special occasions<br>Thanksgiving<br>*Happy birthday!* p58 | Writing a paragraph describing a holiday WB p40 |

| Unit | Grammar | Vocabulary |
|---|---|---|
| **8 How long ago?** p60 | **Past Simple** (2) **Negatives and** *ago*    People didn't watch TV a hundred years ago. p61 **Time expressions**    in 1994, on Saturday, at seven o'clock p63 | Which word is different?    apple, chicken, banana p63 Phonetic symbols    /ˈresəpi/ p63 Relationships    fall in love, get engaged p64 |
| **Stop and check 2** | **Teacher's Book** p140 | |
| **9 Food you like!** p66 | **Count and uncount nouns**    apples, apple juice p66 ***Do you like … ?/Would you like … ?***    Do you like beer? Would you like some now? p67 ***a*** **and** *some*    a cake, some cake p68 ***much*** **and** *many*    There isn't much milk.    There aren't many eggs. p69 | Food and drink    yoghurt, chips    beer, apple juice p66    chopsticks p71 Shops and shopping    a book of stamps    some milk p69 |
| **10 Bigger and better!** p74 | **Comparatives and superlatives**    The country is cheaper than the city. p74    Claridge's is the most expensive hotel. p76 ***have got***    London's got a lot of parks.    I haven't got much money. p75 | City and country adjectives    dirty, noisy    exciting, safe p74 City and country nouns    wood, museum p80 |
| **11 Looking good!** p82 | **Present Continuous**    I'm wearing jeans.    Who is smiling? p82 ***Whose is it?***    Whose is the bike? p84 **Possessive pronouns**    mine, yours, hers p84 | Clothes    hat, coat, shirt p82 Describing people    fair hair, blue eyes p82 Words that rhyme    red, said; laugh, half p88 Phonetic symbols    vowels and diphthongs p88 Tongue twisters p88 |
| **12 Life's an adventure** p90 | ***going to***    I'm going to be a ballet dancer. p90 **Infinitive of purpose**    I'm going to Holland to see the tulips. p92 | Verbs    sneeze, jump, fall p92 The weather    sunny, cloudy    What's the weather like? p96 |
| **Stop and check 3** | **Teacher's Book** p142 | |
| **13 How terribly clever!** p98 | **Question forms**    Why … ? How many … ? How much … ?    Which … ? p98 **Adverbs and adjectives**    quick, quickly, good, well p100 | Describing feelings    bored, worried 101 |
| **14 Have you ever?** p106 | **Present Perfect** ***ever*** **and** *never*    Have you ever been to Paris?    I've never been to Australia. p106 ***yet*** **and** *just*    We haven't been there yet.    They've just had a boat ride. p109 **Present Perfect and Past Simple**    Maria's been to Berlin.    She went there two years ago. p107 | Past participles    cooked, eaten, made p107 At the airport    departure lounge    check in p113 |
| **Stop and check 4** | **Teacher's Book** p144 | |

**Tapescripts** p114          Grammar Reference p124          Word list p135

| Skills work | Everyday English | Writing (in the Workbook) |
|---|---|---|
| **Reading and listening**<br>Three inventors  p62<br>**Speaking**<br>Incredible information  p62<br>**Listening and speaking**<br>How did you two meet?  p64 | What's the date?<br>*the fourth of July*  p65 | Linking words<br>*because, when, until*  WB p47<br>Describing an old friend  WB p47 |
| **Listening and speaking**<br>My favourite food  p72<br>**Reading and speaking**<br>Food around the world<br>Meals in your country  p70 | Polite requests<br>*Could you pass the salt?*<br>*Could I have a glass of water?*<br>*Can you give me the recipe?*<br>*Can I see the menu?*  p73 | Formal letters 2<br>A letter to a hotel  WB p53 |
| **Speaking**<br>I've got more than you!  p76<br>**Reading and speaking**<br>Three musical cities –<br>New Orleans, Vienna, Liverpool<br>Talking about your town  p78 | Directions 2<br>*out of the garage*<br>*over the bridge*  p81 | Linking words<br>*which, where*  WB p58<br>Writing about your capital city  WB p58 |
| **Listening and speaking**<br>Who's at the party?  p84<br>A song – *What a wonderful world!*  p86 | In a clothes shop<br>*What colour are you looking for?*<br>*Can I try it on?*  p89 | Linking words<br>*although, but*  WB p64<br>Describing people<br>WB p64 |
| **Reading and speaking**<br>Dangerous sports<br>Interviews with people who do dangerous sports  p94 | Making suggestions<br>*What shall we do today?*<br>*Let's go to the beach!*  p97 | Writing a postcard  WB p70 |
| **Speaking and listening**<br>Noises in the night  p100<br>**Reading and listening**<br>A story in a story<br>The tale of horribly good Bertha  p104 | Catching a train<br>*A return ticket, please.*  p105 | Adverbs<br>*happy, happily*  WB p75<br>Writing a story<br>*Once upon a time*  WB p75 |
| **Speaking**<br>Things you have done  p106<br>**Reading and speaking**<br>How to live to be 100  p110<br>**Listening**<br>A song – *Leaving on a jet plane*  p112 | At the airport<br>*check in your luggage*<br>*go to gate 4*  p113 | A thank-you letter  WB p80 |

**Appendix 1 – irregular verbs  p142**     **Appendix 2 – verb patterns  p142**     **Phonetic symbols  p143**

# 1 Hello everybody!

*am/is/are* · *my/your/his/her* · Everyday objects · Numbers · Hello and goodbye

**STARTER**

1 Say your names.

*I'm Ali.*  *I'm Tomas.*

2 Stand up in alphabetical order and say your names.

*I'm Ali.*  *I'm Birgit.*  *I'm Tomas.*  *I'm Zak.*

## INTRODUCTIONS
*am/is/are, my/your*

1 **T 1.1** Read and listen.
A Hello. My name's Paula. What's your name?
B Rosa.
A Where are you from, Rosa?
B I'm from Chicago.

**T 1.1** Listen and repeat.

**GRAMMAR SPOT**

name's = name is
what's = what is
I'm = I am

6 Unit 1 · Hello everybody!

**2** Write the conversation.

A Hello. My <u>Name's</u> Richard. What's <u>your</u> name?
B Kurt.
A <u>Where</u> are you from, Kurt?
B <u>I'm</u> from Hamburg. Where <u>are</u> you from?
A <u>I'm from</u> London.

**T 1.2** Listen and check.

**3** Stand up! Talk to the students in the class.

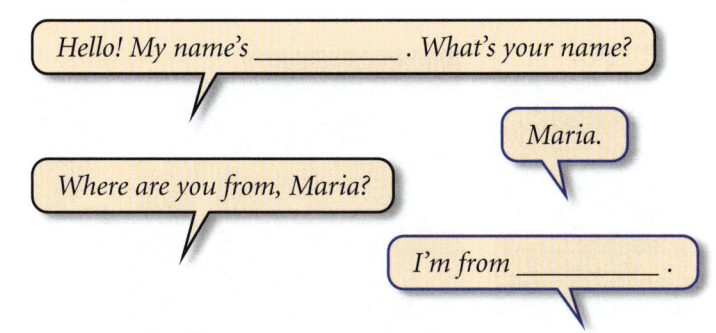

> Hello! My name's _____ . What's your name?

> Maria.

> Where are you from, Maria?

> I'm from _____ .

## Countries, *his/her*

**4** **T 1.3** Listen and repeat.

| | ●• | •● | ●•• |
|---|---|---|---|
| the USA | Egypt | Brazil | Mexico |
| Spain | Russia | Japan | Germany |
| France | England | | Italy |
| | | | Hungary |

**5** Read about the people.

¡Buenos días!

**This is Rafael.**
**He's from Mexico.**

Salem ala goum!

**This is Yasmina.**
**She's from Egypt.**

Hi!

**This is Max and Lisa.**
**They're from the USA.**

**GRAMMAR SPOT**

he's = he is
she's = she is
they're = they are

Unit 1 · Hello everybody! 7

**6** Where are the people from? Write the countries from exercise 4.

> Hello!

**This is Richard.**
He's from England.

> Konnichiwa!

**This is Tomoko.**
She's from Japan.

> Bom dia!

**This is Lena and Miguel.**
They're from Tomoko

> Buongiorno!

**This is Anna.**
She's from Italy

> Privyet!

**This is Irina.**
She's from Hungaries

> Sziasztok!

**This is László and Ilona.**
They're from Hungary

> ¡Buenos días!

**This is María.**
She's from Spain

> Guten Tag!

**This is Kurt.**
He's from Germany

> Bonjour!

**This is Pierre.**
He's from France

**7** Ask and answer questions about the people. Use *he/his* and *she/her*.

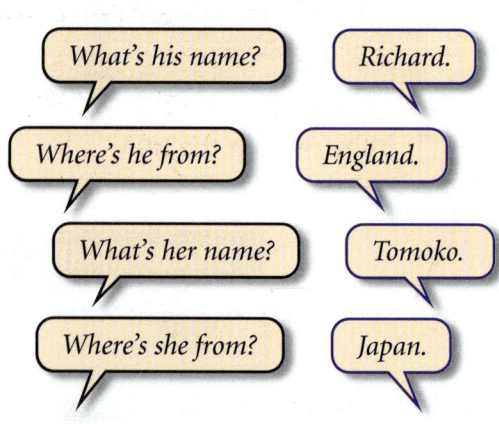

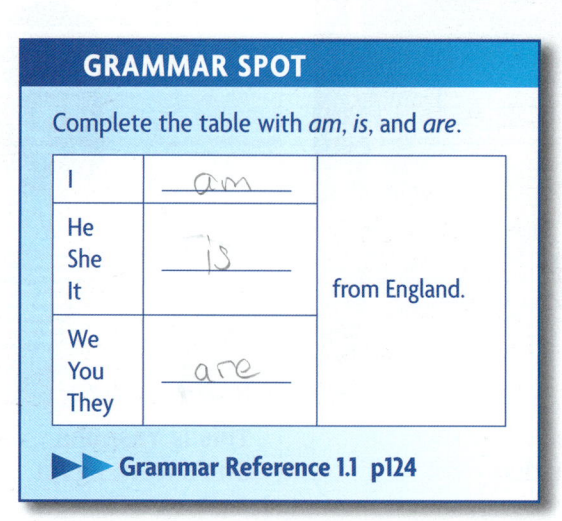

- What's his name? — Richard.
- Where's he from? — England.
- What's her name? — Tomoko.
- Where's she from? — Japan.

### GRAMMAR SPOT

Complete the table with *am*, *is*, and *are*.

| I | am | |
|---|---|---|
| He / She / It | is | from England. |
| We / You / They | are | |

▶▶ Grammar Reference 1.1 p124

8 Unit 1 · Hello everybody!

# PRACTICE

## Talking about you

**1** Ask and answer questions with a partner about the students in your class.

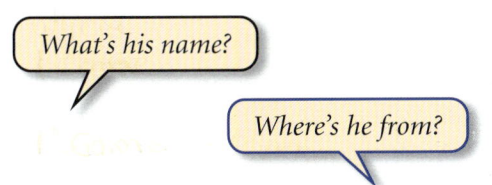

> *What's his name?*

> *Where's he from?*

**2** Introduce your partner to the class.

> *This is Kurt. He's from Hamburg in Germany.*

## Listening and pronunciation

**3** **T 1.4** Listen and tick (✓) the sentence you hear.
1. ☐ She's from Spain.
   ☑ He's from Spain.
2. ☐ What's her name?
   ☑ What's his name?
3. ☑ They're from Brazil.
   ☐ They're in Brazil.
4. ☑ Where's she from?
   ☐ Where's he from?
5. ☐ He's a teacher in Italy.
   ☑ His teacher in Italy.

## Check it

**4** Complete the sentences with *am*, *is*, *are*, *his*, *her*, or *your*.
1. My name _is_ Anna.
2. Where _are_ you from?
3. I _'m_ from Japan.
4. 'What's _your_ name?' 'My name's Tomoko.'
5. Max and Lisa _There_ from Chicago.
6. This _is_ my teacher. _her_ name's Richard.
7. Where _are_ he from?
8. This is my sister. _his_ name's Emma.

## Reading and writing

**5** **T 1.5** Listen and read about Rafael.

> My name's Rafael Ramos and I'm a doctor. I'm 30. I'm married and I have two children. I live in a house in Toluca in Mexico. I want to learn English for my job.

**6** Complete the text about Yasmina.

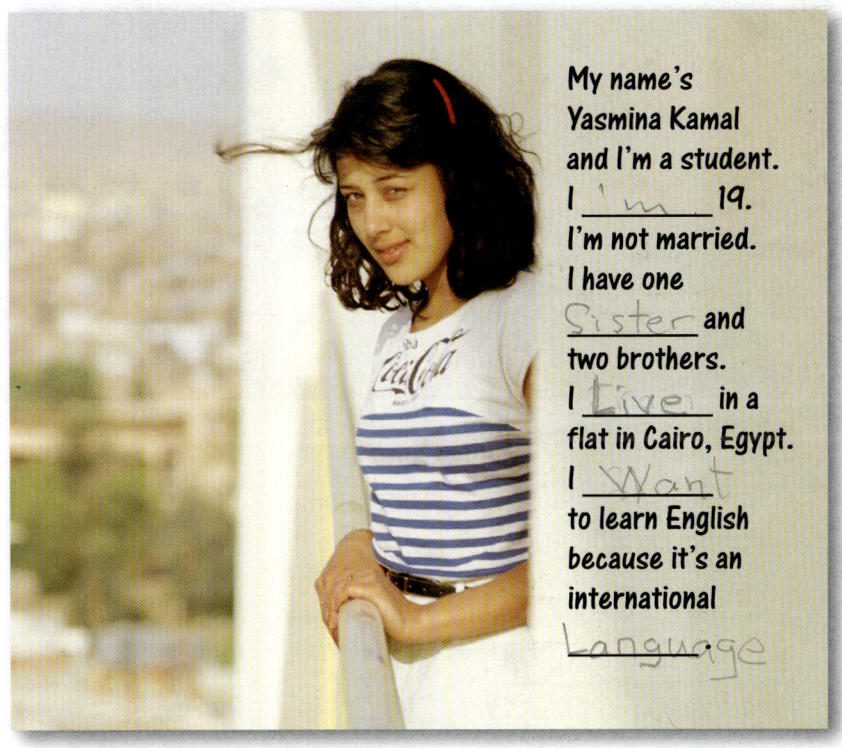

> My name's Yasmina Kamal and I'm a student. I _'m_ 19. I'm not married. I have one _sister_ and two brothers. I _live_ in a flat in Cairo, Egypt. I _want_ to learn English because it's an international _language_.

**T 1.6** Listen and check.

**7** Write about you. Then read it to the class.

Unit 1 · Hello everybody! 9

# VOCABULARY AND PRONUNCIATION
## Everyday objects

1 **T 1.7** Listen to the alphabet song. Say the alphabet as a class.

2 Look at this extract from an English/Spanish dictionary.

the word in English — **apple** /ˈæpl/ n. *manzana* — the part of speech (n. = noun)

the pronunciation — the word in Spanish

3 Match the words and pictures.

| • • | • • • | • • • • | • • • • |
|---|---|---|---|
| a stamp | a camera | a dictionary | a magazine |
| a bag | a ticket | a newspaper | |
| a key | a postcard | | |
| | a letter | | |
| | an apple | | |
| | an orange | | |

a  b  c  d  e  f  g  h  i  j  k  l

**T 1.8** Listen and repeat.

4 Ask and answer questions with a partner.

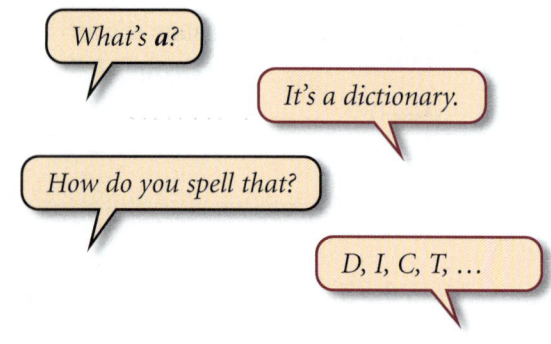

*What's **a**?*

*It's a dictionary.*

*How do you spell that?*

*D, I, C, T, ...*

5 Look at the words. What are *a, e, i, o,* and *u*? When is it *a*? When is it *an*?

*a* bag         *an* apple
*a* ticket      *an* orange
*a* letter      *an* English book

6 Look at the plural words.

two stamps    two apples    two dictionaries

Say the plurals of the other words in exercise 2.

▶▶ **Grammar Reference 1.4 and 1.5  p124**

10  Unit 1 • Hello everybody!

# EVERYDAY ENGLISH
## Hello and goodbye

1  Say the numbers 1–20 round the class.

2  **T 1.9**  Read and listen to the telephone numbers.

| | |
|---|---|
| 682 947 | six eight two    nine four seven |
| 8944 5033 | eight nine *double* four    five 'oh' *double* three |
| 020 7399 7050 | 'oh' two 'oh'    seven three *double* nine    seven 'oh' five 'oh' |

3  **T 1.10**  Listen and write the numbers you hear. Practise them.

4  Ask and answer the question with other students. Write a list.

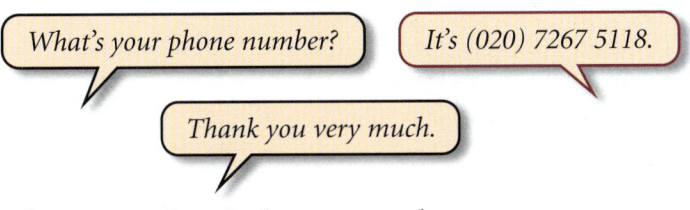

> *What's your phone number?*

> *It's (020) 7267 5118.*

> *Thank you very much.*

5  Write the conversations in the correct order.

1  I'm fine, thank you. And you?
   I'm OK, thanks.
   Hello, Mary. This is Edward. How are you?
   Hello, extension 3442.

   A _____
   B _____
   A _____
   B _____

2  Goodbye, Bianca. Have a nice day.
   Yes, at seven in the cinema.
   Thanks, Marcus. See you this evening!
   Goodbye, Marcus.

   A _____
   B _____
   A _____
   B _____

3  Not bad, thanks. And you?
   Very well. How are the children?
   Hi, Flora! It's me, Leo. How are you?
   They're fine.
   Hello, 270899.

   A _____
   B _____
   A _____
   B _____
   A _____

**T 1.11**  Listen and check.

6  Practise the conversations with other students. Practise again, using your names and numbers.

Unit 1 · Hello everybody!   11

# 2 Meeting people

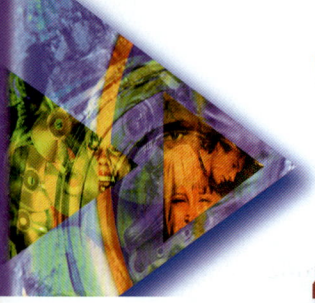

*am/is/are* – questions and negatives • Possessive *'s* • Family • Opposites • In a café

**STARTER**

1 Count from 1–20 round the class.
2 Count in 10s from 10–100 round the class.
   *ten, twenty, thirty . . . one hundred.*
3 How old are you? Ask and answer in groups.

## WHO IS SHE?
### Questions and negatives

1 Read Keesha Anderson's identity card.
2 Complete the questions.

   1 What's __her__ surname?    Anderson.
   2 _What's_ her first name?   Keesha.
   3 _Where_ she from?          London, England.
   4 _What's her_ job?          She's a journalist.
   5 What's _her add_?          42, Muswell Hill Road,
                                London N10 3JD.
   6 _What's her_ phone         020 8863 5741.
     number?
   7 How old _is she_?          Twenty-eight.
   8 Is she _isn't_?            No, she isn't.

   **T 2.1** Listen and check. Practise the questions and answers.

3 Keesha has a brother. Write questions about him. Ask your teacher and complete his card.

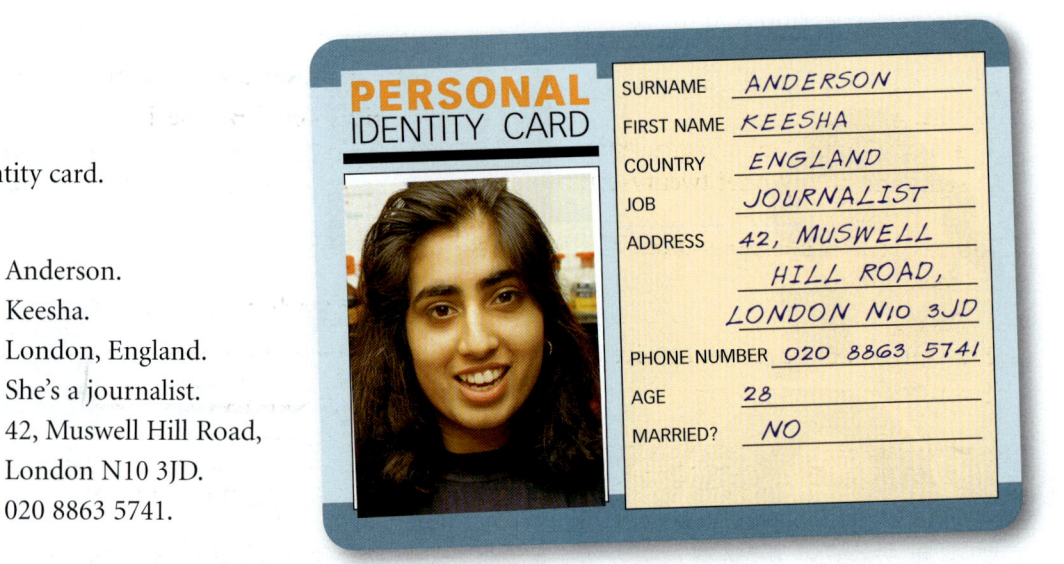

   *What's his surname?*

   *Anderson.*

   *What's his first name?*

**PERSONAL IDENTITY CARD**

SURNAME ANDERSON
FIRST NAME KEESHA
COUNTRY ENGLAND
JOB JOURNALIST
ADDRESS 42, MUSWELL
HILL ROAD,
LONDON N10 3JD
PHONE NUMBER 020 8863 5741
AGE 28
MARRIED? NO

**PERSONAL IDENTITY CARD**

SURNAME ANDERSON
FIRST NAME
COUNTRY
JOB
ADDRESS

PHONE NUMBER
AGE
MARRIED?

12  Unit 2 • Meeting people

## Negatives and short answers

**4** **T 2.2** Read and listen. Then listen and repeat.

*Is she American?*
*No, she isn't.*

*Is she French?*
*No, she isn't.*

*Is she English?*
*Yes, she is.*

Ask and answer *Yes/No* questions about Keesha.
1 a doctor? a teacher? a journalist?
2 eighteen? twenty-one? twenty-eight?

**5** Ask and answer questions about Keesha's brother.
1 Peter? Daniel? Rudi?
2 a journalist? a student? a policeman?
3 sixteen? thirty? twenty-one?

---

### GRAMMAR SPOT

1 Complete the answers to the *Yes/No* questions.
   Is Keesha English?
   Yes, she ____ .
   Is her surname Smith?
   No, it ____ .
   Are you a journalist?
   No, I'm ____ .

2 Look at the negatives.
   She **isn't** married.
   You **aren't** English.
   But: **I'm not** a teacher
   ✗ I ~~amn't~~ a teacher.

▶▶ Grammar Reference 2.1 p125

---

# PRACTICE

### Who is he?

**1** **Student A** Look at the identity card from your teacher.
   **Student B** Look at this identity card.

Ask and answer questions to complete the information.

**RBS INTERNATIONAL IDENTITY CARD**

SURNAME
FIRST NAME   PATRICK
COUNTRY
JOB          ACCOUNTANT
ADDRESS

PHONE NUMBER  1232 4837
AGE
MARRIED?     YES

**2** Ask and answer *Yes/No* questions about Patrick.
1 Smith? Jones? Binchey?
2 from Italy? from England? from Ireland?
3 a policeman? a teacher? an accountant?

### Talking about you

**3** Ask your teacher some questions.

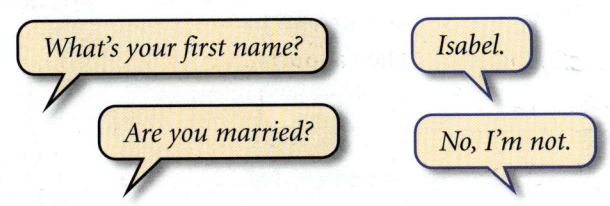

*What's your first name?*
*Isabel.*

*Are you married?*
*No, I'm not.*

**4** Look at the form from your teacher.

Stand up! Ask two students *Yes/No* questions to complete the form. Answer questions about you.

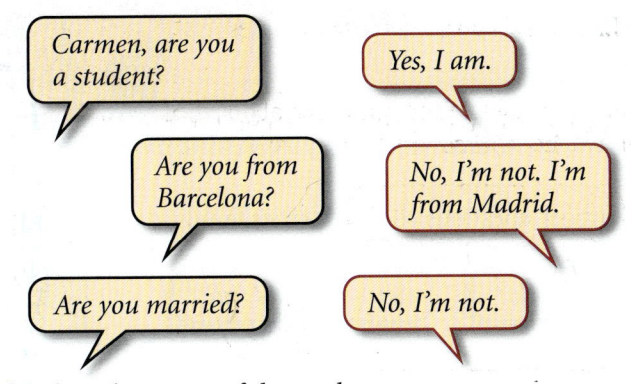

*Carmen, are you a student?*
*Yes, I am.*

*Are you from Barcelona?*
*No, I'm not. I'm from Madrid.*

*Are you married?*
*No, I'm not.*

Tell the class about one of the students.

*Her name's Anna-Maria. She's a student …*

Unit 2 • Meeting people   13

# PATRICK'S FAMILY
## Possessive 's

**1** Write these words in the correct place.

| brother | father | daughter | wife | aunt | grandmother |

| 👨 | boyfriend | husband | Father | son | brother | uncle | grandfather |
|---|---|---|---|---|---|---|---|
| 👩 | girlfriend | wife | mother | daughter | sister | aunt | grandmother |

**2** **T 2.3** Read about Patrick Binchey and listen. Write the names of the people in the correct place.

This is a photo of **Patrick**, his wife, and his children. His wife's name is Brenda. She's a teacher. His daughter's name is Lara. She's twenty-one and she's a nurse. His son's name is Benny. He's nineteen and he's a student. Lara's boyfriend is a nurse, too. His name is Mick.

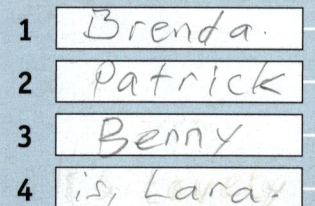

1 Brenda
2 Patrick
3 Benny
4 is Lara
5 is Mick

**3** Ask and answer questions about Patrick's family.

*Who's Brenda?*   *She's Patrick's wife.*

### GRAMMAR SPOT

1 Look at 's.
   She's a teacher:   She's = She is.
   His wife's name:   His wife's name = her name
                      's = possession.
2 Find other examples in the text of possessive 's and 's = is.

▶▶ Grammar Reference 2.2 p125

14 Unit 2 · Meeting people

# PRACTICE

## You and your family

1 Ask your teacher questions about the people in his/her family.

> What's your mother's name?

> What's your sister's name?

2 Write the names of people in your family. Ask and answer questions with a partner.

*Juan   Silvia   María   Fernando   Amelia*

Ask a partner questions about his/her family.

> Who's Juan?

> He's my brother.

> Who's Silvia?

> She's my aunt. She's my mother's sister.

3 Make true sentences with the verb *to be*.

1 I __'m not__ at home.
2 We __'s__ in class.
3 It __'s not a__ Monday today.
4 My teacher's name __he's__ John.
5 My mother and father __It's__ at work.
6 I __'m not__ married.
7 My grandmother __is__ seventy-five years old.
8 Marcus and Carlos __is a__ my brothers.
9 We __is__ in the coffee bar. We __'s is__ in the classroom.

## Check it

4 Tick (✓) the correct sentence.

1 ☒ I'm a doctor.
  ☒ I'm doctor.
2 ☐ I have twenty-nine years old.
  ☒ I am twenty-nine years old.
3 ☒ I no married.
  ☒ I'm not married.
4 ☐ My sister's name is Lara.
  ☒ My sisters name is Lara.
5 ☐ She married.
  ☒ She's married.
6 ☐ I'm an uncle.
  ☒ I'm a uncle.
7 ☒ I have two brother.
  ☐ I have two brothers.
8 ☐ Peter's the son of my sister.
  ☒ Peter's my sister's son.

Unit 2 • Meeting people   15

## VOCABULARY
### Opposites

**1** Match the adjectives with their opposites.

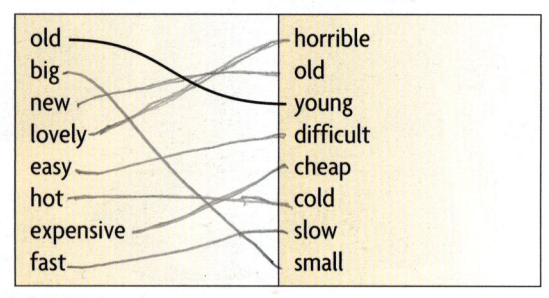

| | |
|---|---|
| old | horrible |
| big | old |
| new | young |
| lovely | difficult |
| easy | cheap |
| hot | cold |
| expensive | slow |
| fast | small |

**2** Write about the pictures, using the adjectives.

1  He's old.   She's young.

2  It's easy ~ e-zi   It's difficult de-fi-cult

3  It's new  rabbit/Bunny   It's old  turtle

4  It's fast   It's slow

5  It's lovely   It's horrible

6  They're hot   They're cold

7  They're cheap gip   They're expensive

8  It's small   It's big

**T 2.4** Listen and check. Practise saying the sentences.

## READING AND LISTENING
### A letter from America

**1** **T 2.5** Dorita is an English student at a school in Queens, New York City. Read and listen to her letter to Miguel, her brother in Argentina.

**2** Match each photograph with part of the letter.

**3** Correct the false (✗) sentences.
1. Dorita is from Argentina. ✓
2. She's in Miami. ✗ No, she isn't. She's in New York.
3. Dorita's happy in New York.
4. She's on holiday.
5. It's a very big class.
6. The students in her class are all from South America.
7. Annie and Marnie are both students.
8. The subway is easy to use.

**4** Write the questions about Dorita's letter.
1. Where's Dorita from?
   Argentina.
2. They're all from ?
   Japan, Brazil, Switzerland, Poland, and Italy.
3. What she's Name ?
   Isabel.
4. She's Live Dorita ?
   They are sisters. They live with Dorita.
5. How old annie and Marnie ?
   Annie's twenty and Marnie's eighteen.
6. Isn't New York very big ?
   Yes, it is.

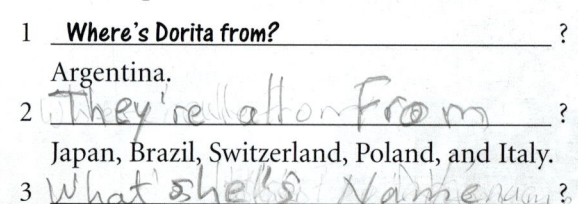

**5** **T 2.6** Listen to three conversations. Where is Dorita? Who is she with?

### Writing

**6** Write a letter about *your* class.

16  Unit 2 • Meeting people

41 46th Street
Sunnyside, New York 11104
February 12

Dear Miguel,

How are you? I'm fine. Here's a letter in English. It's good practice for you and me!

I have classes in English at La Guardia Community College. I'm in a class with eight students. They're all from different countries: Japan, Brazil, Switzerland, Poland, and Italy. Our teacher's name is Isabel. She's very nice and a very good teacher.

I live in an apartment with two American girls, Annie and Marnie Kass. They are sisters. Annie's twenty years old and a dancer. Marnie's eighteen and a student. They're very friendly, but it isn't easy to understand them. They speak very fast!

New York is very big, very exciting but very expensive! The subway isn't difficult to use and it's cheap. It's very cold now but Central Park is lovely in the snow. I'm very happy here.

Write to me soon.
Love,
Dorita

Unit 2 · Meeting people

# EVERYDAY ENGLISH
## In a café

**1**  1  **T 2.7**  Read and listen to the prices.

| | | |
|---|---|---|
| £1.00  one pound | 50p  fifty p /piː/ | £10.75  ten pounds seventy-five |
| £5.00  five pounds | £7.50  seven pounds fifty | |

2  **T 2.8**  Write the prices you hear. Practise saying them.

**2**  Read the menu. Match the food and pictures.

## Baker Street Snack Bar

### Menu

| | |
|---|---|
| Hamburger & chips | £3.50 |
| Chicken & chips | £3.90 |
| Tuna & egg salad | £4.25 |
| Pizza | £3.75 |
| Ice-cream | £1.50 |
| Chocolate cake | £1.75 |
| Coffee | £1.00 |
| Tea | 60p |
| Orange juice | 90p |
| Mineral water | 70p |

18  Unit 2 · Meeting people

**3** **T 2.9** Listen and repeat. Then ask and answer questions with a partner.

*How much is a hamburger and chips?*  *Three pounds fifty.*

*How much is a hamburger and chips and an orange juice?*  *Four pounds forty.*

**4** **T 2.10** Listen and complete the conversations.

**A** Good morning.
**B** Good _morning_. Can I have _an_ , please?
**A** Here you are. Anything else?
**B** No, thanks.
**A** _19_ p, please.
**B** Thanks.
**A** Thank you.

**A** Hi. Can I help?
**B** Yes. Can I have a _egg_ salad, please?
**A** Anything to drink?
**B** Yeah. A _water_, please.
**A** OK. Here you are.
**B** _How much_ is that?
**A** _4_ pounds _95_, please.
**B** Thanks.

**5** Practise the conversations with your partner. Make more conversations.

Unit 2 · Meeting people 19

# 3 The world of work

Present Simple 1 – *he/she/it* • Questions and negatives • Jobs • What time is it?

**STARTER**   What are the jobs of the people in your family? Tell the class.

*My father is a doctor.*   *My mother is a …*   *My brother …*

## THREE JOBS
**Present Simple** *he/she/it*

1  **T 3.1**  Listen and read about Ali and Bob.

**Ali** is a scientist. She comes from Cambridge in England but now she lives in Switzerland. She works three days a week at the Institute of Molecular Biology in Geneva. She speaks three languages: English, French, and German. She's married and has a daughter. She likes skiing in winter and going for walks in summer.

**Alison Hauser**

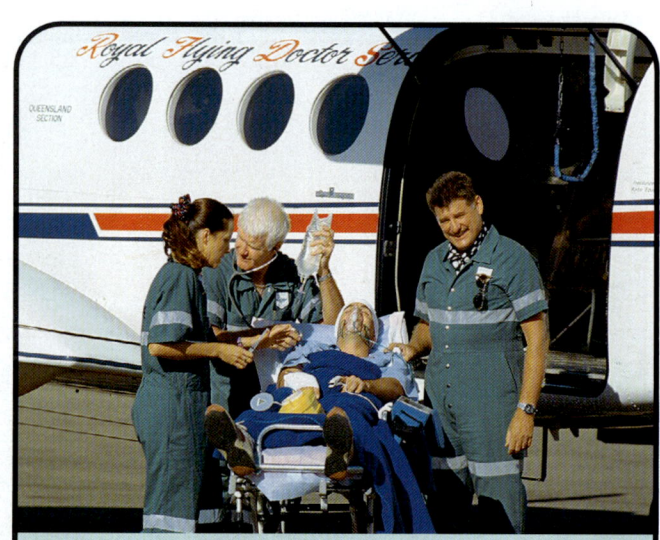

**Bob** is a doctor. He's English but now he lives in Australia in the small town of Alice Springs. He isn't an ordinary doctor, he's a *flying* doctor. Every day, from 8 a.m. to 10 a.m. he speaks to people on his radio, then he flies to help them. He works 16 hours a day non-stop but he loves his job. He isn't married. He has no free time.

**Bob Nelson**

### GRAMMAR SPOT

1  Underline all the verbs in the texts.   *is*   *comes*
2  What is the last letter of these verbs?
3  Practise saying the verbs. Read the texts aloud.

**2** Complete the sentences about Ali and Bob.

1 She's a scientist. He 's a doctor.
2 Alison comes from England. Bob comes from England, too.
3 She lives in a big city, but he lives in a small town.
4 She works three days a week. He works 16 hours a day non stop.
5 He speaks to sick people on his radio. She speaks three languages.
6 She loves her job and he loves his job, too.
7 She has a daughter. He isn't married.
8 She likes skiing and going for walks in her free time. He never has free time.

**T 3.2** Listen and check.

# PRACTICE

## Talking about people

**1** Read the information about Philippe.

**Philippe Ballon**

| | |
|---|---|
| Job | a barman |
| Country | France |
| Town | Paris |
| Place of work | in the centre of Paris |
| Languages | French, a little English |
| Married? | no |
| Family | a dog (!) |
| Free time | walking his dog, playing football |

**2** Talk about Phillippe.

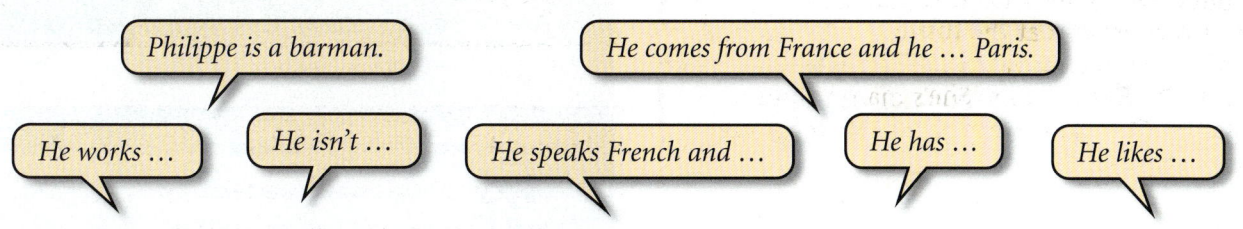

*Philippe is a barman.*

*He comes from France and he ... Paris.*

*He works ...*

*He isn't ...*

*He speaks French and ...*

*He has ...*

*He likes ...*

**3** Write about a friend or a relative. Talk to a partner about him/her.
**My friend Anna is a student. She lives in ...**

Unit 3 • The world of work 21

## WHAT DOES SHE DO?
### Questions and negatives

1 **T 3.3** Read and listen. Complete the answers. Practise the questions and answers.

Where does Alison come from?   Cambridge, _in_ England.
What does she do?   She's _a_ scientist.
Does she speak French?   _Yes_, she does.
Does she speak Spanish?   _not_, she doesn't.

> **GRAMMAR SPOT**
>
> 1 What does she/he do? = What's her/his job?
> 2 Complete these sentences with the correct form of *come*.
>    **Positive**
>    She _come_ from England.
>    **Negative**
>    She _don't_ from America.
>    **Question**
>    Where _doesnt_ she _are_ from?
> 3 Notice the pronunciation of *does* and *doesn't*.
>    /dəz/       /dʌz/       /'dʌznt/
>    **Does** he speak French? Yes he **does**./No, he **doesn't**.
>
> ▶▶ Grammar Reference 3.1 p.126

2 Complete the questions and answers.
  1 Where _does_ Bob _come_ from?
    England.
  2 What _does_ he _do_?
    He's a doctor.
  3 _Does_ he fly to help people?
    Yes, he _does_.
  4 _Does_ he _speak_ French and German?
    No, he _doesn't_.

  **T 3.4** Listen and check.

3 Write similar questions about Philippe the barman. Ask and answer with a partner.

> *Where does Philippe come from?*
>
> *Paris.*

## PRACTICE
### Asking about people

1 Read the information about Keiko or Mark.

| Keiko Wilson | |
|---|---|
| Job | an interpreter |
| Country | Japan |
| Town | New York |
| Place of work | at the United Nations |
| Languages | Japanese, English, and French |
| Family | married to an American, two sons |
| Free time | skiing |

2 Talk to a partner.

> *Keiko's an interpreter. She comes from Japan. She lives …*

Unit 3 · The world of work

**3** Write questions about Keiko or Mark.
- Where/come from?
  **Where does Keiko come from?**
- Where/live?
- What/do?
- Where/work?
- Does he/she speak French/Spanish . . . ?
- What . . . in his/her free time?
- . . . listen to music?
- How many children . . . ?
- . . . a dog?

**4** Don't look at the information. Ask and answer questions with your partner.

**5** Now ask your partner the same questions about a friend or relative.

## Listening and pronunciation

**6** **T 3.5** Listen to the sentences about Philippe, Keiko, and Mark. Correct the wrong sentences.

*Philippe comes from Paris.*

*Yes, that's right.*

*Philippe lives in London.*

*No, he doesn't. He lives in Paris.*

**7** **T 3.6** Tick (✓) the sentence you hear.
1. ☐ He likes his job.
   ☐ She likes her job.
2. ☐ She loves walking.
   ☐ She loves working.
3. ☐ He's married.
   ☐ He isn't married.
4. ☐ Does she have three children?
   ☐ Does he have three children?
5. ☐ What does he do?
   ☐ Where does he go?

## Check it

**8** Tick (✓) the correct sentence.
1. ☐ She comes from Japan.
   ☐ She come from Japan.
2. ☐ What he do in his free time?
   ☐ What does he do in his free time?
3. ☐ Where lives she?
   ☐ Where does she live?
4. ☐ He isn't married.
   ☐ He doesn't married.
5. ☐ Does she has two sons?
   ☐ Does she have two sons?
6. ☐ He doesn't play football.
   ☐ He no plays football.
7. ☐ She doesn't love Peter.
   ☐ She doesn't loves Peter.
8. ☐ What's he's address?
   ☐ What's his address?

### Mark König

| | |
|---|---|
| Job | a journalist for the BBC |
| Country | England |
| Town | Moscow |
| Place of work | in an office |
| Languages | English, Russian, and German |
| Family | married, three daughters |
| Free time | listening to music |

Unit 3 · The world of work

## READING AND LISTENING
Seumas McSporran – the man with thirteen jobs!

1 **Seumas McSporran** /ˈʃeɪməs məkˈspɒrən/ comes from Scotland. Look at the photographs of some of the things he does every day.

# The man with thirteen jobs

2 Match a sentence with a photograph.
1 He **helps** in the shop.
2 He **makes** breakfast for the hotel guests.
3 He **serves** petrol.
4 He **delivers** the beer to the pub.
5 He **collects** the post from the boat.
6 He **drives** the children to school.
7 He **delivers** the letters.
8 He **has** a glass of wine.
9 He **works** as an undertaker.

24 Unit 3 · The world of work

**Seumas McSporran** is a very busy man. He is 60 years old and he has thirteen jobs. He is a postman, a policeman, a fireman, a taxi driver, a school-bus driver, a boatman, an ambulance man, an accountant, a petrol attendant, a barman, and an undertaker. Also, he and his wife, Margaret, have a shop and a small hotel.

Seumas lives and works on the island of Gigha in the west of Scotland. Only 120 people live on Gigha but in summer 150 tourists come by boat every day.

Every weekday Seumas gets up at 6.00 and makes breakfast for the hotel guests. At 8.00 he drives the island's children to school. At 9.00 he collects the post from the boat and delivers it to all the houses on the island. He also delivers the beer to the island's only pub. Then he helps Margaret in the shop.

He says: 'Margaret likes being busy, too. We never have holidays and we don't like watching television. In the evenings Margaret makes supper and I do the accounts. At 10.00 we have a glass of wine and then we go to bed. Perhaps our life isn't very exciting, but we like it.'

10.00 p.m.

**3** Read about Seumas. Answer the questions.
1 Where does Seumas live?
2 How old is he?
3 How many jobs does he have?
4 What's his wife's name?
5 What does she do?
6 How many people live on Gigha?
7 How many tourists visit Gigha in summer?
8 What does Seumas do in the morning?
9 What do he and Margaret do in the evening?

**4** Look at the photos. Ask and answer questions with a partner about times in Seumas's day.

*What does he do at 6 o'clock?*

*He gets up and makes breakfast.*

**5** **T 3.7** Listen to four conversations from Seumas's day. After each one answer these questions.
1 Is it morning, afternoon, or evening?
2 Who are the people? Where are they?
3 What is Seumas's job?

**6** Complete the conversations.
1 A  Good _____ . Can I _____ two ice-creams, please?
   B  Chocolate or vanilla?
   A  One chocolate, one vanilla please.
   B  That's _____ . Anything _____ ?
   A  No, thank you.

2 A  Only _____ letters for you this _____ , Mrs Craig.
   B  Thank you very much, Mr McSporran. And _____ 's Mrs McSporran this _____ ?
   A  Oh, she's very well, thank you. She's _____ in the shop.

3 A  A glass of _____ before bed, my dear?
   B  Oh, yes please.
   A  _____ you are.
   B  Thank you, my dear. I'm very _____ this _____ .

4 A  Hello, Mr McSporran!
   B  Good _____ , boys and girls. Hurry up, we're late.
   A  Can I sit here, Mr McSporran?
   C  No, no, I _____ to sit there.
   B  Be quiet _____ of you, and SIT DOWN!

Practise the conversations with your partner.

# VOCABULARY AND PRONUNCIATION
## Jobs

1 Use your dictionary and match a picture with a job in column **A**.

| A | B |
|---|---|
| a  A pilot | designs buildings. |
| b  An interpreter | delivers letters. |
| c  A nurse | looks after people in hospital. |
| d  A barman | looks after money. |
| e  An accountant | writes for a newspaper. |
| f  A journalist | translates things. |
| g  A postman | sells things. |
| h  An architect | flies planes. |
| i  A shopkeeper | serves drinks. |

2 Match a job in **A** with a line in **B**.

3 Look at the phonetic spelling of some of the words. Practise saying them.

1 /nɜːs/   2 /ˈpəʊsmən/   3 /əˈkaʊntənt/   4 /ˈʃɒpkiːpə/   5 /ˈɑːkɪtekt/   6 /ˈbɑːmən/

4 Memorize the jobs. Close your books. Ask and answer questions with a partner.

*What does a pilot do?*   *He/She flies planes.*

Unit 3 · The world of work

# EVERYDAY ENGLISH
## What time is it?

**1** Look at the clocks. Write the times. Practise saying them.

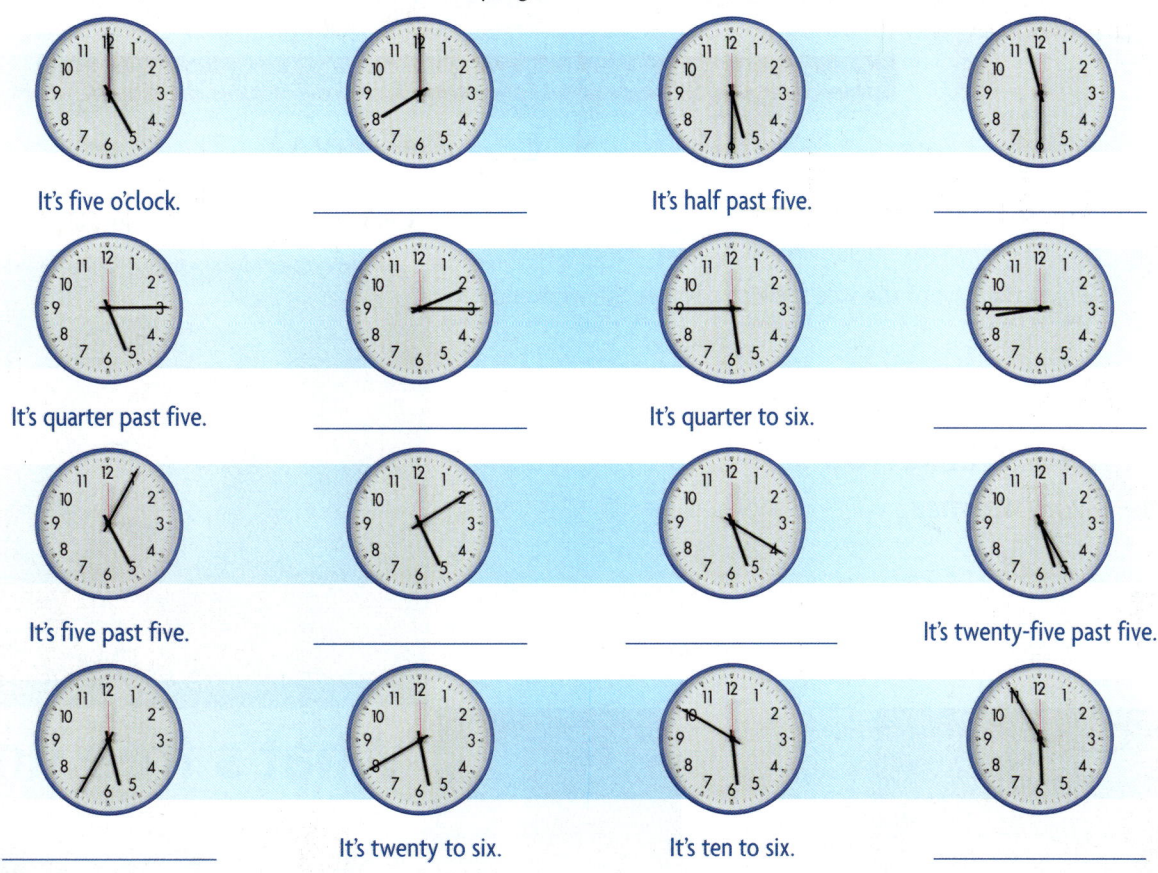

It's five o'clock.  _____  It's half past five.  _____

It's quarter past five.  _____  It's quarter to six.  _____

It's five past five.  _____  _____  It's twenty-five past five.

_____  It's twenty to six.  It's ten to six.  _____

**T 3.8** Listen and check.

**2** Look at the times.

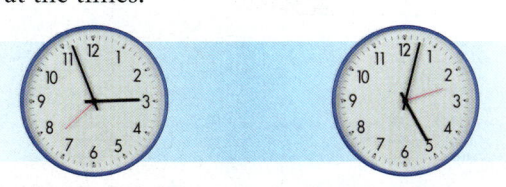

It's about three o'clock.   It's about five o'clock.

What time is it now? What time does the lesson end?

**3** **T 3.9** Listen and practise the conversations.

**Conversation 1**

*Excuse me. Can you tell me the time, please?*

*Yes, of course. It's (about) six o'clock.*

*Thanks.*

**Conversation 2**

*Excuse me. Can you tell me the time, please?*

*I'm sorry, I don't know. I don't have a watch.*

*Never mind.*

With a partner, draw clocks on a piece of paper. Make more conversations.

# 4 Take it easy!

**Present Simple 2 – I/you/we/they • Leisure activities • Social expressions**

**STARTER**

1 What year is it? What month is it? What day is it today?
2 Say the days of the week. Which days are the weekend?

## WEEKDAYS AND WEEKENDS
### Present Simple I/you/we/they

1 Read about Bobbi Brown's weekends. Complete the text with the verbs.

| gets up   lives   is   loves   works   doesn't work   interviews   starts |

'What's free time?'
says Bobbi Brown.

### Bobbi's weekends

Bobbi Brown _lives_ in New Jersey. She _is_ thirty-four and _works_ for SKY TV in New York City. But she _doesn't_ work on weekdays, she only works at weekends. She _____ famous people for an early morning news programme called *The World This Weekend*. On Saturdays and Sundays she _gets up_ at 3.00 in the morning because she _starts_ work at 6.30! She _loves_ her job because it is exciting.

28  Unit 4 • Take it easy!

**2** **T 4.1** Now read and listen to what Bobbi says about her weekdays.

> "My weekends are fast and exciting. My weekdays are fast and domestic! I _have_ two sons, Dylan, 7, and Dakota, 5. Every morning I _get up_ one hour before them, at 6.00, and I _go_ to the gym. I _come_ home and I _make_ breakfast, then I _like_ them to school. On Mondays I always _go_. I _shop_ all the food for the week. I often _cook_ dinner in the evenings, but not every day because I don't _like_ cooking. Fortunately, my husband, Don, _loves_ cooking. On Tuesdays and Thursdays I _visit_ my father. He _____ on the next block. Every afternoon I _pick up_ the kids from school. In the evenings Don and I usually _relax_ but sometimes we _visit_ friends. We never _go out_ on Friday evenings because I _start_ work so early on Saturdays."

**3** Complete the text with the correct form of the verbs in the box. Look up new words in your dictionary.

| love | relax | have | like | go | live | start | come |
| visit x2 | go shopping | pick up | go out | get up | take |
| buy | make | cook |

**T 4.1** Listen again and check. Read the text aloud.

## Questions and negatives

**4** **T 4.2** Read and listen. Complete Bobbi's answers. Practise the questions and answers.

Where do you work?                    _is_ New York.
Do you like your work?                Yes, I _____.
Do you relax at weekends?             No, I _____.
Why don't you relax at weekends?      _____ I work.

**5** Work in pairs. One of you is Bobbi Brown. Ask and answer questions about your life.
- Where . . . you live/work?
- Are . . . married?
- Do . . . have children?
- What time . . . get up/Saturday morning/Monday morning?
- Why . . . get up at . . . ? Because I . . .
- . . . like your work?
- Why . . . like it? Because it . . .
- . . . like cooking?
- . . . your husband like cooking?
- Who . . . you visit on Tuesdays and Thursdays?
- Where . . . your father live?
- . . . go out on Friday evenings? Why not?
- . . . have a busy life?

### GRAMMAR SPOT

1 Complete the table for the Present Simple.

|  | Positive | Negative |
| --- | --- | --- |
| I | work | don't work |
| You | work | don't work |
| He/She | works | doesn't work |
| It | works | doesn't work |
| We | work | don't work |
| They | work | don't work |

2 Complete the questions and answers.
Where _don't_ you work?
Where _don't_ she work?
_____ you work in New York? Yes, I _____.
_____ he work in New York? No, he _____.

3 Find the words in the text:
*always  usually  often  sometimes  never*

▶▶ Grammar Reference 4.1 and 4.2 p127

# PRACTICE

## Talking about you

1  Make the questions. Then match the questions and answers.

| Questions | | Answers | |
|---|---|---|---|
| 1 What time | do you like your job? | a | My mother and sisters. |
| 2 Where | do you travel to school? | b | To Spain or Portugal. |
| 3 What | do you go on holiday? | c | After dinner. |
| 4 When | do you go to bed? | d | At 11 o'clock. |
| 5 Who | you go out on Friday evenings? | e | I always relax. |
| 6 Why | do you live with? | f | Because it's interesting. |
| 7 How | do you do on Sundays? | g | By bus. |
| 8 Do | do you do your homework? | h | Yes, I do sometimes. |

**T 4.3** Listen and check.

2  Ask and answer the questions with a partner. Give true answers.

3  Tell the class about you and your partner.

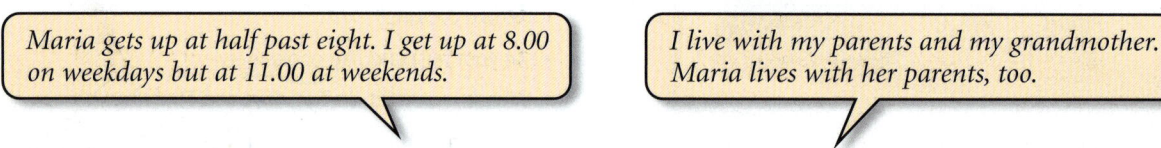

> *Maria gets up at half past eight. I get up at 8.00 on weekdays but at 11.00 at weekends.*

> *I live with my parents and my grandmother. Maria lives with her parents, too.*

## Listening and pronunciation

4  **T 4.4** Tick (✓) the sentence you hear.

1. ☐ What does he do on Sundays?
   ☐ What does she do on Sundays?
2. ☐ Do you stay home on Tuesday evenings?
   ☐ Do you stay home on Thursday evenings?
3. ☐ He lives here.
   ☐ He leaves here.
4. ☐ Where do you go on Saturday evenings?
   ☐ What do you do on Saturday evenings?
5. ☐ I read a lot.
   ☐ I eat a lot.
6. ☐ Why do you like your job?
   ☐ Why don't you like your job?

## A questionnaire

5  Read the questionnaire on p31. Answer the questions about you. Put ✓ or ✗ in column 1.

6  Ask your teacher the questions, then ask two students. Complete columns 2, 3, and 4.

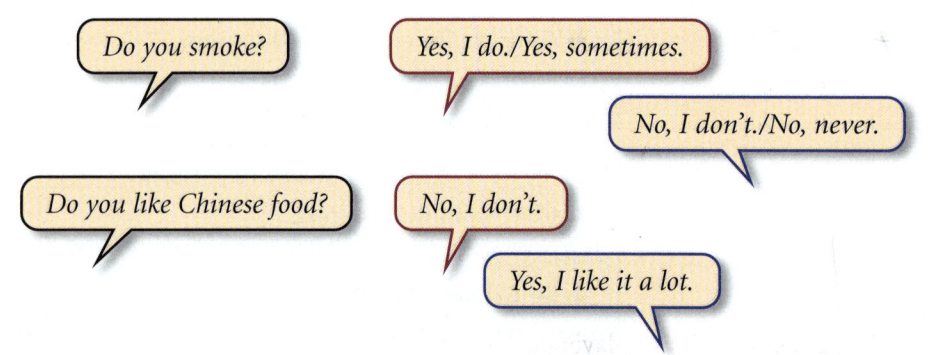

> *Do you smoke?*

> *Yes, I do./Yes, sometimes.*

> *No, I don't./No, never.*

> *Do you like Chinese food?*

> *No, I don't.*

> *Yes, I like it a lot.*

7  Use the information in the questionnaire. Write about you and your teacher.
**I don't get up early on weekdays, but my teacher does. We don't play tennis ...**

# A Questionnaire

## HOW DO YOU LIVE?

**Do you ...?**

|  | Me | T | S1 | S2 |
|---|---|---|---|---|
| get up early on weekdays |  |  |  |  |
| play tennis |  |  |  |  |
| smoke |  |  |  |  |
| drink wine |  |  |  |  |
| like Chinese food |  |  |  |  |
| watch TV a lot |  |  |  |  |
| have a big breakfast |  |  |  |  |
| have a computer |  |  |  |  |

### Positives and negatives

**8** Make the sentences opposite.

1 She's French.  **She isn't French.**
2 I don't like cooking.  **I like cooking.**
3 She doesn't speak Spanish.
4 They want to learn English.
5 We're tired and want to go to bed.
6 Roberto likes watching football on TV, but he doesn't like playing it.
7 I work at home because I have a computer.
8 Amelia isn't happy because she doesn't have a new car.
9 I smoke, I drink, and I don't go to bed early.
10 He doesn't smoke, he doesn't drink, and he goes to bed early.

Unit 4 · Take it easy!  31

## READING AND LISTENING
### My favourite season

**1**  1  What season is it now? What are the seasons?
   2  What month is it now? Say the months of the year.
   3  When are the different seasons in your country?

**2**  Look at the photographs. Which season is it? What colours do you see?

**3**  **T 4.5**  Read and listen to three people from different countries.

### AL WHEELER
### from Canada

We have long, cold winters and short, hot summers. We have a holiday home near a lake, so in summer I go sailing a lot and I play baseball, but in winter I often play ice hockey and go ice-skating. My favourite season is autumn, or fall, as we say in North America. I love the colours of the trees – red, gold, orange, yellow, and brown.

### MANUELA DA SILVA
### from Portugal

People think it's always warm and sunny in Portugal, but January and February are often cold, wet, and grey. I don't like winter. I usually meet friends in restaurants and bars and we chat. Sometimes we go to a Brazilian bar. I love Brazilian music. But then suddenly it's summer and at weekends we drive to the beach, sunbathe, and go swimming. I love summer.

32   Unit 4 · Take it easy!

**TOSHI SUZUKI from Japan**

*I work for Pentax cameras, in the export department. I don't have a lot of free time, but I have one special hobby – taking photographs, of course! I like taking photographs of flowers, especially in spring. Sometimes, after work, I relax in a bar near my office with friends. My friend, Shigeru, likes singing pop songs in the bar. This has a special name, 'karaoke'. I don't sing – I'm too shy!*

**4** Answer the questions.
1 Do they all play sports?
2 What do Al and Manuela do in winter?
3 Do Manuela and Toshi like going to bars?
4 Where is Al's holiday home?
5 When does Toshi like taking photographs of flowers?
6 What do Manuela and her friends do in summer?
7 Do you know all their jobs?
8 Why does Al like autumn?
9 Why doesn't Toshi sing in the bar?
10 Which colours are in the texts?

**5** There are six mistakes about Al, Manuela, and Toshi. Correct them.

| **Al** comes from Canada. In winter he plays ice hockey and goes skiing. He has a holiday home near the sea. | **Manuela** comes from Brazil. She likes sunbathing and sailing in summer. | **Toshi** comes from Japan. He has a lot of free time. He likes taking photographs and singing pop songs in bars. |
|---|---|---|

**6** **T 4.6** Listen to the conversations. Is it Al, Manuela, or Toshi? Where are they? How do you know? Discuss with a partner.

### What do you think?

- What is *your* favourite season? Why?
- What do you do in the different seasons?

Unit 4 • Take it easy! 33

## VOCABULARY AND SPEAKING
**Leisure activities**

1 Match the words and pictures. Tick (✓) the things that *you* like doing.

- ☐ playing football
- ☐ dancing
- ☐ skiing
- ☐ watching TV
- ☐ going to the gym
- ☐ taking photographs
- ☐ cooking
- ☐ playing computer games
- ☐ sailing
- ☐ listening to music
- ☐ swimming
- ☐ reading
- ☐ eating in restaurants
- ☐ going to the cinema
- ☐ jogging
- ☐ sunbathing

2 Discuss in groups what you think your teacher likes doing. Choose *five* activities.

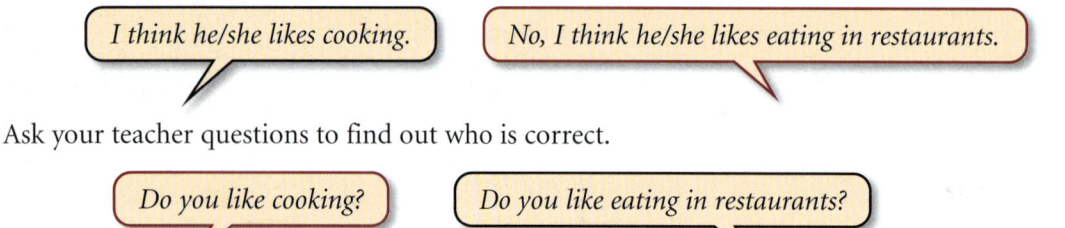

*I think he/she likes cooking.*

*No, I think he/she likes eating in restaurants.*

Ask your teacher questions to find out who is correct.

*Do you like cooking?*

*Do you like eating in restaurants?*

3 Tell the other students what you *like* doing and what you *don't like* doing from the list. Ask questions about the activities.

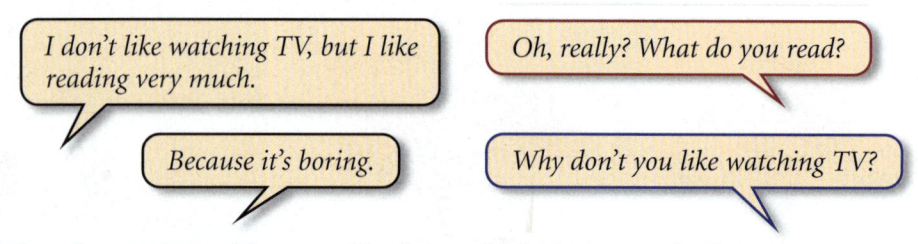

*I don't like watching TV, but I like reading very much.*

*Oh, really? What do you read?*

*Because it's boring.*

*Why don't you like watching TV?*

4 Tell the other students things you like doing which are *not* on the list.

# EVERYDAY ENGLISH
## Social expressions

**1** Complete the conversations with the expressions.

| | |
|---|---|
| 1  A  _____. The traffic is bad today.<br>B  _____. Come and sit down. We're on page 25. | Don't worry.<br>I'm sorry I'm late. |
| 2  A  _____.<br>B  Yes?<br>A  Do you have a dictionary?<br>B  _____ I don't. It's at home.<br>A  _____. | I'm sorry,<br>Excuse me.<br>That's OK. |
| 3  A  It's very hot in here. _____?<br>B  _____? I'm quite cold.<br>A  OK. _____. | Really?<br>Can I open the window?<br>It doesn't matter. |
| 4  A  _____!<br>B  Can I help you?<br>A  Can I have a film for my camera?<br>B  How many exposures?<br>A  _____?<br>B  How many *exposures*?<br>A  _____?<br>B  How many pictures? 24? 36? 40?<br>A  Ah! _____! 40, please. | Pardon?<br>Now I understand!<br>Excuse me!<br>What does 'exposures' mean? |

**T 4.7**  Listen and check.

**2** Practise the conversations with a partner.

Unit 4 · Take it easy!  35

# 5 Where do you live?

*There is/are • Prepositions • some/any • this/that • Furniture • Directions 1*

**STARTER**

1 Write the words in the correct column.

an armchair   a fridge   a television
a coffee table   a shelf   a plant   a stereo
a lamp   a cooker   a washing machine
a telephone   a cupboard   a cup   a sofa

2 What's in your living room?
Tell a partner.

| The living room | The kitchen | both |
|---|---|---|
|  |  |  |

## WHAT'S IN THE LIVING ROOM?
*There is/are*, prepositions

1 Helen has a new flat. Describe her living room on p37.

> *There's a telephone.*

> *There are two plants.*

2 **T 5.1** Read and listen. Complete the answers.
Practise the questions and answers.

Is there a television?        Yes, there _____ .
Is there a radio?             No, there _____ .
Are there any books?          Yes, there _____ .
How many books are there?     There _____ a lot.
Are there any photographs?    No, there _____ .

### GRAMMAR SPOT

Complete the tables.

**Positive**

| There | _____ | a television. |
|---|---|---|
|  | _____ | some books. |

**Negative**

| There | _____ | a radio. |
|---|---|---|
|  | _____ | any photos. |

**Question**

| _____ | there | a television? |
|---|---|---|
|  |  | any books? |

▶▶ **Grammar Reference 5.1 and 5.2  p127**

3 Ask and answer questions about these things.

| a dog | a cat | a computer |
|---|---|---|
| a fire | a mirror | a clock |
| a rug |  |  |

| plants | pictures | bookshelves |
|---|---|---|
| lamps | newspapers | photos |
| flowers |  |  |

> *Is there a cat?*

> *Yes, there is.*

4 Look at the picture of Helen's living room.
Complete the sentences with a preposition.

| on | under | next to | in front of |
|---|---|---|---|

1 The television is _____ the cupboard.
2 The coffee table is _____ the sofa.
3 There are some magazines _____ the table.
4 The television is _____ the stereo.
5 There are two pictures _____ the walls.
6 The cat is _____ the rug _____ the fire.

**Helen's living room**

# PRACTICE

### What's in your picture?

1 Work with a partner. Look at the pictures from your teacher. There's a picture of another living room and lots of things that go in it. *Don't* look at your partner's picture.

| **Student A** Your picture is not complete. Ask Student B questions and find out where the things go. Draw them on your picture. | **Student B** Your picture is complete. Answer Student A's questions and help him/her complete the picture. |
|---|---|
| *Where's the lamp? Where exactly?* | *It's on the table. Next to the book.* |

2 **T 5.2** Look at the complete picture together. Listen to someone describing it. There are *five* mistakes in the description. Say 'Stop!' when you hear a mistake.

*Stop! There aren't three people! There are four people!*

Unit 5 · Where do you live?   37

# WHAT'S IN THE KITCHEN?
some/any, this/that/these/those

**1** This is the kitchen in Helen's new flat. Describe it.

**Helen's kitchen**

**2** **T 5.3** Listen and complete the conversation between Helen and her friend, Bob.

**Helen** And this is the kitchen.
**Bob** Mmm, it's very nice.
**Helen** Well, it's not very big, but there _____ a _____ of cupboards. And _____'s a new fridge, and a cooker. That's new, too.
**Bob** But what's *in* all these cupboards?
**Helen** Well, not a lot. There are some cups, but there aren't any plates. And I have _____ knives and forks, but I don't have _____ spoons!
**Bob** Do you have _____ glasses?
**Helen** No. Sorry.
**Bob** Never mind. We can drink this champagne from those cups! Cheers!

**3** What is there in your kitchen? How is your kitchen different from Helen's?

## GRAMMAR SPOT

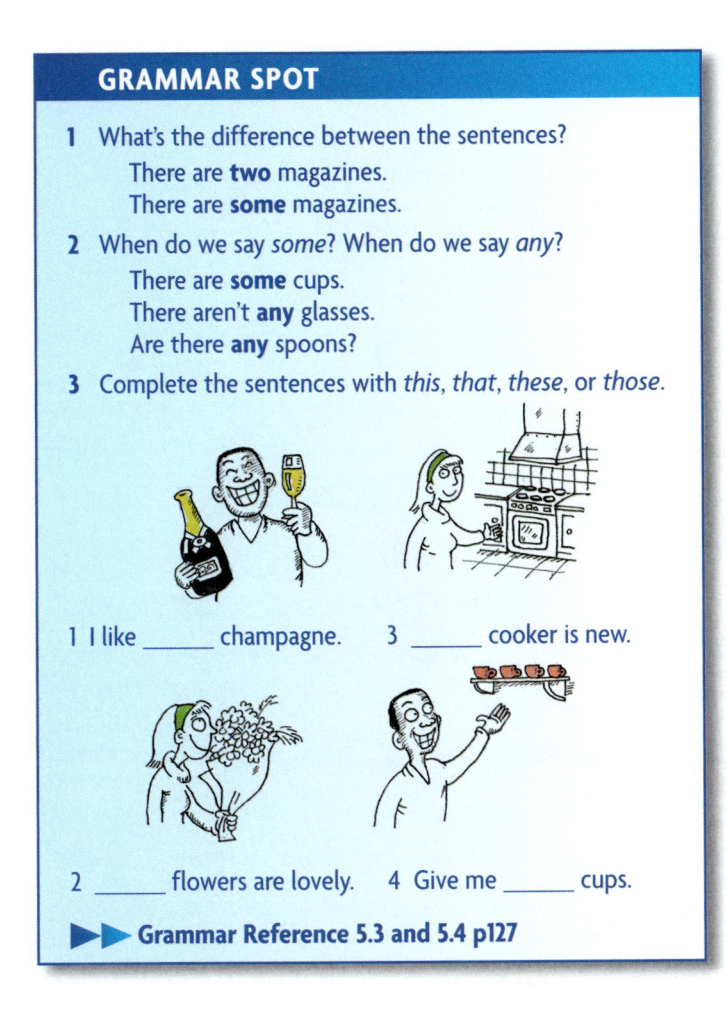

1 What's the difference between the sentences?
   There are **two** magazines.
   There are **some** magazines.

2 When do we say *some*? When do we say *any*?
   There are **some** cups.
   There aren't **any** glasses.
   Are there **any** spoons?

3 Complete the sentences with *this*, *that*, *these*, or *those*.

1 I like _____ champagne.    3 _____ cooker is new.

2 _____ flowers are lovely.   4 Give me _____ cups.

▶▶ Grammar Reference 5.3 and 5.4 p127

# PRACTICE

### In our classroom

1 Complete the sentences with *some* or *any*.
   1 In our classroom there are _____ books on the floor.
   2 There aren't _____ plants.
   3 Are there _____ Spanish students in your class?
   4 There aren't _____ Chinese students.
   5 We have _____ dictionaries in the cupboard.
   6 There aren't _____ pens in my bag.

2 What is there in your classroom? Describe it.

3 Talk about things in your classroom, using *this/that/these/those*. Point to or hold the things.

   *This is my favourite pen.*    *I like that bag.*

   *These chairs are nice.*    *Those windows are dirty.*

### What's in Pierre's briefcase?

4 **T 5.4** Pierre is a Frenchman on business in Boston. Listen to him describe what's in his briefcase. Tick (✓) the things in it.

☐ a newspaper
☐ a dictionary
☐ a sandwich
☐ pens
☐ a notebook
☐ keys
☐ a bus ticket
☐ a letter
☐ photos
☐ a mobile phone
☐ stamps
☐ an address book

5 Look in your bag. Ask and answer questions about your bags with a partner.

   *Is there a dictionary in your bag?*

   *Are there any stamps?*    *How many stamps are there?*

### Check it

6 Tick (✓) the correct sentence.
   1 ☐ There aren't some sandwiches.
     ☐ There aren't any sandwiches.
   2 ☐ Do you have some good dictionary?
     ☐ Do you have a good dictionary?
   3 ☐ I have some photos of my dog.
     ☐ I have any photos of my dog.
   4 ☐ I have lot of books.
     ☐ I have a lot of books.
   5 ☐ How many students are there in this class?
     ☐ How many of students are there in this class?
   6 ☐ Next my house there's a park.
     ☐ Next to my house there's a park.
   7 ☐ Look at this house over there!
     ☐ Look at that house over there!
   8 ☐ Henry, that is my mother. Mum, that is Henry.
     ☐ Henry, this is my mother. Mum, this is Henry.

# READING AND SPEAKING
## At home on a plane

**1** Write the words in the correct place on the picture. What other things are there on a plane?

| steps   a cockpit   a flight attendant   the first class section   emergency exit   windows   door   toilet |

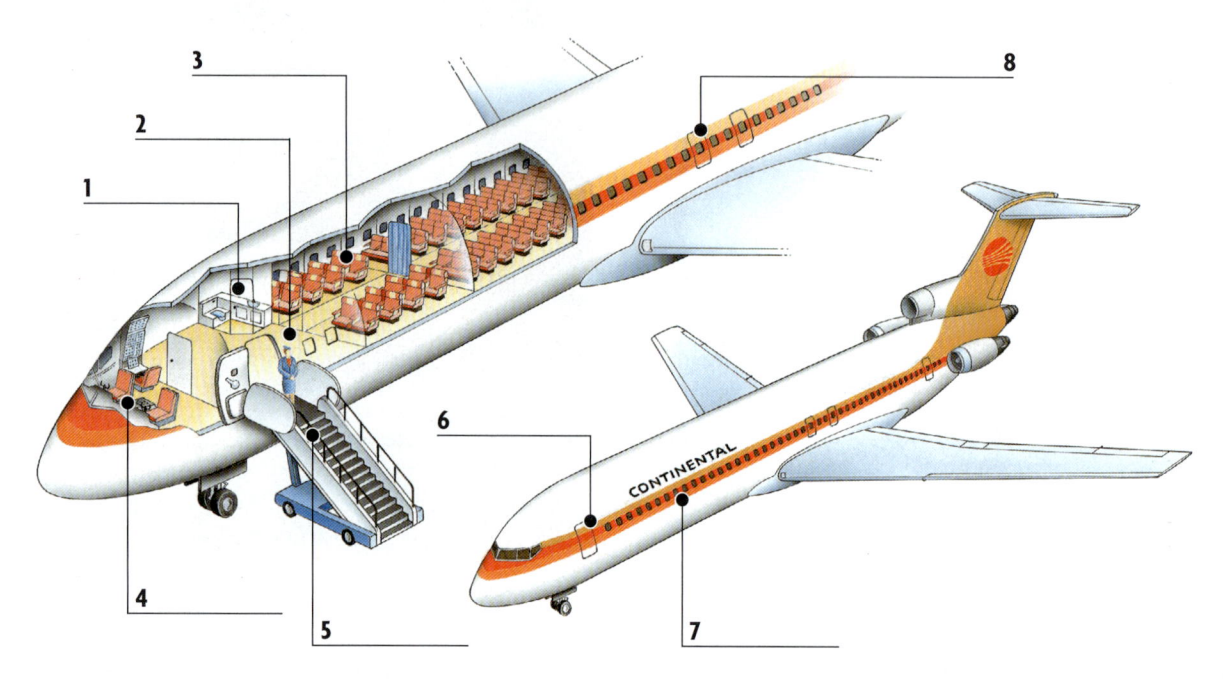

**2** Read about Joanne Ussery and answer the questions.
1. How old is she?
2. Where does she live?
3. How old is her home?
4. How many grandsons does she have?
5. How many bedrooms are there?
6. How many toilets are there?

**3** Are the sentences true (✓) or false (✗)?
1. Joanne loves her home.
2. You need a ticket when you visit her.
3. The bathroom is next to the living room.
4. Joanne sometimes opens the emergency exit doors.
5. There is a photo of the plane in the living room.
6. It's very warm in summer because she doesn't have air conditioning.
7. Her friends love her parties because flight attendants serve the drinks.
8. She doesn't want to buy another plane.

**4** Work with a partner. Ask and answer questions about Joanne's home.

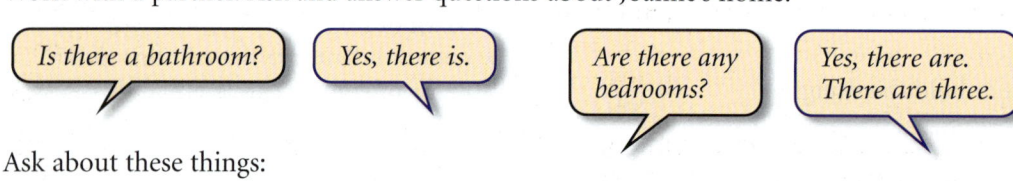

*Is there a bathroom?*

*Yes, there is.*

*Are there any bedrooms?*

*Yes, there are. There are three.*

Ask about these things:
- a telephone
- a dishwasher
- toilets
- flight attendants
- an upstairs bedroom

**What do you think?**

What do you like about Joanne's home? What don't you like?

40   Unit 5 · Where do you live?

# The lady who lives on a plane

Joanne Ussery, 54, from Mississippi is a big favourite with her two grandsons because she lives on a jet plane. Her home is a Boeing 727, so a visit to grandma is very special.

Joanne's front door is at the top of the plane's steps, but you don't need a ticket or a passport when you visit. There are three bedrooms, a living room, a modern kitchen, and a luxury bathroom. The bathroom is in the cockpit, with the bath under the windows. Next to this is Joanne's bedroom in the first class section of the plane. Then there's the living room with four emergency exit doors, which she opens on summer evenings. On the wall there's a photo of the plane flying for Continental Airlines from Florida to the Caribbean. There are also four toilets, all with No Smoking signs.

'The plane is 27 years old and it's the best home in the world,' says Joanne. 'It has all the things you want in a home: a telephone, air conditioning, a cooker, a washing machine, even a dishwasher. It's always very warm, even in winter, and it's very big, 42 metres long. My grandchildren love running up and down. And my friends love parties here, but there aren't any flight attendants to serve them their drinks!'

The plane cost Joanne just $2,000. 'Next time,' she says, 'I want a Boeing 747, not a 727, because they have an upstairs and a downstairs, and I want to go upstairs to bed!'

## LISTENING AND SPEAKING
### Homes around the world

1 Match the places and the photos. What do you know about them?
   ☐ Lisbon   ☐ Toronto   ☐ Malibu   ☐ Samoa

2 **T 5.5** Listen to some people from these places. Complete the chart.

| | Manola from LISBON | Ray and Elsie from TORONTO | Brad from MALIBU | Alise from SAMOA |
|---|---|---|---|---|
| House or flat? | | | | |
| Old or modern? | | | | |
| Where? | | | | |
| How many bedrooms? | | | | |
| Live(s) with? | | | | |
| Extra information | | | | |

3 Talk about where you live.

   *Do you live in a house or a flat?*
   *Where is it?*
   *How many rooms are there?*
   *Do you have a garden?*
   *Who do you live with?*

4 Write a paragraph about where you live.

Unit 5 · Where do you live?

# EVERYDAY ENGLISH
## Directions 1

**1** Look at the street map. Where can you buy these things?

> some aspirin    a CD    a plane ticket    a newspaper    a book    some stamps

**2** **T 5.6** Listen to the conversations and complete them.

1. **A** Excuse me! Is _____ a chemist _____ here?
   **B** Yes. It's over _____ .
   **A** Thanks.

2. **A** _____ me! Is there a _____ near here?
   **B** Yes. _____ _____ Church Street. Take the first _____ _____ _____ right. It's _____ _____ the music shop.
   **A** Oh yes. Thanks.

3. **A** Excuse me! Is there a _____ near here?
   **B** There's a Chinese one in Park Lane _____ _____ the bank, and there's an Italian one in Church Street next to the _____ _____ .
   **A** Is that one _____ ?
   **B** No. Just two minutes, that's all.

4. **A** Is there a post office near here?
   **B** Go straight ahead, and it's _____ _____ left, _____ _____ the pub.
   **A** Thanks a lot.

Practise the conversations with a partner.

**3** Make more conversations with your partner. Ask and answer about these places:
- a bookshop
- a cinema
- a bank
- a phone box
- a public toilet
- a music shop
- a supermarket
- a bus stop
- a park
- a swimming pool
- a post box
- a pub

**4** Talk about where *you* are. Is there a chemist near here? Is it far? What about a bank/a post office/ a supermarket?

Unit 5 · Where do you live?   43

# 6 Can you speak English?

can/can't/could/couldn't • was/were • Words that sound the same • On the phone

**STARTER**

1 Where do people speak these languages?

French   Spanish   German   Italian   Portuguese   Japanese   English

> They speak French in France and also in Canada.

2 Which languages can you speak? Tell the class.

> I can speak English and a little Spanish. And of course, I can speak my language.

## WHAT CAN YOU DO?
can/can't

1 **T 6.1** Match the sentences and pictures. Then listen and check.

1  He can ski really well.
2  She can use a computer.
3  'Can dogs swim?' 'Yes, they can.'
4  'Can you speak Japanese?' 'No, I can't.'
5  I can't spell your name.
6  We can't understand the question.

### GRAMMAR SPOT

1 Say all persons of *can* and *can't*.
   I can, you can, he ... she ... it ... we ... they ...
   I can't, you ..., etc.
   What do you notice?

2 **T 6.2** Listen and repeat these sentences.
   I can speak French.
   Can you speak French?   = /kən/
   Yes, I can.              = /kæn/
   No, I can't.             = /kɑ:nt/

3 Say these sentences.
   • • •              • • •
   We can swim.    She can't cook.

▶▶ Grammar Reference 6.1 p128

a  b  c  d  e  f

44  Unit 6 • Can you speak English?

**2** **T 6.3** Listen and complete the sentences with *can* or *can't* + verb.

1 I ____ ____ ____ , but I ____ ____ ____ .
2 He ____ ____ , but he ____ ____ .
3 '____ you ____ ?' 'Yes, I ____ .'
4 They ____ ____ , but they ____ ____ .
5 We ____ ____ and we ____ ____ .
6 '____ she ____ ?' 'No, she ____ .'

## PRACTICE

**Tina can't cook. Can you?**

**1** **T 6.4** Listen to Tina and complete the chart. Put ✓ or ✗.

| Can . . . ? | Tina | you | your partner |
|---|---|---|---|
| drive a car | | | |
| speak French | | | |
| speak Italian | | | |
| cook | | | |
| play tennis | | | |
| ski | | | |
| swim | | | |
| play the piano | | | |
| use a computer | | | |

**2** Complete the chart about you.

**3** Complete the chart about your partner. Ask and answer the questions.

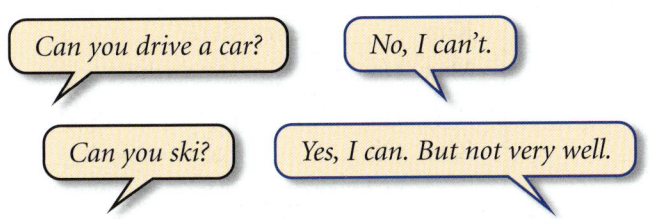

*Can you drive a car?*

*No, I can't.*

*Can you ski?*

*Yes, I can. But not very well.*

Tell the class about you and your partner.

*Louis can ski, but I can't.*

## What can computers do?

**4** Talk about computers with a partner. What can they do? What can't they do?

*They can translate, but they can't speak English.*

*Yes, they can.*

## COMPUTERS

### Can they . . . ?

- translate
- write poetry
- speak English
- laugh
- play chess
- hear
- check spellings
- feel
- make music
- think
- have conversations
- fall in love

**5** What can people do that computers can't do?

# WHERE WERE YOU YESTERDAY?
*was/were, can/could*

Read the questions. Complete the answers.

| | Present | Past |
|---|---|---|
| 1 | What day is it today?<br>It's _____ . | What day was it yesterday?<br>It was _____ . |
| 2 | What month is it now?<br>It's _____ . | What month was it last month?<br>It was _____ . |
| 3 | Where are you now?<br>I'm in/at _____ . | Where were you yesterday?<br>I was in/at _____ . |
| 4 | Are you in England?<br>_____ , I am.<br>_____ , I'm not. | Were you in England in 1999?<br>_____ , I was.<br>_____ , I wasn't. |
| 5 | Can you swim?<br>_____ , I can.<br>_____ , I can't. | Could you swim when you were five?<br>_____ , I could.<br>_____ , I couldn't. |
| 6 | Can your teacher speak three languages?<br>Yes, _____ can.<br>No, _____ can't. | Could your teacher speak English when he/she was seven?<br>Yes, _____ could.<br>No, _____ couldn't. |

> **GRAMMAR SPOT**
>
> 1 Complete the table with the past of *to be*.
>
> | | Positive | Negative |
> |---|---|---|
> | I | was | wasn't |
> | You | were | weren't |
> | He/She/It | _____ | _____ |
> | We | _____ | _____ |
> | They | _____ | _____ |
>
> 2 **T 6.5** Listen and repeat.
>
> /wəz/        /wə/
> It was Monday yesterday. We were at school.
> In short answers the pronunciation is different.
>                              /wɒz/
> 'Was it hot?'      'Yes, it was.'
>                              /wɜː/
> 'Were you tired?'    'Yes, we were.'
>
> 3 What is the past of *can*?
> Positive _____    Negative _____
>
> ▶▶ Grammar Reference 6.1 and 6.2 p128

# PRACTICE

**Talking about you**

1 Ask and answer questions with a partner.
Where were you ... ?
- at eight o'clock this morning
- at half past six yesterday evening
- at two o'clock this morning
- at this time yesterday
- at ten o'clock last night
- last Saturday evening

2 Complete the conversation, using *was*, *were*, *wasn't*, *weren't*, or *couldn't*.

Kim  _____ you at Charlotte's party last Saturday?
Max  Yes, I _____ .
Kim  _____ it good?
Max  Well, it _____ OK.
Kim  _____ there many people?
Max  Yes, there _____ .
Kim  _____ Henry there?
Max  No, he _____ . And where _____ you? Why _____ you there?
Kim  Oh ... I _____ go because I _____ at Mark's party! It _____ brilliant!

**T 6.6** Listen and check. Listen for the pronunciation of *was* and *were*. Practise with a partner.

46 Unit 6 · Can you speak English?

**Four geniuses!**

**3** The people in the photos were all geniuses. Who are they?

**4** Look at these sentences.

> I was born in London in 1973. I could read when I was four.
> My sister couldn't read until she was seven.

Match lines in **A**, **B**, and **C** and make similar sentences about the four geniuses.

| A | B | C |
|---|---|---|
| Mozart / born in | Siberia / 1938 | paint / one |
| Picasso / born in | Germany / 1879 | dance / two |
| Nureyev / born in | Austria / 1756 | play the piano / three |
| Einstein / born in | Spain / 1881 | couldn't speak / eight |

**5** Ask and answer questions with a partner about the geniuses.

*When was Mozart born?*

*Where was he born?*

*How old was he when he could … ?*

**6** Work in groups. Ask and answer questions about you.
1. Where were you born?
2. When were you born?
3. How old were you when you could … ?
   - walk
   - talk
   - read
   - swim
   - ride a bike
   - use a computer
   - speak a foreign language

**Check it**

**7** Tick (✓) the correct sentence.
1. ☐ I don't can use a computer.
   ☐ I can't use a computer.
2. ☐ Was they at the party?
   ☐ Were they at the party?
3. ☐ I'm sorry. I can't go to the party.
   ☐ I'm sorry. I no can go to the party.
4. ☐ She was no at home.
   ☐ She wasn't at home.
5. ☐ He could play chess when he was five.
   ☐ He can play chess when he was five.
6. ☐ I can to speak English very well.
   ☐ I can speak English very well.

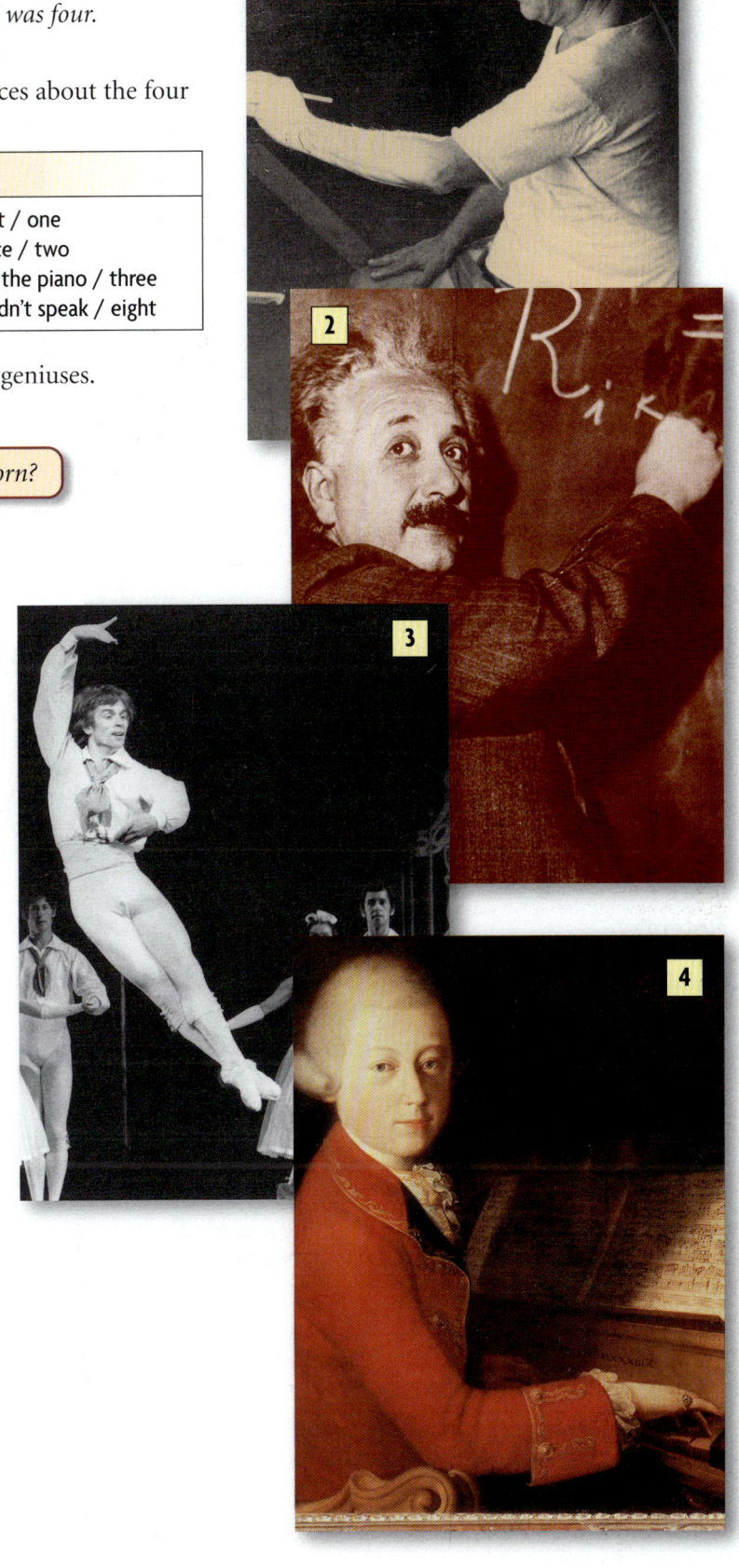

Unit 6 • Can you speak English? 47

# READING AND SPEAKING
## Super Kids

1 Look at the children in the photographs. How old are they? What can they do?

2 Work in two groups.
   **Group A** Read about little Miss Picasso.
   **Group B** Read about the new Mozart.

3 Answer the questions about Alexandra or Lukas.
   1 How old is she/he?
   2 Why is she/he special?
   3 Where was she/he born?
   4 Where does she/he live now?
   5 Who does she/he live with?
   6 Does she/he go to school?
   7 What could she/he do when she/he was very young?
   8 Does she/he have much free time? Why not?
   9 Is she/he poor?
   10 Where was she/he last year?

4 Find a partner from the other group. Tell your partner about your child, using your answers.

5 What is the same about Alexandra and Lukas? What is different? Discuss with your partner.

*They are both geniuses.*

*Alexandra is a painter, and Lukas is a pianist.*

### Roleplay

6 Work with a partner.
   **Student A** is a journalist.
   **Student B** is Alexandra or Lukas.

   Ask and answer questions, using the questions in exercise 3 to help you.

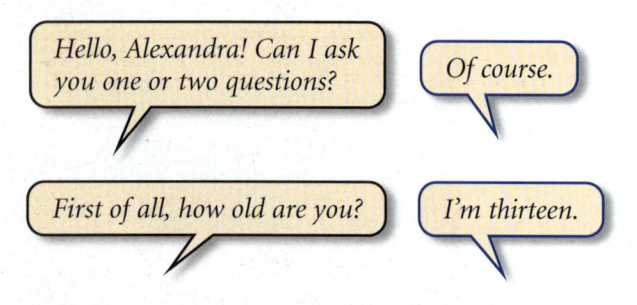

*Hello, Alexandra! Can I ask you one or two questions?*

*Of course.*

*First of all, how old are you?*

*I'm thirteen.*

# The New Mozart

Ten-year-old **Lukas Vondracek** is very shy, but every year he travels the world and meets hundreds of people. Lukas is a brilliant pianist and he gives lots of concerts. Last year he was in Washington, Chicago, and London. He is sometimes called 'the new Mozart'. He says 'I'm shy, but I love giving concerts.'

Lukas was born in **Opava** in the **Czech Republic** but now he lives with his parents in **Vienna**, where he practises the piano six hours a day. He goes to school two days a week. Lukas could play the piano when he was two and he could read music before he could read books. Now he can write music, too.

Lukas doesn't just play the piano, he plays football and ice hockey. He says: 'Mozart was poor and he couldn't play football, so I'm not like him at all!'

# Little Miss Picasso

**Alexandra Nechita** is thirteen and she is called 'the new Picasso'. She paints large pictures in cubist style and sells them for between $10,000 and $80,000.

She was born in **Romania** but now she lives in **Los Angeles** with her family. She could paint very well when she was only four but her parents couldn't understand her pictures. Alexandra says: 'I paint how I feel, sometimes I'm happy and sometimes sad. I can't stop painting.' Every day after school she does her homework, plays with her little brother, then paints for two or three hours until bedtime.

Alexandra doesn't spend her money, she saves it: 'We were very poor when we were first in America. We couldn't buy many things, but now I can buy a big house for my family and we can travel the world. Last year we were in London, Paris, and Rome. It was fantastic!'

## VOCABULARY AND PRONUNCIATION
### Words that sound the same

**1** Look at the sentences. What do you notice about these words?

I have a black **eye**.
**No**, he doesn't **know** the answer.

**2** Find the words in **B** that have the same pronunciation as the words in **A**.

**A** hear, write, wear, there, eye, hour, see, for, by, too, son, know

**B** sun, four, I, our, sea, where, buy, here, no, right, two, their

**3** Correct the two spelling mistakes in each sentence.
1. I can here you, but I can't sea you.
2. Their are three bedrooms in hour house.
3. I don't no wear Jill lives.
4. My sun lives near the see.
5. Don't where that hat, by a new one!
6. Know, eye can't come to your party.
7. You were write. Sally and Peter can't come four dinner.
8. There daughter could right when she was three.
9. I no my answers are write.

**4** Look at the phonetic symbols. Write the two words with the same pronunciation.
1. /nəʊ/ _____ _____
2. /sʌn/ _____ _____
3. /tuː/ _____ _____
4. /raɪt/ _____ _____
5. /hɪə/ _____ _____
6. /weə/ _____ _____

## EVERYDAY ENGLISH
### On the phone

**1** When you do not know someone's telephone number, you can phone Directory Enquiries. In Britain you ring 153 for international numbers. Here are the names and addresses of some people you want to phone.

**WILSON ASSOCIATES**
Nancy Wilson
302 Erindale Road
PERTH 6034
Australia
Tel: _____
e-mail: n.wilson@connect.com.au

Heißesonnig
BERLIN
Franziska Novak
Karl Marx Allee 99
10265 BERLIN
Deutschland
e-mail: nordk@bz_berlin.de
Tel/fax: _____

Avenida Vitória 713
SÃO PAULO – SP
Brasil
Tel: _____
Fax: _____
E-mail: ferreira_m@dpret.com.br
**Mauricio Ferreira**

**T 6.7** Listen to the operator and answer her questions. Get Nancy's telephone number.

**Operator** International Directory Enquiries. Which country, please?
**You** _Australia_ .
**Operator** And which town?
**You** _____ .
**Operator** Can I have the last name, please?
**You** _____ .
**Operator** And the initial?
**You** _____ .
**Operator** What's the address?
**You** _____ .
**Recorded message** The number you require is _____ .

**2** Work with a partner. Look at the numbers from your teacher. Ask and answer to get the telephone and fax numbers of Franziska and Mauricio.

**3** Read the lines below. They are all from telephone conversations.
What do you think the lines before and/or after are? Discuss with a partner.

1 This is Jo.
2 Can I take a message?
3 Great! See you on Sunday at ten, then. Bye!
4 Oh, never mind. Perhaps next time. Bye!
5 No, it isn't. I'll just get her.
6 I'll ring back later.
7 There's a party at my house on Saturday. Can you come?
8 Can I speak to the manager, please?

> ! I'll = I will
> will = an offer or promise
> I'll help you

**4** Complete the conversations with a line from exercise 3.

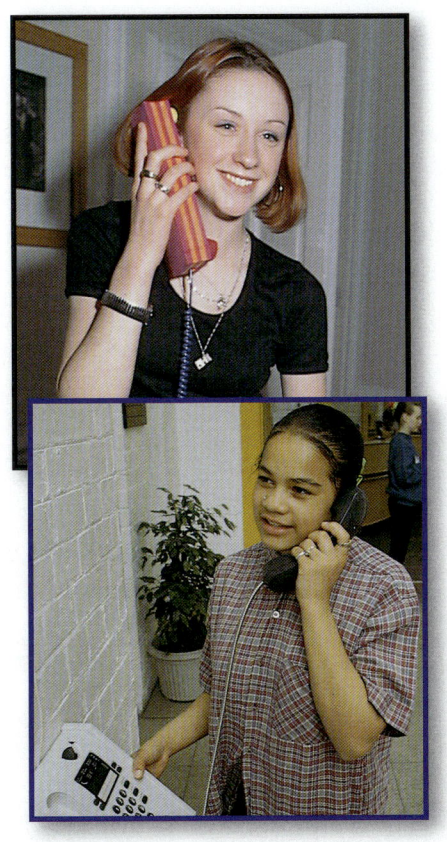

1 A Hello.
  B Hello. Can I speak to Jo, please?
  A _____ .
  B Oh! Hi, Jo. This is Pat. Is Sunday still OK for tennis?
  A Yes, that's fine.
  B _____ !
  A Bye!

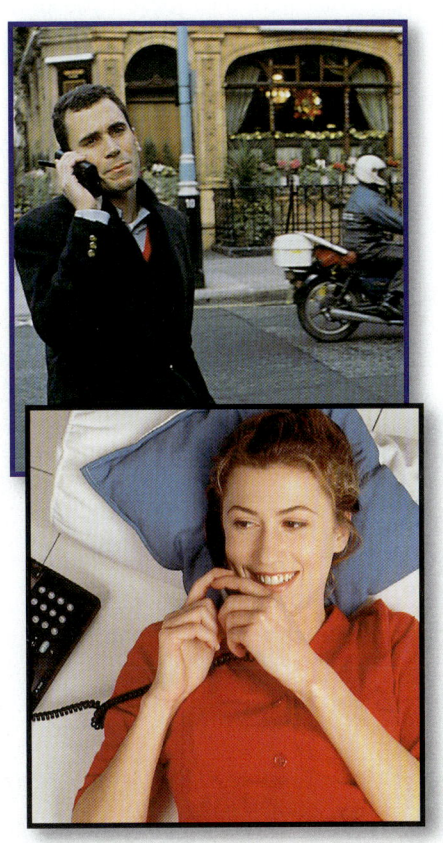

2 A Hello.
  B Hello. Is that Liz?
  A _____ .
  ...
  C Hello, Liz here.
  B Hi, Liz. It's Tom. Listen! _____ ?
  C Oh sorry, Tom. I can't. It's my sister's wedding.
  B _____ !
  C Bye!

3 A Good morning. Barclays Bank, Watford. How can I help you?
  B Good morning. _____ ?
  A I'm afraid Mr Smith isn't in his office at the moment. _____ ?
  B Don't worry. _____ .
  A All right. Goodbye.
  B Goodbye.

**T 6.8** Listen and check. Practise the conversations.

Make similar conversations with your partner.

# 7 Then and now

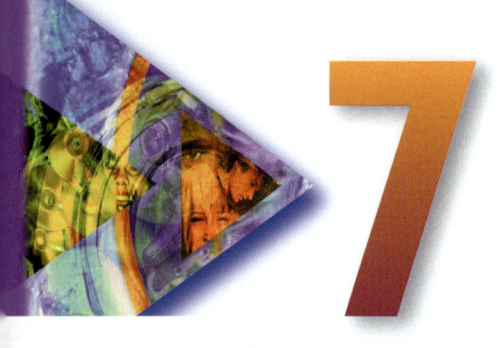

Past Simple 1 – regular verbs • Irregular verbs • Silent letters • Special occasions

**STARTER** When were your grandparents and great-grandparents born? Where were they born? Do you know all their names? What were their jobs? If you know, tell the class.

## WHEN I WAS YOUNG
Past Simple – regular verbs

1 **T 7.1** Read and listen to Mattie Smith's life now. Complete text A with the verbs you hear.

**A**

**Mattie Smith** is 91 years old. She ____ alone in Atlanta, Georgia. She ____ her day at 7.30. First she ____ a bath, next she ____ the house, and then she ____ outside on her verandah and ____ about her past life. Then she ____ poems about it.

**B**

Mattie was never at school. She lived with her mother and four sisters. She started work when she was eight. She worked in the cotton fields from 6.00 in the morning to 10.00 at night. She couldn't read or write but she could think, and she created poems in her head.

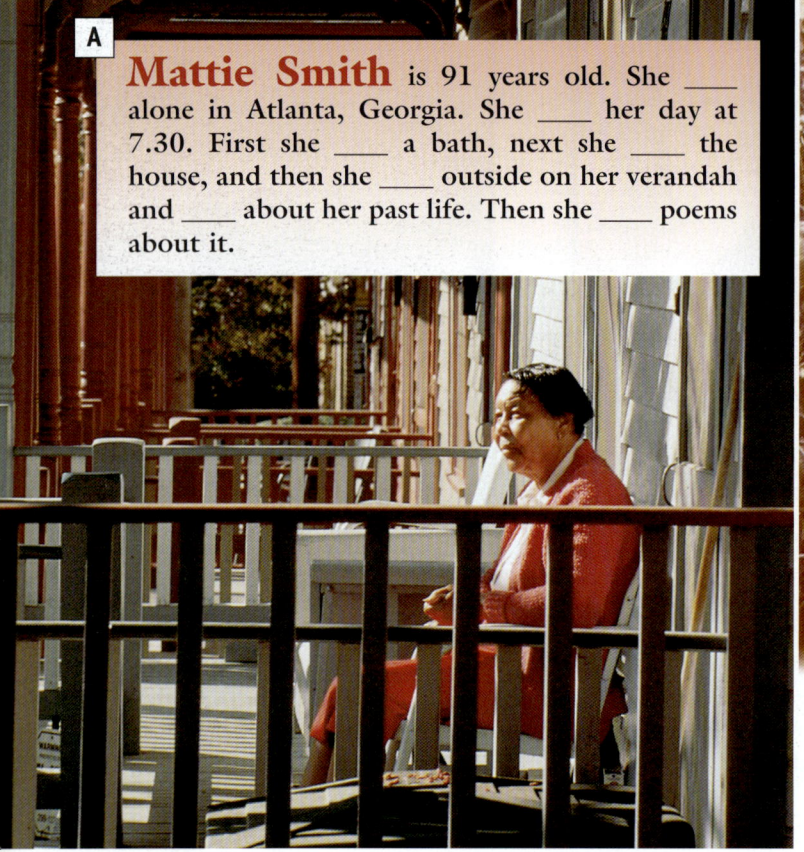

2 **T 7.2** Read and listen to text B about Mattie's life a long time ago.

### GRAMMAR SPOT

1 Find examples of the past of *is* and *can* in text **B**.
2 Complete the sentence with *live* in the correct form.
   Now she _____ alone, but when she was a child she _____ with her mother and sisters.
3 Find the Past Simple of *start*, *work*, and *create* in text **B**. How do we form the Past Simple of regular verbs?

▶▶ Grammar Reference 7.1 p129

**3** **T 7.3** What is the past form of these verbs? Listen and practise saying them.

| look   work   love   learn   earn   marry   die   hate   want |

**4** **T 7.4** Read and listen to Mattie talking about her past life. Complete the text, using the Past Simple form of the verbs in exercise 3.

'I _____ from 6.00 in the morning until 10.00 at night. Sixteen hours in the cotton fields and I only _____ $2 a day. I sure _____ that job but I _____ the poems in my head. I really _____ to learn to read and write. When I was sixteen I _____ Hubert, and soon there were six children, five sons, then a daughter, Lily. Hubert _____ just before she was born. That was sixty-five years ago. So I _____ after my family alone. There was no time for learning, but my children, they all _____ to read and write – that was important to me. And when did I learn to read and write? I didn't learn until I was 86, and now I have three books of poems.'

### GRAMMAR SPOT

1 Find a question and a negative in the last part of the text about Mattie.

2 Look at these questions.
   Where **does** she live now?
   Where **did** she live in 1950?

   *Did* is the past of *do* and *does*. We use *did* to form a question in the Past Simple.

3 We use **didn't** (= did not) to form the negative.
   She **didn't** learn to read until she was 86.

▶▶ Grammar Reference 7.2 p129

**5** Complete the questions about Mattie.

1 When _did_ she **start** work?   When she was eight years old.
2 Where ____ she ____ ?   In the cotton fields.
3 Who ____ she ____ with?   Her mother and sisters.
4 How many hours ____ she ____ ?   Sixteen hours a day.
5 How much ____ she ____ ?   $2 a day.
6 Who ____ she ____ ?   Hubert.
7 When ____ Hubert ____ ?   Sixty-five years ago.
8 When ____ she ____ to read?   She didn't learn until she was 86.

**T 7.5** Listen and check. Practise the questions and answers with a partner.

# PRACTICE

## Talking about you

**1** Complete the sentences with *did*, *was*, or *were*.

1 Where _____ you born? Where _____ your mother born?
2 When _____ you start school?
3 When _____ you learn to read and write?
4 Who _____ your first teacher?
5 What _____ your favourite subject?
6 Where _____ you live when you _____ a child?
7 _____ you live in a house or a flat?

**2** Stand up! Ask two or three students the questions in exercise 1.

**3** Tell the class some of the information you learned.

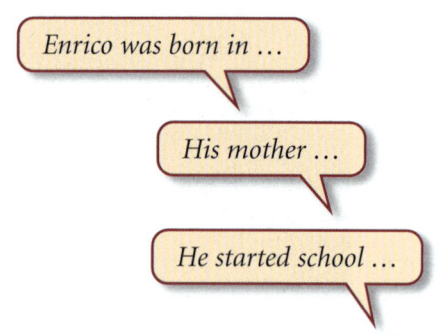

> *Enrico was born in …*
>
> *His mother …*
>
> *He started school …*

## Pronunciation

**4** **T 7.6** The *-ed* ending of regular verbs has three different pronunciations. Listen to the examples. Then put the verbs you hear in the correct column.

| /t/ | /d/ | /ɪd/ |
|---|---|---|
| worked | lived | started |

# THE END OF THE 20TH CENTURY

## Irregular verbs

**1** Look at the list of irregular verbs on p142. Write the Past Simple form of the verbs in the box. Which verb isn't irregular?

| have _____ | begin _____ | come _____ | go _____ | do _____ |
| leave _____ | get _____ | study _____ | become _____ | |
| win _____ | lose _____ | buy _____ | meet _____ | |

**2** **T 7.7** Listen and repeat the Past Simple forms.

**3** **T 7.8** How old were you in 2000? Simon was twenty-four. Listen to him and complete the sentences.

### What did Simon do?

He _____ school in 1994. He _____ to university where he _____ graphic design. Then, in 1997, he _____ a job with Saatchi and Saatchi, an advertising agency in London. He _____ his girlfriend, Zoë, in 1998, and the next year they _____ a flat together.

### What happened in the world?

**Sport**
France _____ the World Cup in 1998.
Brazil _____ .

**Politics**
Tony Blair _____ Britain's Prime Minister in 1997. Bill Clinton _____ a lot of problems in his last years in the White House. Eleven countries in Europe (but not Britain) _____ to use the Euro in 1999.

**Famous people**
Princess Diana _____ in a car crash in Paris in 1997. Millions of people _____ to London for her funeral.

Listen again and check.

**4** Work with a partner. Ask and answer questions about Simon.

1 When/Simon/leave school?
2 What/study at university?
3 When/a job with Saatchi and Saatchi?
4 When/meet Zoë?
5 What/Zoë and Simon do in 1999?

**5** What did you do in the last years of the 20th century? What can you remember? Write about it. Tell the class.

## PRACTICE

### When did it happen?

1 Work in small groups. What important dates in the 20th century can you remember? What happened in the world? What happened in your country? Make a list of events. Then make questions to ask the other groups.

*When did the First World War begin/end?*

*When did the first person walk on the moon?*

### What did you do?

2 Look at these phrases.

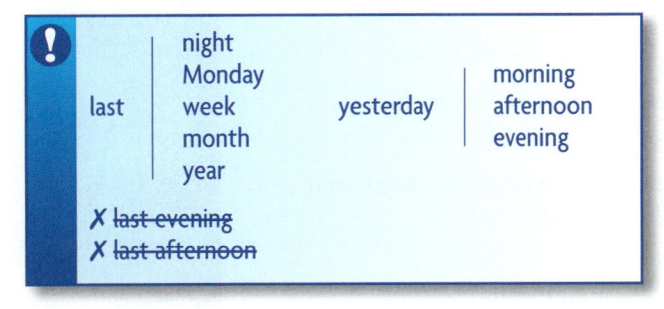

| last | night / Monday / week / month / year | yesterday | morning / afternoon / evening |

✗ last evening
✗ last afternoon

3 Work with a partner. Ask and answer questions with *When did you last … ?* Ask another question for more information.

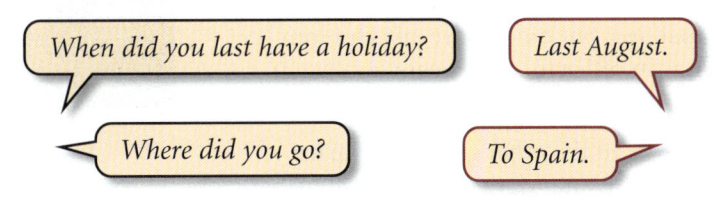

*When did you last have a holiday?* — *Last August.*
*Where did you go?* — *To Spain.*

- have a holiday
- see a video
- go shopping
- give someone a kiss
- take a photograph
- go to a party
- lose something
- write a letter
- get a present
- have dinner in a restaurant

Tell the class some things you learned about your partner.

*Yukio had a holiday last August and she went to Italy.*

### Check it

4 Tick (✓) the correct sentence.

1. ☐ He bought some new shoes.
   ☐ He buyed some new shoes.
2. ☐ Where did you go yesterday?
   ☐ Where you went yesterday?
3. ☐ You see Jane last week?
   ☐ Did you see Jane last week?
4. ☐ Did she get the job?
   ☐ Did she got the job?
5. ☐ I went out yesterday evening.
   ☐ I went out last evening.
6. ☐ He studied French at university.
   ☐ He studyed French at university.
7. ☐ What had you for breakfast?
   ☐ What did you have for breakfast?
8. ☐ I was in New York the last week.
   ☐ I was in New York last week.

Unit 7 • Then and now   55

# READING AND SPEAKING
## Two famous firsts

1. Translate these words.

   | nouns |
   |---|
   | grocer   slaves   politician   twins   widow   (in) tears |
   | **verbs** |
   | agree   bomb   grow   fight   own   resign   survive |

2. Look at the photographs and complete these sentences.

   George Washington was the first _____ .
   Margaret Thatcher was the first _____ .

   What else do you know about these people?

3. Work in two groups.

   **Group A** Read about George Washington.
   **Group B** Read about Margaret Thatcher.

4. Are the sentences true (✓) or false (✗) about your person? Correct the false sentences.

   1. He/She came from a rich family.
   2. He/She loved being a politician.
   3. He/She worked hard.
   4. He/She had a lot of other interests.
   5. He/She had a good education.
   6. He/She married, but didn't have any children.
   7. He/She was in office for eight years.
   8. Finally he/she was tired of politics and resigned.

5. Find a partner from the other group. Compare George Washington and Margaret Thatcher, using your answers.

6. Complete the questions about the other person. Then ask and answer them with your partner.

   **About George Washington**
   1. How many jobs did he … ?
   2. When did he … President?
   3. What did he … doing in his free time?
   4. Did George and Martha have any … ?
   5. What … he build?
   6. How long … he President?

   **About Margaret Thatcher**
   7. What … her father's job?
   8. When did she … Denis?
   9. How many children did they … ?
   10. How much sleep … she need?
   11. When did the terrorists … her hotel?
   12. How long … she Prime Minister?

## What do you think?

Who were famous leaders in your country?
What did they do?

Unit 7 · Then and now

# Two Famous Firsts

## George Washington (1732–1799)

He was the first President of the United States. He became President in 1789, eight years after the American War of Independence.

### His early life

George was born in Virginia. His family owned a big farm and had slaves. George didn't have much education. During his life he had three jobs: he was a farmer, a soldier, and a politician. He loved the life of a farmer. He grew tobacco and owned horses. He worked hard but he also liked dancing and going to the theatre. In 1759 he married a widow called Martha Custis. They were happy together, but didn't have any children.

### His later life

He was Commander-in-Chief of the army and fought the British in the War of Independence. When the war ended in 1781 he was happy to go back to the farm, but his country wanted him to be President. Finally, in 1789, he became President, and gave his name to the new capital city. He started the building of the White House, but he never lived in it. By 1797 he was tired of politics. He went back to his farm and died there two years later.

## Margaret Thatcher (1925– )

She was the first woman prime minister in Europe. She became Prime Minister of Britain in 1979.

### Her early life

She was born above a shop in the small English town of Grantham. Her father, Alfred Roberts, was a grocer. He worked very hard for little money. Margaret also worked hard, and she went to Oxford University, where she studied chemistry. In 1951 she married Denis Thatcher, a rich businessman. They had twins, a girl and a boy. The love of her life was politics. She didn't have much time for other interests. She said she only needed four hours' sleep a night.

### Her later life

She became a politician in 1959, leader of the Conservative Party in 1975, and Prime Minister of Britain four years after that. She had a strong personality. A lot of people were afraid of her, and she was called 'The Iron Lady'. In 1984 Irish terrorists bombed her hotel, but she survived. She was Prime Minister for eleven years. She finally resigned in 1990, but she didn't want to, and she was in tears when she left 10 Downing Street.

## VOCABULARY AND PRONUNCIATION
### Spelling and silent letters

**1** There are many silent letters in English words. Here are some words from the reading texts on p57. Practise saying them.

bom**b** /bɒm/    wido**w** /ˈwɪdəʊ/
har**d** /hɑːd/    fou**gh**t /fɔːt/

Cross out the silent letters in these words.

1 wa~~l~~k      7 work
2 listen       8 war
3 know        9 island
4 write       10 build
5 eight       11 resign
6 farm        12 daughter

**T 7.9** Listen and check. Practise saying the words.

**2** Look at the phonetic spelling of these words from exercise 1. Write the words.

1 /wɜːk/     __work__
2 /fɑːm/     _____
3 /ˈlɪsən/   _____
4 /bɪld/     _____
5 /raɪt/     _____
6 /ˈdɔːtə/   _____

**3** Write the words. They all have silent letters.

1 /bɔːn/     _____
2 /bɔːt/     _____
3 /wɜːld/    _____
4 /ˈɑːnsə/   _____
5 /naɪvz/    _____
6 /rɒŋ/      _____
7 /ˈkʌbəd/   _____
8 /ˈkrɪsməs/ _____

**T 7.10** Listen and practise saying the words.

## EVERYDAY ENGLISH
### Special occasions

**1** Look at the list of days. Which are special? Match the special days with the pictures. Do you have the same customs in your country?

birthday
Monday
wedding day
Christmas Day
yesterday
New Year's Eve
Easter Day
tomorrow
Mother's Day
today
Thanksgiving
Valentine's Day
Friday
Hallowe'en

**2** Complete the conversations. What are the occasions?

1 **A** Ugh! Work again! I hate _____ mornings!
   **B** Me, too. Did you have a nice weekend?
   **A** Yes. It was brilliant.

2 Happy _____ to you.
   Happy _____ to you.
   Happy _____ , dear Tommy,
   Happy _____ to you.

3 **A** Did you get any _____ cards?
   **B** Yes, I did. Listen to this.
      *Roses are red. Violets are blue.*
      *You are my _____*
      *And I love you.*
   **A** Oooh-er! Do you know who it's from?
   **B** No idea!

4 **A** Congratulations!
   **B** Oh … thank you very much.
   **A** When's the happy day?
   **B** Pardon?
   **A** Your _____ day. When is it?
   **B** Oh! We're not sure. Perhaps some time in June.

5 **A** It's midnight! Happy _____ everybody!
   **B** Happy _____ !
   **C** Happy _____ !

6 **A** Thank goodness! It's _____ !
   **B** Yeah. Have a nice weekend!
   **A** Same to you.

**T 7.11** Listen and check. Practise the conversations with a partner.

**3** **T 7.12** Listen and answer.

Unit 7 · Then and now 59

# 8 How long ago?

Past Simple 2 – negatives/*ago* • Which word is different? • What's the date?

**STARTER**  What is the Past Simple of these verbs? Most of them are irregular.

eat   drink   drive   fly   listen to   make   ride   take   watch   wear

## FAMOUS INVENTIONS
Past Simple negatives/*ago*

1 Match the verbs from the Starter with the photographs.

1 Coca-Cola
2 photographs
3 records
4 planes
5 jeans

60  Unit 8 • How long ago?

6 | hamburgers

7 | cars

8 | phone calls

9 | television

10 | bikes

**2** Work in groups. What year was it one hundred years ago? Ask and answer questions about the things in the pictures. What did people do? What didn't they do?

*Did people drive cars one hundred years ago?*

*Yes, I think they did.*

*I'm not sure.*

*No, they didn't.*

**3** Tell the class the things you think people did and didn't do.

*We think people drove cars, but they didn't watch TV.*

**4** Your teacher knows the exact dates when these things were invented. Ask your teacher about them. Write down the dates. How many years ago was it?

S  When were cars invented?
T  In 1893.
S  That's … years ago.

### GRAMMAR SPOT

Write the Past Simple forms.

| Present Simple | Past Simple |
|---|---|
| I live in London. | I lived in London. |
| He lives in London. | _____ |
| Do you live in London? | _____ |
| Does she live in London? | _____ |
| I don't live in London. | _____ |
| He doesn't live in London. | _____ |

▶▶ Grammar Reference 8.1 and 8.2  p129

Unit 8 • How long ago?

# PRACTICE

## Three inventors

1  **T 8.1**  The dates in the texts are *all* incorrect. Read and listen, and correct the dates.

> *They didn't make the first jeans in 1923. They made them in 1873.*

### Jeans

Two Americans, Jacob Davis and **Levi Strauss**, made the first jeans in 1923. Davis bought cloth from Levi's shop. He told Levi that he had a special way to make strong trousers for workmen. The first jeans were blue. In 1965 jeans became fashionable for women after they saw them in *Vogue* magazine. In the 1990s, Calvin Klein earned $12.5 million a week from jeans.

### Television

A Scotsman, **John Logie Baird**, transmitted the first television picture on 25 November, 1905. The first thing on television was a boy who worked in the office next to Baird's workroom in London. In 1929 Baird sent pictures from London to Glasgow. In 1940 he sent pictures to New York, and also produced the first colour TV pictures.

### Aspirin

**Felix Hofman**, a 29-year-old chemist who worked for the German company Bayer, invented the drug Aspirin in April 1879. He gave the first aspirin to his father for his arthritis. By 1940 it was the best-selling painkiller in the world, and in 1959 the Apollo astronauts took it to the moon. The Spanish philosopher, José Ortega y Gasset, called the 20th century 'The Age of Aspirin'.

2  Make these sentences negative. Then give the correct answers.
   1  Two Germans made the first jeans.
      ***Two Germans didn't make the first jeans. Two Americans made them.***
   2  Davis sold cloth in Levi's shop.
   3  Women saw pictures of jeans in *She* magazine.
   4  Baird sent pictures from London to Paris.
   5  Felix Hofman gave the first aspirin to his mother.
   6  A Spanish philosopher called the 19th century 'The Age of Aspirin'.

   **T 8.2**  Listen and check. Practise the stress and intonation.

## Did you know that?

3  **T 8.3**  Read and listen to the conversations. Then listen and repeat.

   A  Did you know that Marco Polo brought spaghetti back from China?
   B  Really? He didn't! That's incredible!
   A  Well, it's true!

   C  Did you know that Napoleon was afraid of cats?
   D  He wasn't! I don't believe it!
   C  Well, it's true!

4  Work with a partner. Look at the lists of more incredible information from your teacher. Have similar conversations.

Unit 8 · How long ago?

**Time expressions**

5 Make correct time expressions.

|    |    |                       |
|----|----|-----------------------|
|    |    | seven o'clock         |
|    |    | the morning           |
|    |    | Saturday              |
| in |    | Sunday evening        |
| on |    | night                 |
| at |    | September             |
|    |    | weekends              |
|    |    | summer                |
|    |    | 1994                  |
|    |    | the twentieth century |

6 Work with a partner. Ask and answer questions with *When ... ?* Use a time expression and *ago* in the answer.

*When did you get up?*

*At seven o'clock, three hours ago.*

*When did this term start?*

*In September, two months ago.*

When did . . . ?
- you get up
- you have breakfast
- you arrive at school
- you start learning English
- you start at this school
- this term start
- you last use a computer
- you learn to ride a bicycle
- your parents get married
- you last eat a hamburger
- you last have a coffee break

7 Tell the class about your day so far. Begin like this.

*I got up at seven o'clock, had breakfast, and left the house at ...*

## VOCABULARY AND PRONUNCIATION
### Which word is different?

1 Which word is different? Why?
 1 orange   apple   ~~chicken~~   banana
    **Chicken is different because it isn't a fruit.**
 2 hamburger   sandwich   pizza   recipe
 3 television   dishwasher   vacuum cleaner   washing machine
 4 wrote   kissed   threw   found
 5 fax   e-mail   CD player   mobile phone
 6 brown   green   delicious   blue
 7 face   eye   mouth   leg
 8 talk   speak   chat   laugh
 9 century   clock   season   month
 10 funny   shy   nervous   worried
 11 fall in love   get married   get engaged   go to a party

2 Look at the phonetic spelling of these words from exercise 1. Practise saying them.

 1 /ˈresəpi/            6 /ˈwʌrɪd/
 2 /tʃæt/               7 /dɪˈlɪʃəs/
 3 /ʃaɪ/                8 /ˈsænwɪdʒ/
 4 /ˈfʌni/              9 /məˈʃiːn/
 5 /feɪs/              10 /ˈsentʃəri/

**T 8.4** Listen and check.

3 Complete the sentences with a word from exercise 1.
 1 A Why didn't you _____ at my joke?
    B Because it wasn't very _____ . That's why!
 2 A Hello. Hello. I can't hear you. Who is it?
    B It's me, Jonathon ... JONATHON! I'm on my _____ .
    A Oh, Jonathon! Hi! Sorry, I can't _____ now. I'm in a hurry.
 3 A Good luck in your exams!
    B Oh, thank you. I always get so _____ before exams.
 4 A Mmmmm! Did you make this chocolate cake?
    B I did. Do you like it?
    A Like it? I *love* it. It's _____ . Can I have the _____ ?
 5 A Come on, Tommy. Say hello to Auntie Mavis. Don't be _____ .
    B Hello, Auntie Mavis.

**T 8.5** Listen and check. Practise the conversations.

## LISTENING AND SPEAKING
### How did you two meet?

**1** Put the sentences in the correct order. There is more than one answer!

☐ They got married.
☐ They fell in love.
☒ Wilma and Carl met at a party.
☐ He invited her to meet his parents.
☐ They chatted for a long time.
☐ They had two children.
☐ They kissed.
☐ They got engaged.

**2** Look at the four people and discuss the questions.

The people are:
- **Vincent Banks** from America
- **Debbie Grant** from England
- **Per Olafson** from Norway
- **Rosa Randeiro** from Spain

1 Who do you think is who? Why?
2 Who do you think are husband and wife? Why?
3 How do you think they met?

**3** Read the introductions to the stories of how they met. What do you think happened next?

### LOVE ON THE INTERNET
Nowadays love on the Internet is big business. Millions try to find true love there every day. Per Olafson from Bergen in Norway, and Debbie Grant from Banbury in England, looked for love that way ...

### LOVE IN A BOTTLE
Fisherman Vincent Banks from Cape Cod in America couldn't find a wife, so he wrote a letter, put it in a bottle and threw it into the sea. Ten years later and five thousand miles away in Spain, Rosa Randeiro found the bottle on the beach ...

**4** `T 8.6` Now listen to them talking. Were your ideas correct?

**5** Answer the questions about Per and Debbie, and Vincent and Rosa.
1 When did they meet?
2 Why does Debbie like to chat on the Internet?
3 Where was Vincent's letter? What did it say?
4 Why couldn't Rosa read the letter?
5 Do both couples have children?
6 Who says these sentences? Write P, D, V, R in the boxes.
a ☐ I'm really quite shy.
☐ I was very shy.
b ☐ I find it difficult to talk to people face to face.
☐ I flew to America and we met face to face.
c ☐ I stood on something.
☐ I stood there with some flowers.
d ☐ We chatted on the Internet for a year.
☐ We wrote every week for six months.

## Speaking

**6** Imagine you are one of the people. Tell the story of how you met your husband/wife.

**7** Look at the questions. Tell a partner about you and your family.
1 Are you married or do you have a girlfriend/boyfriend? How did you meet?
2 When did your parents or grandparents meet? Where? How?

## EVERYDAY ENGLISH

### What's the date?

**1** Write the correct word next to the numbers.

| fourth | twelfth | sixth | twentieth | second | thirtieth | thirteenth |
| thirty-first | fifth | seventeenth | tenth | sixteenth | first | third | twenty-first |

1st _____   6th _____   17th _____
2nd _____   10th _____  20th _____
3rd _____   12th _____  21st _____
4th _____   13th _____  30th _____
5th _____   16th _____  31st _____

`T 8.7` Listen and practise saying the ordinals.

**2** Ask and answer questions with a partner about the months of the year.

*Which is the first month?*   *January.*

> We write: 3/4/1999 or 3 April 1999
> We say: 'The third of April, nineteen ninety-nine.'
> or 'April the third, nineteen ninety-nine.'
> Notice how we say these years:
> 1900   nineteen hundred
> 1905   nineteen oh five
> 2001   two thousand and one

**3** Practise saying these dates:
1 April   2 March   17 September   19 November   23 June
29/2/76   19/12/83   3/10/99   31/5/2000   15/7/2004

`T 8.8` Listen and check.

**4** `T 8.9` Listen and write the dates you hear.

**5** Ask and answer the questions with your partner.
1 What's the date today?
2 When did this school course start? When does it end?
3 When's Christmas Day?
4 When's Valentine's Day?
5 When's Mother's Day this year?
6 When's American Independence Day?
7 What century is it now?
8 What are the dates of public holidays in your country?
9 When were you born?
10 When's your birthday?

# 9 Food you like!

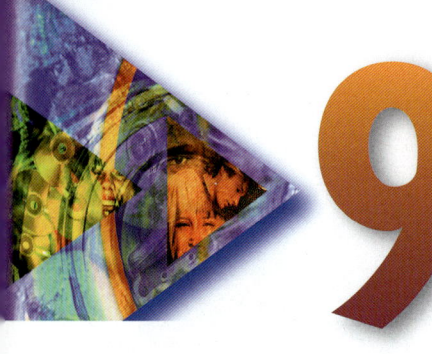

Count and uncount nouns • I like/I'd like • much/many • Food • Polite requests

**STARTER**  What's your favourite • fruit? • vegetable? • drink?
Write your answers. Compare them with a partner, then with the class.

## FOOD AND DRINK
### Count and uncount nouns

1 Match the food and drink with the pictures.

| A | B |
|---|---|
| ☐ tea | ☐ apples |
| ☐ coffee | ☐ oranges |
| ☐ wine | ☐ bananas |
| ☐ beer | ☐ strawberries |
| ☐ apple juice | ☐ peas |
| ☐ spaghetti | ☐ carrots |
| ☐ yoghurt | ☐ tomatoes |
| ☐ pizza | ☐ hamburgers |
| ☐ cheese | ☐ chips |
| ☐ chocolate | ☐ biscuits |

### GRAMMAR SPOT

1 Which list in exercise 1 has plural nouns, **A** or **B**?
2 Look at the pairs of sentences. What is the difference?

| A | B |
|---|---|
| Chocolate **is** delicious. | Strawberries **are** delicious. |
| Apple juice **is** good for you. | Apples **are** good for you. |

3 Can we count apple juice?    Can we count apples?

▶▶ Grammar Reference 9.1 p130

66  Unit 9 • Food you like!

**2** **T 9.1** Listen to Daisy and Tom talking about what they like and don't like. Tick (✓) the food and drink in the lists on p66 that they both like.

Who says these things? Write D or T.

- ☐ I don't like wine but I like beer.
- ☐ I really like apple juice. It's delicious.
- ☐ I quite like peas.
- ☐ I don't like tomatoes very much.
- ☐ I don't like cheese at all.

**3** Talk about the lists of food and drink with a partner. What do you like? What do you quite like? What don't you like?

## *I like* . . . and *I'd like* . . .

**1** **T 9.2** Read and listen to the conversation.

A Would you like some tea or coffee?
B I'd like a cold drink, please, if that's OK.
A Of course. Would you like some orange juice?
B Yes, please. I'd love some.
A And would you like a biscuit?
B No, thanks. Just orange juice is fine.

### GRAMMAR SPOT

1 Look at the sentences. What is the difference?

| A | B |
|---|---|
| Do you like tea? | Would you like some tea? |
| I like biscuits. | I'd like a biscuit. (I'd = I would) |

Which sentences, **A** or **B**, mean *Do you want/I want* . . . ?

2 Look at these sentences.
  I'd like some bananas. (plural noun)
  I'd like some mineral water. (uncount noun)

  We use *some* with both plural and uncount nouns.

3 Look at these questions.
  Would you like *some* chips?
  Can I have *some* tea?
**but** Are there *any* chips?
  Is there *any* tea?

We use *some* not *any* when we request and offer things.
We use *any* not *some* in other questions and negatives.

▶▶ Grammar Reference 9.2 p130

**2** Practise the conversation in exercise 1 with a partner. Then have similar conversations about other food and drink.

*Would you like some tea?*

*No, thanks. I don't like tea very much.*

## PRACTICE

### *a* or *some*?

**1** Write *a*, *an*, or *some*.

1. __a__ strawberry
2. __some__ fruit
3. _____ mushroom
4. _____ bread
5. _____ milk
6. _____ meat
7. _____ apple
8. _____ rice
9. _____ money
10. _____ dollar
11. _____ notebook
12. _____ homework

**2** Write *a*, *an*, or *some*.

1. _____ egg
2. _____ eggs 
3. _____ (cup of) coffee 
4. _____ coffee 
5. _____ cake 
6. _____ cake 
7. _____ ice-cream 
8. _____ ice-cream 

### Questions and answers

**3** Choose *Would/Do you like … ?* or *I/I'd like …* to complete the conversations.

1. ☐ Would you like  
   ☐ Do you like  } a cigarette?  
   No, thanks. I don't smoke.

2. ☐ Do you like  
   ☐ Would you like  } your teacher?  
   Yes. She's very nice.

3. ☐ Do you like  
   ☐ Would you like  } a drink?  
   Yes, please. Some Coke, please.

4. Can I help you?  
   ☐ Yes. I like  
   ☐ Yes. I'd like  } a book of stamps, please.

5. What sports do you do?  
   ☐ Well, I'd like  
   ☐ Well, I like  } swimming very much.

6. Excuse me, are you ready to order?  
   ☐ Yes. I like  
   ☐ Yes. I'd like  } a steak, please.

**T 9.3** Listen and check. Practise the conversations with a partner.

**4** **T 9.4** Listen to the questions and choose the correct answers.

1. ☐ I like all sorts of fruit.  
   ☐ Yes. I'd like some fruit, please.

2. ☐ I'd like a book by John Grisham.  
   ☐ I like books by John Grisham.

3. ☐ I'd like a new bike.  
   ☐ I like riding my bike.

4. ☐ I'd like a cat but not a dog.  
   ☐ I like cats, but I don't like dogs.

5. ☐ I like French wine, especially red wine.  
   ☐ We'd like a bottle of French red wine.

6. ☐ No, thanks. I don't like ice-cream.  
   ☐ I'd like some ice-cream, please.

**T 9.5** Listen and check. Practise the conversations with your partner.

# GOING SHOPPING
## some/any, much/many

**1** What is there in Miss Potts's shop? Talk about the picture. Use *some/any*, and *not much/not many*.

*There's some yoghurt.*

*There aren't any carrots.*

*There isn't much coffee.*

*There aren't many eggs.*

### GRAMMAR SPOT

1 We use *many* with count nouns in questions and negatives.
   **How many** eggs are there?
   There **aren't many** eggs.

2 We use *much* with uncount nouns in questions and negatives.
   **How much** coffee is there?
   There **isn't much** coffee.

▶▶ **Grammar Reference 9.3 p130**

**2** Ask and answer questions about what there is in the shop with a partner.

*Are there any eggs?*

*Yes, there are some, but there aren't many.*

*Is there any coffee?*

*Yes, there is some, but there isn't much.*

**3** **T 9.6** Look at Barry's shopping list. Listen and tick (✓) the things he buys. Why doesn't he buy the other things?

**THINGS TO BUY**
Orange juice   Cheese   Apples
Milk           Pizza
Coffee         Bread

Unit 9 • Food you like!   69

## PRACTICE

### much or many?

**1** Complete the questions using *much* or *many*.

1. How _____ people are there in the room?
2. How _____ money do you have in your pocket?
3. How _____ cigarettes do you smoke?
4. How _____ petrol is there in the car?
5. How _____ apples do you want?
6. How _____ wine is there in the fridge?

**2** Choose an answer for each question in exercise 1.

a. A kilo.
b. There are two bottles.
c. Ten a day.
d. Just fifty pence.
e. Twenty. Nine men and eleven women.
f. It's full.

### Check it

**3** Correct the sentences.

1. How ~~much~~ apples do you want? ✗
   **How many apples do you want?**
2. I don't like an ice-cream.
3. Can I have a bread, please?
4. I'm hungry. I like a sandwich.
5. I don't have many milk left.
6. I'd like some fruits, please.
7. How many money do you have?
8. We have lot of homework today.

### Roleplay

**4** Work with a partner. Make a shopping list each and roleplay conversations between Miss Potts and a customer.

- Can I help you?
- Here you are. Anything else?
- Yes, please. I'd like a/some …
- Yes. Can I have a/some … ?
- How much is that?
- That's … , please.

## READING AND SPEAKING
### Food around the world

**1** Which food and drink comes from your country? Which foreign food and drink is popular in your country?

**2** Can you identify any places or nationalities in the photographs? What else can you see?

**3** Read the text. Write the correct question heading for each paragraph.

WHERE DOES OUR FOOD COME FROM?
WHAT DO WE EAT?
HOW DO WE EAT?

**4** Answer the questions.

1. When did human history start? Was it about 10,000 years ago or was it about 1 million years ago?
2. Do they eat much rice in the south of China?
3. Why do the Scandinavians and the Portuguese eat a lot of fish?
4. Why don't the Germans eat much fish?
5. Which countries have many kinds of sausages?
6. How many courses are there in China?
7. How do people eat in the Middle East?
8. Why can we eat strawberries at any time of the year?

### Speaking

**5** Work in small groups and discuss these questions about your country.

1. What is a typical breakfast?
2. What does your family have for breakfast?
3. Is lunch or dinner the main meal of the day?
4. What is a typical main meal?

### Writing

**6** Write a paragraph about meals in your country.

# FOOD AROUND THE WORLD

For 99% of human history, people took their food from the world around them. They ate all that they could find, and then moved on. Then about 10,000 years ago, or for 1% of human history, people learned to farm the land and control their environment.

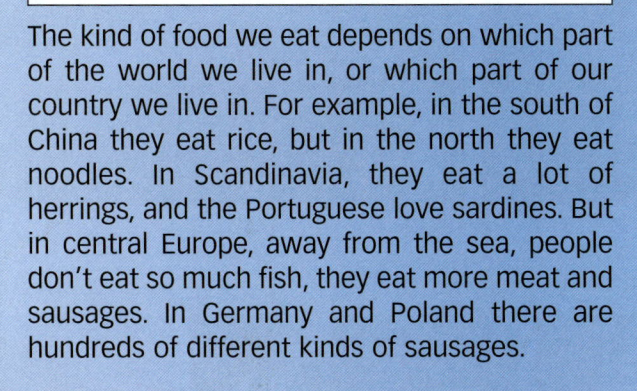

The kind of food we eat depends on which part of the world we live in, or which part of our country we live in. For example, in the south of China they eat rice, but in the north they eat noodles. In Scandinavia, they eat a lot of herrings, and the Portuguese love sardines. But in central Europe, away from the sea, people don't eat so much fish, they eat more meat and sausages. In Germany and Poland there are hundreds of different kinds of sausages.

In North America, Australia, and Europe there are two or more courses to every meal and people eat with knives and forks.

In China there is only one course, all the food is together on the table, and they eat with chopsticks.

In parts of India and the Middle East people use their fingers and bread to pick up the food.

Nowadays it is possible to transport food easily from one part of the world to the other. We can eat what we like, when we like, at any time of the year. Our bananas come from the Caribbean or Africa; our rice comes from India or the USA; our strawberries come from Chile or Spain. Food is very big business. But people in poor countries are still hungry, and people in rich countries eat too much.

## LISTENING AND SPEAKING
My favourite food

1 Look at the photographs of different food. Where is it from? Which do you like?

2 **T 9.7** Listen and match each person with their favourite food.

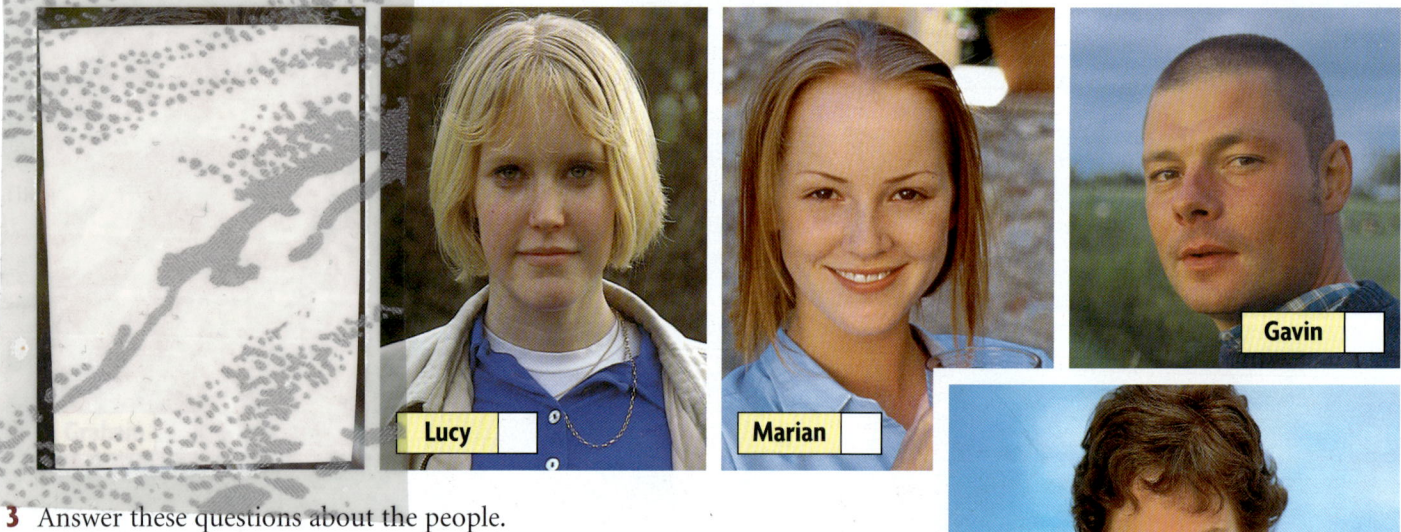

Lucy     Marian     Gavin     Sally

3 Answer these questions about the people.
Who . . . ?
- travels a lot
- likes sweet things
- had her favourite food on holiday
- prefers vegetables
- likes food from his own country

4 What's your favourite food? Is it from your country or from another country?

72  Unit 9 · Food you like!

# EVERYDAY ENGLISH
## Polite requests

**1** What can you see in the photograph?

**2** Match the questions and responses.

| | |
|---|---|
| Would you like some more carrots? | Black, no sugar, please. |
| Could you pass the salt, please? | Yes, of course. I'm glad you like it. |
| Could I have a glass of water, please? | Do you want fizzy or still? |
| Does anybody want more dessert? | Yes, please. They're delicious. |
| How would you like your coffee? | Yes, of course. Here you are. |
| This is delicious! Can you give me the recipe? | Yes, please. I'd love some. It's delicious. |
| Do you want help with the washing-up? | No, of course not. We have a dishwasher. |

> ❗ We use *Can/Could I ... ?* to ask for things.
> Can I have a glass of water?
> Could I have a glass of water?
>
> We use *Can/Could you ... ?* to ask other people to do things for us.
> Can you give me the recipe?
> Could you pass the salt?

**T 9.8** Listen and check. Practise the questions and responses with a partner.

**3** Complete these requests with *Can/Could I ... ?* or *Can/Could you ... ?*

1 _____ have a cheese sandwich, please?
2 _____ tell me the time, please?
3 _____ take me to school?
4 _____ see the menu, please?
5 _____ lend me some money, please?
6 _____ help me with my homework, please?
7 _____ borrow your dictionary, please?

**4** Practise the requests with a partner. Give an answer for each request.

> Can I have a cheese sandwich, please?

> Yes, of course. That's £1.75.

**T 9.9** Listen and compare your answers.

Unit 9 · Food you like!

# 10 Bigger and better!

Comparatives and superlatives · *have got* · Town and country · Directions 2

**STARTER**  Work with a partner. Who is taller? Who is older? Tell the class.

*I'm taller and older than Maria. She's smaller and younger than me.*

## CITY LIFE
### Comparative adjectives

1 Match an adjective with its opposite.
   Which adjectives describe life in the city?
   Which describe life in the country?

| Adjective | Opposite |
|---|---|
| fast | cheap |
| big | slow |
| dirty | friendly |
| dangerous | clean |
| noisy | quiet |
| modern | old |
| unfriendly | safe |
| exciting | boring |
| expensive | small |

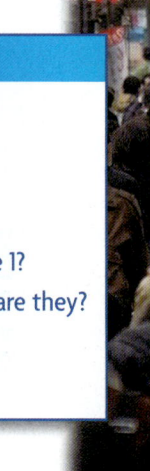

2 Make sentences comparing life in the city and country.

| | | |
|---|---|---|
| The city is | cheaper | |
| The country is | safer | than the country. |
| | noisier | than the city. |
| | dirtier | |
| | more expensive | |
| | more exciting | |

3 **T 10.1** Listen and repeat. Be careful with the sound /ə/.
   /ə/       /ə/ /ə/   /ə/  /ə/  /ə/
   *The country is cheaper and safer than the city.*

4 What do you think? Tell the class.

   *I think it's safer in the country, but the city's more exciting.*

### GRAMMAR SPOT

1 Complete these comparatives. What are the rules?
   I'm _____ (old) than you.
   Your class is _____ (noisy) than my class.
   Your car was _____ (expensive) than my car.

2 What are the comparatives of the adjectives in exercise 1?

3 The comparatives of *good* and *bad* are irregular. What are they?
   good _____      bad _____

▶▶ Grammar Reference 10.1 p131

# PRACTICE

**Much more than . . .**

1 Complete the conversations with the correct form of the adjectives.

1 A Life in the country is _slower than_ city life. (slow)
  B Yes, the city's much _faster_ . (fast)
2 A New York is _____ _____ London. (safe)
  B No, it isn't. New York is much _____ _____ . (dangerous)
3 A Paris is _____ _____ Madrid. (big)
  B No, it isn't! It's much _____ . (small)
4 A Madrid is _____ _____ _____ Rome. (expensive)
  B No, it isn't. Madrid is much _____ . (cheap)
5 A The buildings in Rome are _____ _____ _____ the buildings in New York. (modern)
  B No, they aren't. They're much _____ . (old)
6 A The Underground in London is _____ _____ the Metro in Paris. (good)
  B No! The Underground is much _____ . (bad)

**T 10.2** Listen and check. Practise with a partner.

2 Work with a partner. Compare two towns or cities that you both know. Which do you like better? Why?

# COUNTRY LIFE
*have got*

1 **T 10.3** Mel moved to Seacombe, a small country town near the sea. Read and listen to Mel's conversation with her friend Tara. Complete it with the correct adjectives.

T  Why did you leave London? You had a _____ job.
M  Yes, but I've got a _____ job here.
T  And you had a _____ flat in London.
M  Well, I've got a _____ flat here.
T  Really? How many bedrooms has it got?
M  Three. And it's got a garden. It's _____ than my flat in London and it's _____ .
T  But you haven't got any friends!
M  I've got a lot of friends here. People are much _____ than in London.
T  But the country's so _____ .
M  No, it isn't. It's much _____ _____ than London. Seacombe has got shops, a cinema, a theatre, and a park. And the air is _____ and the streets are _____ .
T  OK. Everything is _____ ! So when can I visit you?

### GRAMMAR SPOT

1 *Have* and *have got* both express possession. We often use *have got* in spoken British English.

I have a dog. = I've got a dog. (I've = I have)
He has a car. = He's got a car. (He's = He has)
Do you have a dog? = Have you got a dog?
Does she have a car? = Has she got a car?
They don't have a flat. = They haven't got a flat.
It doesn't have a garden. = It hasn't got a garden.

2 The past of both *have* and *have got* is *had*.
3 Find examples of *have got* and *had* in the conversation.

▶▶ Grammar Reference 10.2 p131

2 Practise the conversation with a partner.

Unit 10 • Bigger and better! 75

# PRACTICE

## have/have got

1 Write the sentences again, using the correct form of *have got*.

1 London has a lot of parks.
   *London's got a lot of parks.*
2 I don't have much money.
   *I haven't got much money.*
3 I have a lot of homework tonight.
4 Do you have any homework?
5 Our school has a library, but it doesn't have any computers.
6 My parents have a new stereo.
7 Does your sister have a boyfriend?
8 I don't have a problem with this exercise.

## I've got more than you!

2 Work with a partner. You are both multi-millionaires. Your teacher has more information for you. Ask and answer questions to find out who is richer!

**Millionaire A**     **Millionaire B**

*I've got four houses. How many have you got?*

*Five. I've got two in France, one in Miami, one in the Caribbean, and a castle in Scotland.*

*Well, I've got thirty cars!*

*That's nothing! I've got …*

# THE WORLD'S BEST HOTELS
## Superlative adjectives

1 Read about the three hotels.

### Claridge's
London
- 100 years old
- 292 rooms
- £315–£2,500 a night
- 35 mins Heathrow Airport
- no swimming pool

### The Mandarin Oriental
Hong Kong
- 36 years old
- 542 rooms
- £300–£2,000 a night
- 30 mins Chek Lap Kok Airport
- swimming pool

### The Plaza
New York
- 94 years old
- 812 rooms
- £200–£500 a night
- 45 mins Kennedy Airport
- no swimming pool

2 Correct the false sentences. How many correct sentences (✓) are there? What do you notice about them?

1 The Mandarin Oriental is cheaper than the Plaza. ✗
   *No, it isn't. It's more expensive.*
2 The Plaza is the cheapest. ✓
3 Claridge's is the most expensive hotel.
4 The Mandarin Oriental is older than the Plaza.
5 Claridge's is the oldest hotel.
6 The Plaza is the biggest hotel.
7 The Mandarin Oriental is smaller than Claridge's.
8 The Plaza has got a swimming pool.
9 Claridge's is nearer the airport than the Mandarin.
10 The Mandarin is the nearest to the airport.
11 The Plaza is the furthest from the airport.

3 Which is the best hotel in or near your town? What has it got?

### GRAMMAR SPOT

1 Complete these superlative sentences. What's the rule?
   The Green Palace is the _____ (cheap) hotel in New York.
   The Four Seasons is the _____ _____ (expensive).

2 Dictionaries often show irregular comparative and superlative forms of adjectives. Look at this:
   **good** /gʊd/ adj. (**better, best**)
   Complete these irregular forms:
   **bad** /bæd/ adj. ( _____ , _____ )
   **far** /fɑː/ adj. ( _____ , _____ )

▶▶ **Grammar Reference 10.1 p131**

## PRACTICE

### The biggest and best!

1 Complete the conversations using the superlative form of the adjective.

1 That house is very big.
   Yes, _it's the biggest house_ in the village.
2 Claridge's is a very expensive hotel.
   Yes, _____ in London.
3 Castle Combe is a very pretty village.
   Yes, _____ in England.
4 New York is a very cosmopolitan city.
   Yes, _____ in the world.
5 Tom Hanks is a very popular film star.
   Yes, _____ in America.
6 Miss Smith is a very funny teacher.
   Yes, _____ in our school.
7 Anna is a very intelligent student.
   Yes, _____ in the class.
8 This is a very easy exercise.
   Yes, _____ in the book.

**T 10.4** Listen and check.

2 **T 10.5** Close your books. Listen to the first lines in exercise 1 and give the answers.

### Talking about your class

3 How well do you know the other students in your class? Describe them using these adjectives and others.

   tall   small   old   young   intelligent   funny

*I think Roger is the tallest in the class. He's taller than Carl.*

*Maria's the youngest.*

*I'm the most intelligent!*

4 Write the name of your favourite film star. Read it to the class. Compare the people. Which film star is the most popular in your class?

### Check it

5 Tick (✓) the correct sentence.
   1 ☐ Yesterday was more hot than today.
     ☐ Yesterday was hotter than today.
   2 ☐ She's taller than her brother.
     ☐ She's taller that her brother.
   3 ☐ I'm the most young in the class.
     ☐ I'm the youngest in the class.
   4 ☐ Last week was busier than this week.
     ☐ Last week was busyer than this week.
   5 ☐ He hasn't got any sisters.
     ☐ He doesn't got any sisters.
   6 ☐ Do you have any bread?
     ☐ Do you got any bread?
   7 ☐ My homework is the baddest in the class.
     ☐ My homework is the worst in the class.
   8 ☐ This exercise is the most difficult in the book.
     ☐ This exercise is most difficult in the book.

## READING AND SPEAKING
### Three musical cities

1 **T 10.6** Listen to three types of music. What kind of music is it? Which music goes with which city?

   New Orleans     Vienna     Liverpool

2 Where are these cities? What do you know about them? Each sentence is about one of them. Write NO, V, or L.
   1. ☐ Its music, theatre, museums, and parks make it a popular tourist centre.
   2. ☐ It stands on the banks of the Mississippi River.
   3. ☐ It stands on the banks of the River Danube.
   4. ☐ It is an important port for travel to Ireland.
   5. ☐ In 1762, Louis XV gave it to his cousin Carlos of Spain.
   6. ☐ Its university, founded in 1365, is one of the oldest in Europe.
   7. ☐ It became an important trade centre for sugar, spices, and slaves.
   8. ☐ Many Irish immigrants live there.

3 Work in three groups.

   **Group 1** Read about **New Orleans**.
   **Group 2** Read about **Vienna**.
   **Group 3** Read about **Liverpool**.

   Which sentences in exercise 2 are about your city?

4 Answer the questions about your city.
   1. How many people live there?
   2. What is the name of its river?
   3. Why is it a tourist centre?
   4. What are some important dates in its history?
   5. Which famous people lived there?
   6. What kind of music is it famous for?
   7. What is world famous about the city?
   8. Which of these things can you do in the city you read about?
      - go by ship to Ireland
      - see Sigmund Freud's house
      - see a famous carnival
      - walk round the French Quarter
      - listen to a famous orchestra
      - visit the homes of a famous rock group

5 Find partners from the other two groups. Compare the cities, using your answers.

### Your home town

6 Write some similar information about your city, town, or village. Tell a partner or the class.

## New Orleans

New Orleans is the largest city in Louisiana, USA. It stands on the banks of the Mississippi River and is a busy port and tourist centre. Its population of about 550,000 is very cosmopolitan, with immigrants from many countries. Every year people from all over the world visit New Orleans to see its famous Mardi Gras carnival.

### Its history

In 1682 the French named Louisiana after the French King, Louis XIV. They built New Orleans in 1718. In 1762, Louis XV gave it to his cousin Carlos of Spain. Then, in 1800, it became French again until Napoleon sold it to the USA in 1803. The French Quarter in New Orleans still has many old buildings and excellent restaurants.

### Its music

New Orleans is the home of jazz. Jazz is a mixture of blues, dance songs, and hymns. Black musicians started to play jazz in the late 19th century. Louis Armstrong and Jelly Roll Morton came from the city. New Orleans is most famous for its jazz, but it also has a philharmonic orchestra.

# Vienna

Vienna, or Wien in German, is the capital of Austria. It stands on the banks of the River Danube and is the gateway between east and west Europe. Its music, theatre, museums, and parks make it a popular tourist centre. It has a population of over 1,500,000.

## Its history

Vienna has a rich history. Its university opened in 1365, and is one of the oldest in Europe. From 1558 to 1806 it was the centre of the Holy Roman Empire and it became an important cultural centre for art and learning in the 18th and 19th centuries. The famous psychiatrist, Sigmund Freud, lived and worked there.

## Its music

Vienna was the music capital of the world for many centuries. Haydn, Mozart, Beethoven, Brahms, Schubert, and the Strauss family all came to work here. It is now the home of one of the world's most famous orchestras, the Vienna Philharmonic. Its State Opera House is also world famous.

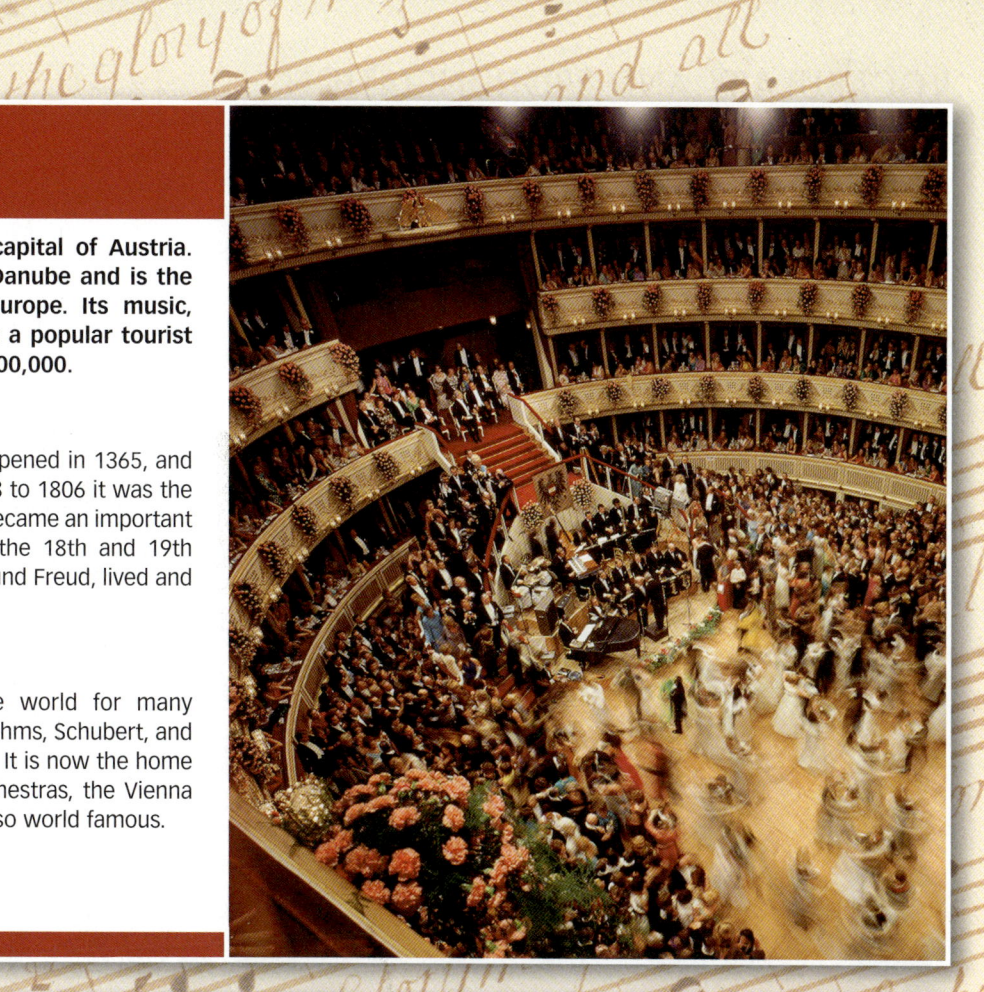

# Liverpool

Liverpool is Britain's second biggest port, after London. It stands on the banks of the River Mersey in north-west England. It is an important passenger port for travel to Ireland and many Irish immigrants live there. It has a population of nearly 500,000.

## Its history

King John named Liverpool in 1207. The city grew bigger in the 18th century, when it became an important trade centre for sugar, spices, and slaves between Africa, Britain, the Americas, and the West Indies.

## Its music

Liverpool's most famous musicians are the Beatles. In the 1960s this British rock group was popular all over the world. They had 30 top ten hits. They were all born in Liverpool and started the group there in 1959. They first played at a night club called the Cavern and then travelled the world. One of them, Paul McCartney, is now the richest musician in the world. Many tourists visit Liverpool to see the homes of the Beatles.

## VOCABULARY AND PRONUNCIATION
### Town and country words

| Town | Country | Both |
|------|---------|------|
|      |         |      |

**1** Find these words in the picture. Which things do you usually find in towns? Which in the country? Which in both? Put the words into the correct columns.

wood   park   museum   church   cathedral   farm   bridge   car park   port   factory   field   theatre
night club   lake   village   hill   mountain   cottage   building   river bank   tractor

**2** Complete the sentences with a word from exercise 1.

1. Everest is the highest _____ in the world.
2. The Golden Gate _____ in San Francisco is the longest _____ in the USA.
3. The Caspian Sea isn't a sea, it's the largest _____ in the world.
4. Rotterdam is the busiest _____ in Europe. Ships from all over the world stop there.
5. The Empire State _____ in New York was the tallest _____ in the world for over 40 years.
6. A church is much smaller than a _____ .

**3** Write these words from exercise 1.

/wʊd/ _____   /ˈθɪətə/ _____   /fɑːm/ _____   /ˈvɪlɪdʒ/ _____
/ˈfæktəri/ _____   /ˈkɒtɪdʒ/ _____   /fiːld/ _____   /tʃɜːtʃ/ _____

**T 10.7** Listen and repeat.

**4** Do you prefer the town or the country? Divide into two groups. Play the game. Which group can continue the longest?

**Group 1  A walk in the country**

Continue one after the other.

S1  I went for a walk in the country and I saw a farm.
S2  I went for a walk in the country and I saw a farm and some cows.
S3  I went for …

**Group 2  A walk in the town**

Continue one after the other.

S1  I went for a walk in the town and I saw some shops.
S2  I went for a walk in the town and I saw some shops, and a cathedral.
S3  I went for …

# EVERYDAY ENGLISH
## Directions 2

1. **T 10.8** Listen to the directions to the lake. Mark the route on the map. Then fill in the gaps.

   'Drive _____ Park Road and turn _____ . Go _____ the bridge and _____ the pub. Turn _____ up the hill, then drive _____ the hill to the river. _____ _____ after the farm and the lake is _____ _____ right. It takes twenty minutes.'

2. **T 10.9** Complete the text with the prepositions. Listen to Norman talking about his drive in the country. Check your answers.

   | along | down | into | out of | over | past | through | under | up |

## NORMAN'S DRIVE IN THE COUNTRY

Norman drove
_____ the garage,
_____ the road, and
_____ the bridge.

Then he drove
_____ the pub,
_____ the hill, and
_____ the hill.

Next he drove
_____ the river,
_____ the hedge,
and _____ the lake!

3. Cover the text. Look at the pictures and tell Norman's story.
4. Work with a partner. **Student A** Think of a place near your school. Give your partner directions, but don't say what the place is!
   **Student B** Listen to the directions. Where are you?

# 11 Looking good!

**Present Continuous • Whose? • Clothes • Words that rhyme • In a clothes shop**

**STARTER**

1 Look around the classroom. Can you see any of these clothes?

a hat   a coat   a jumper   a shirt   a T-shirt   a dress   a skirt   a jacket
a suit   trousers   jeans   shorts   shoes   trainers   boots

2 What are you wearing?
What is your teacher wearing?
Tell the class.

*I'm wearing blue jeans and a white T-shirt.*

*You're wearing a dress.*

## DESCRIBING PEOPLE
### Present Continuous

1 Look at the photographs. Describe the people.
Who ... ?
• is tall   • isn't very tall   • is pretty   • good-looking   • handsome

Who's got ... ?

| long  |      |       |      |
|-------|------|-------|------|
| short |      | blue  |      |
| fair  | hair | brown | eyes |
| dark  |      |       |      |
| grey  |      |       |      |

*Becca's got dark hair and brown eyes.*

2 What are they doing?
Who ... ?
• is smiling       • is cooking
• is talking       • is standing up
• is writing       • is playing
• is laughing      • is running
• is eating        • is sitting down

*Jane's smiling.*   *Angela's running.*

3 What are they wearing?

*Rudi's wearing a brown T-shirt.*

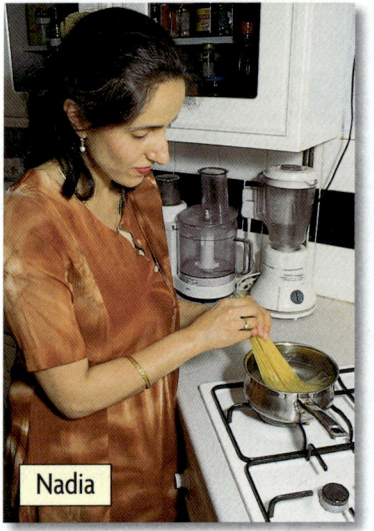

Ruth, Cathy, and Jane

Nadia

Rudi

82 Unit 11 • Looking good!

## GRAMMAR SPOT

1 *Am/is/are* + adjective describes people and things.
   She **is** young/tall/pretty.

2 *Am/is/are* + verb + *-ing* describes activities happening *now*.
   Complete the table.

   | I        | _____ | learning English.      |
   |----------|-------|------------------------|
   | You      | _____ | sitting in a classroom.|
   | He/She   | _____ | listening to the teacher.|
   | We       | _____ |                        |
   | They     | _____ |                        |

   This is the Present Continuous tense. What are the questions and the negatives?

3 What is the difference between these sentences?
   He speaks Spanish.
   He's speaking Spanish.

▶▶ Grammar Reference 11.1 and 11.2 p132

## PRACTICE

### Who is it?

1 Work with a partner.

   **Student A** Choose someone in the classroom, but don't say who.
   **Student B** Ask *Yes/No* questions to find out who it is!

   *Is it a girl?*   *Yes, it is.*

   *Is she sitting near the window?*   *No, she isn't.*

   *Has she got fair hair?*   *No, she hasn't.*

2 Write sentences that are true for you at the moment.
   1 I/wearing a jacket
   **I'm not wearing a jacket, I'm wearing a jumper.**
   2 I/wearing jeans
   3 I/standing up
   4 I/looking out of the window
   5 It/raining
   6 teacher/writing
   7 We/working hard
   8 I/chewing gum

   Tell a partner about yourself.

## Who's at the party?

**3** [T 11.1] Oliver is at Monica's party, but he doesn't know anyone. Monica is telling him about the other guests. Listen and write the names above the people.

**4** Listen again and complete the table.

|  | Present Continuous | Present Simple |
|---|---|---|
| Harry | He's sitting down and he's talking to Mandy. | He works in LA. |
| Mandy |  |  |
| Fiona |  |  |
| George |  |  |
| Roz and Sam |  |  |

**5** Work with a partner. Look at the pictures of a party from your teacher. Don't show your picture! There are *ten* differences. Talk about the pictures to find them.

*In my picture three people are dancing.*

*In my picture four people are dancing.*

*There's a girl with fair hair.*

*Is she wearing a black dress?*

# A DAY IN THE PARK
## Whose is it?

**1** Find these things in the picture.

> a baseball cap   a bike   a football   roller blades
> trainers   a dog   sunglasses   a radio   a skateboard
> an umbrella   flowers

**2** [T 11.2] Listen to the questions. Complete the answers with *his*, *hers*, or *theirs*.

1 Whose is the baseball cap?    It's ____ .
2 Whose are the roller blades?  They're ____ .
3 Whose is the dog?             It's ____ .

Practise the questions and answers with a partner. Then ask about about the other things in exercise 1.

**3** Give something of yours to the teacher. Ask and answer questions about the objects. Use these possessive pronouns.

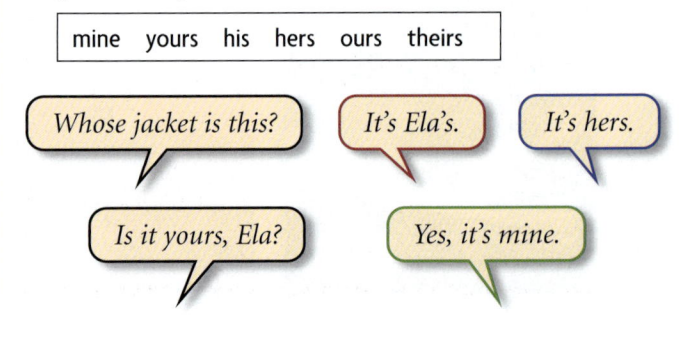

> mine   yours   his   hers   ours   theirs

*Whose jacket is this?*   *It's Ela's.*   *It's hers.*

*Is it yours, Ela?*   *Yes, it's mine.*

84   Unit 11 · Looking good!

## PRACTICE

### who's or whose?

**1** Choose the correct word. Compare your answers with a partner.

1. I like *your / yours* house.
2. *Ours / Our* house is smaller than *their / theirs*.
3. And *their / theirs* garden is bigger than *our / ours*, too.
4. *My / Mine* children are older than *her / hers*.
5. *Whose / Who's* talking to *your / yours* sister?
6. This book isn't *my / mine*. Is it *your / yours*?
7. '*Whose / Who's* dictionary is this?' 'It's *his / him*.'
8. '*Whose / Who's* going to the party tonight?' 'I'm not.'
9. '*Whose / Who's* dog is running round *our / ours* garden?'

**2** **T 11.3** Listen to the sentences.
If the word is *Whose?* shout **1**! If the word is *Who's?* shout **2**!

### What a mess!

**3** **T 11.4** The house is in a mess! Complete the conversation. Listen and check.

A  _____ is this tennis racket?
B  It's _____ .
A  What's it doing here?
B  I'm _____ tennis this afternoon.

> ❗ The Present Continuous can also describe activities happening in the near future.
> **I'm playing** tennis this afternoon.
> **We're having** pizza for dinner tonight.

**4** Make more conversations with a partner.

1. these football boots? / John's / playing football later
2. these ballet shoes? / Mary's / going dancing tonight
3. this suitcase? / mine / going on holiday tomorrow
4. this coat? / Jane's / going for a walk soon
5. this plane ticket? / Jo's / flying to Rome this afternoon
6. all these glasses? / ours / having a party tonight

### Check it

**5** Correct the sentences.

1. Alice is tall and she's got long, black hairs.
2. Who's boots are these?
3. I'm wearing a jeans.
4. Look at Roger. He stands next to Jeremy.
5. He's work in a bank. He's the manager.
6. What is drinking Suzie?
7. Whose that man in the garden?
8. Where you going tonight?
9. What you do after school today?

### GRAMMAR SPOT

1. Complete the table.

| Subject | Object | Adjective | Pronoun |
|---------|--------|-----------|---------|
| I | me | my | mine |
| You | you | ____ | ____ |
| He | ____ | his | ____ |
| She | ____ | ____ | hers |
| We | us | our | ____ |
| They | them | ____ | ____ |

2. *Whose . . . ?* asks about possession.
Whose hat is this?
Whose is this hat?        It's mine. = It's my hat.
Whose is it?

3. **Careful!**
Who's your teacher?        Who's = Who is

▶▶ Grammar Reference 11.3 p132

Unit 11 · Looking good!

## LISTENING AND SPEAKING
### What a wonderful world!

1 Look out of the window. What can you see? Buildings? Hills? Fields? Can you see any people? What are they doing? Describe the scene.

2 These words often go together. Match them. Can you see any of them in the photos?

| | |
|---|---|
| shake | clouds |
| babies | roses |
| sunny | hands |
| starry | trees |
| blue | day |
| red | night |
| white | cry |
| green | bloom |
| flowers | of the rainbow |
| colours | skies |

3 Read the song by Louis Armstrong. Can you complete any of the lines? Many of the words are from exercise 2.

4 **T 11.5** Listen and complete the song.

### What do you think?

Make a list of things that you think are wonderful in the world. Compare your list with a partner.

# What a Wonderful World

I see \_\_\_\_ of green
red \_\_\_\_ too
I see them \_\_\_\_ for me and you
and I think to myself
what a wonderful world.
I see \_\_\_\_ of blue
and \_\_\_\_ of white
the bright \_\_\_\_ day
and the dark \_\_\_\_ night
and I think to myself
what a wonderful world.
The \_\_\_\_ of the rainbow
so pretty in the sky
are also on the \_\_\_\_
of the people going by.
I see friends shaking \_\_\_\_
saying, 'How do you do?'
They're really saying
'I \_\_\_\_ you.'
I hear \_\_\_\_ cry
I watch them grow.
They'll \_\_\_\_ much more
than you'll ever know
and I think to myself
what a wonderful world.
Yes, I think to myself
what a wonderful world.

## VOCABULARY AND PRONUNCIATION
### Words that rhyme

1 Match the words that rhyme.

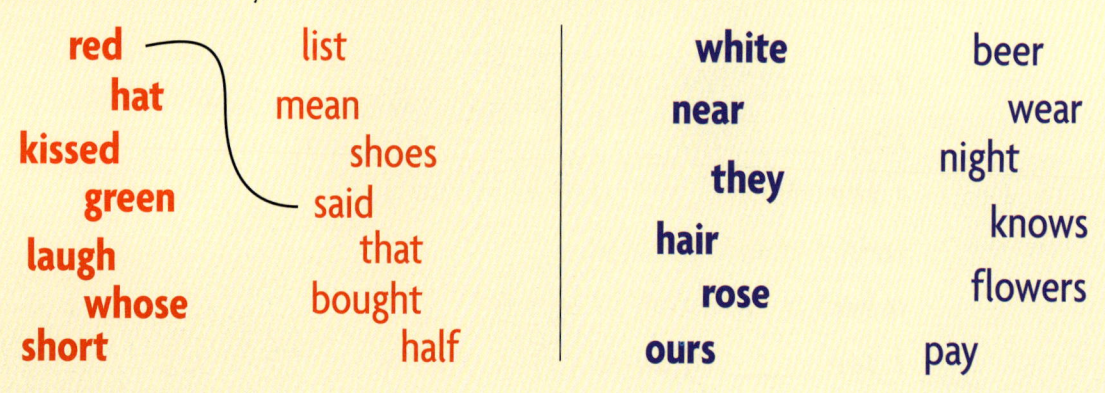

| | | | |
|---|---|---|---|
| red | list | white | beer |
| hat | mean | near | wear |
| kissed | shoes | they | night |
| green | said | hair | knows |
| laugh | that | rose | flowers |
| whose | bought | ours | pay |
| short | half | | |

(red — said)

2 Write two of the words on each line according to the sound.

**Vowels**
1 /e/ _red_  _said_
2 /æ/ _____ _____
3 /ɪ/ _____ _____
4 /iː/ _____ _____
5 /ɑː/ _____ _____
6 /uː/ _____ _____
7 /ɔː/ _____ _____

**Diphthongs**
1 /aɪ/ _white_ _____
2 /ɪə/ _____ _____
3 /eɪ/ _____ _____
4 /eə/ _____ _____
5 /əʊ/ _____ _____
6 /aʊ/ _____ _____

**T 11.6** Listen and check.

3 Can you add any more words to the lists? Practise saying the words in rhyming pairs.

### Tongue twisters

4 **T 11.7** Tongue twisters are sentences that are difficult to say. They are good pronunciation practice. Listen, then try saying these quickly to a partner.

1 Four fine fresh fish for you

2 Six silly sisters selling shiny shoes

3 If a dog chews shoes, whose shoes does he choose?

4 I'm looking back,
To see if she's looking back,
To see if I'm looking back,
To see if she's looking back at me!

5 Choose two tongue twisters and learn them. Say them to the class.

# EVERYDAY ENGLISH
## In a clothes shop

1 Read the lines of conversation in a clothes shop. Who says them, the customer or the shop assistant?
Write **C** or **SA**.

a ☐ Can I help you? **SA**

b ☐ Oh yes. I like that one much better. Can I try it on? **C**

c ☐ £39.99. How do you want to pay?

d ☐ Yes, please. I'm looking for a shirt to go with my new suit.

e ☐ Blue.

f ☐ Yes, of course. The changing rooms are over there.

g ☐ OK. I'll take the white. How much is it?

h ☐ Can I pay by credit card?

i ☐ What colour are you looking for?

j ☐ No, it isn't the right blue.

k ☐ No, it's a bit too big. Have you got a smaller size?

l ☐ That's the last blue one we've got, I'm afraid. But we've got it in white.

m ☐ Well, what about this one? It's a bit darker blue.

n ☐ What about this one? Do you like this?

o ☐ Is the size OK?

p ☐ Credit card's fine. Thank you very much.

2 Can you match any lines?

> *Can I help you?*

> *Yes, please. I'm looking for a shirt to go with my new suit.*

> *What about this one? Do you like this?*

> *No, it's not the right blue.*

3 Work with a partner and put the all the lines in the correct order.

**T 11.8** Listen and check.

4 Practise the conversation with your partner. Make more conversations in a clothes shop. Buy some different clothes.

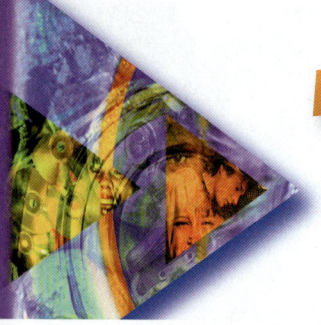

# 12 Life's an adventure!

going to future • Infinitive of purpose • The weather • Making suggestions

**STARTER**

1 How many sentences can you make?

| | |
|---|---|
| I'm going to Florida | soon. |
| I went to Florida | when I was a student. |
| | next month. |
| | in a year's time. |
| | two years ago. |
| | when I retire. |

2 Make similar true sentences about you. Tell the class.

## FUTURE PLANS
*going to*

**When I grow up ...**

1 Rosie and her teacher Miss Bishop both have plans for the future.
Read their future plans. Which do you think are Rosie's? Which are Miss Bishop's? Write **R** or **MB**.
1. [R] I'm going to be a ballet dancer.
2. [ ] I'm going to travel all over the world.
3. [ ] I'm going to learn Russian.
4. [ ] I'm going to learn to drive.
5. [ ] I'm going to open a school.
6. [ ] I'm not going to marry until I'm thirty-five.
7. [ ] I'm not going to wear skirts and blouses.
8. [ ] I'm going to wear jeans and T-shirts all the time.
9. [ ] I'm going to write a book.
10. [ ] I'm going to become a TV star.

**T 12.1** Listen and check. Were you correct?

2 Talk first about Rosie, then about Miss Bishop. Use the ideas in exercise 1.

*Rosie's going to be a ballet dancer.*

*She's going to ...*   *She isn't going to ...*

Which two plans are the same for both of them?

*They're both going to ...*

Rosie, aged 11

90 Unit 12 • Life's an adventure!

**3** **T 12.2** Listen and repeat the questions and answers about Rosie.

*Is she going to be a ballet dancer?*

*Yes, she is.*

*What's she going to do?*

*Travel all over the world.*

### GRAMMAR SPOT

1 The verb *to be* + *going to* expresses future plans. Complete the table.

| I | _____ | |
| You | _____ | |
| He/She | _____ | going to leave tomorrow. |
| We | _____ | |
| They | _____ | |

What are the questions and the negatives?

2 Is there much difference between these two sentences?
I'm leaving tomorrow.   I'm going to leave tomorrow.

▶▶ Grammar Reference 12.1 p133

*When I retire ...*

Miss Bishop, aged 59

## PRACTICE

### Questions about Rosie

**1** With a partner, make more questions about Rosie. Then match them with an answer.

**Questions**
1 Why/she/learn French and Russian?
2 When/marry?
3 How many children/have?
4 How long/work?
5 What/teach?

**Answers**
a Until she's seventy-five.
b Two.
c Dancing.
d Not until she's thirty-five.
e Because she wants to dance in Paris and Moscow.

**2** **T 12.3** Listen and check. Practise the questions and answers with your partner.

### Questions about you

**3** Are you going to do any of these things after the lesson? Ask and answer the questions with a partner.
1 watch TV

*Are you going to watch TV?*

*Yes, I am./No, I'm not.*

2 have a coffee
3 catch a bus
4 eat in a restaurant
5 meet some friends
6 cook a meal
7 go shopping
8 wash your hair
9 do your homework

**4** Tell the class some of the things you and your partner *are* or are *not* going to do.

*We're both going to have coffee.*

*I'm going to catch a bus, but Anna isn't. She's going to walk home.*

Unit 12 • Life's an adventure!  91

**I'm going to sneeze!**

> We also use *going to* when we can see *now* that something is sure to happen in the future.

**5** What is going to happen? Use these verbs.

| have   sneeze   win   jump   be late   kiss   rain   fall |

1  It _____
2  You _____
3  I _____
4  They _____
5  She _____
6  He _____
7  He _____
8  They _____

**6** Put a sentence from exercise 5 into each gap.

1  Take an umbrella. _____ .
2  Look at the time! _____ for the meeting.
3  Anna's running very fast. _____ .
4  Look! Jack's on the wall! _____ .
5  Look at that man! _____ .
6  _____ . It's due next month.
7  There's my sister and her boyfriend! Yuk! _____ .
8  'Oh dear. _____ . Aaattishooo!' 'Bless you!'

**T 12.4** Listen and check.

# I WANT TO TRAVEL THE WORLD
## Infinitive of purpose

**1** Match a country or a city with an activity. What can you see in the photographs?

| | |
|---|---|
| Holland | visit the pyramids |
| Spain | fly over the Grand Canyon |
| Moscow | see Mount Fuji |
| Egypt | see the tulips |
| Kenya | walk along the Great Wall |
| India | watch flamenco dancing |
| China | take photographs of the lions |
| Japan | sunbathe on Copacabana beach |
| the USA | walk in Red Square |
| Rio | visit the Taj Mahal |

**2** Miss Bishop is going to visit all these countries. She is telling her friend, Harold, about her plans. Read their conversation and complete the last sentence.

**Miss Bishop**  First I'm going to Holland.
**Harold**  Why?
**Miss Bishop**  To see the tulips, of course!
**Harold**  Oh yes! How wonderful! Where are you going after that?
**Miss Bishop**  Well, then I'm going to Spain to …

**T 12.5** Listen and check. Practise the conversation with a partner.

### GRAMMAR SPOT

1  With the verbs *to go* and *to come*, we usually use the Present Continuous for future plans.
   I'm going to Holland tomorrow.
   ✗ I'm going to go to Holland tomorrow.
   She's coming this evening.
   ✗ She's going to come this evening.

2  Do these sentences mean the same?
   I'm going to Holland to see the tulips.
   I'm going to Holland because I want to see the tulips.
   The infinitive can tell us why something happens.
   I'm going to America to learn English.

▶▶ Grammar Reference 12.2 p133

## PRACTICE

### Roleplay

1 Work with a partner. **Student A** is Harold, **Student B** is Miss Bishop. Ask and answer questions about the places.

| Harold | Why are you going to Holland? |
|---|---|
| Miss Bishop | To see the tulips, of course! |
| Harold | How wonderful! |

2 Talk about Miss Bishop's journey. Use *first, then, next, after that*.

*First she's going to Holland to see the tulips. Then she's ...*

### Why and When?

3 Write down the names of some places you went to in the past. Ask and answer questions about the places with a partner.

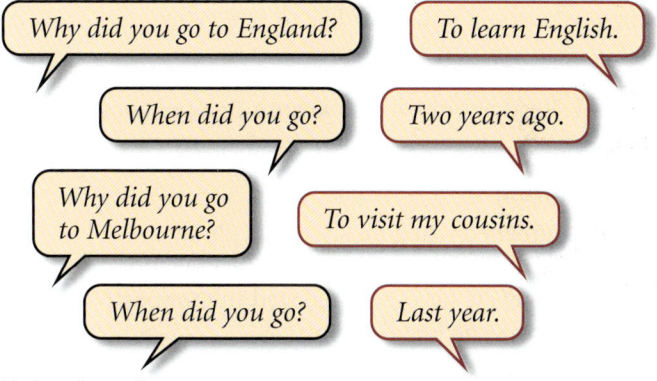

*Why did you go to England?*   *To learn English.*

*When did you go?*   *Two years ago.*

*Why did you go to Melbourne?*   *To visit my cousins.*

*When did you go?*   *Last year.*

Tell the class about your partner.

4 Write down the names of some places you are going to in the *future* and do the same.

*Why are you going to Paris?*   *To go shopping.*

*When are you going?*   *In two weeks' time.*

### Check it

5 Tick (✓) the correct sentence.
1. ☐ Is going to rain.
   ☐ It's going to rain.
2. ☐ Do you wash your hair this evening?
   ☐ Are you going to wash your hair this evening?
3. ☐ She's going to have a baby.
   ☐ She's going to has a baby.
4. ☐ I'm going to the Post Office to buy some stamps.
   ☐ I'm going to the Post Office for buy some stamps.
5. ☐ I'm going home early this evening.
   ☐ I'm go home early this evening.
6. ☐ I opened the window to get some fresh air.
   ☐ I opened the window for to get some fresh air.

Unit 12 • Life's an adventure!   93

## READING AND SPEAKING
### Living dangerously

**1** Match a verb with a noun or phrase.

| | |
|---|---|
| have | sick |
| win | an accident |
| feel | in water |
| float | top marks |
| get | a race |

**2** Which of these sports do you think is the most dangerous? Put them in order 1–6. 1 is the *most* dangerous. Compare your ideas with a partner and then the class.

☐ skiing ☐ football ☐ motor racing
☐ windsurfing ☐ golf ☐ sky-diving

**3** Look at the photos of Clem Quinn and Sue Glass. Which of their sports would you most like to try? Why?

Work in two groups.

**Group A** Read about Clem.   **Group B** Read about Sue.

Answer the questions about your person. Check your answers with your group.

1 What happened when he/she was a child?
2 What job did he/she do when she/he grew up?
3 How did he/she become interested in the sport?
4 Why does he/she like the sport?
5 Does he/she think it is a dangerous sport?
6 Does he/she teach the sport?
7 What are his/her future plans?
8 When is he/she going to stop doing it?
9 These numbers are in your text. What do they refer to?
   5   6   20   100

**4** Work with a partner from the other group. Compare Clem and Sue, using your answers.

### Interviews

**1** **Group A** You are Clem. Make questions about Sue.
1 Why/not like driving?
2 Why/Julian Swayland take you to Brands Hatch?
3 Why/do well on the motor racing course?
4 Why/stop motor racing?
5 What/do next year?

**Group B** You are Sue. Make questions about Clem.
1 What/do when you were five?
2 When/do your first parachute jump?
2 Why /move to the country?
3 Why/love sky-diving?
4 What/do next July?

**2** Work with a partner from the other group. Interview each other.

## Clem Quinn
### SKY-DIVER

**Clem Quinn** was always interested in flying. When he was five, he tried to fly by jumping off the garden shed with a golf umbrella, but when he grew up he didn't become a pilot, he became a taxi driver. Then 20 years ago he did a parachute jump and loved it. He decided that being a taxi driver in London was a lot more dangerous than jumping out of a plane, so he moved to the country to learn parachute jumping and sky-diving. He is now a full-time teacher of sky-diving. He says:

'I love sky-diving because the world looks so good – blue sky, green fields, white clouds. You float through the air, it's like floating in water. You can see forever, all the way to the French coast. The views are fantastic. You can forget all your worries. People think it is dangerous but it's very safe. Football is much more dangerous. Footballers often have accidents. When did you last hear of a sky-diving accident? Next July I'm going to do a sky-dive with 100 people from six planes. That's a record. I'm never going to retire. I'm going to jump out of planes until I'm an old man.'

## Sue Glass

### RACING DRIVER

**Sue Glass** had a car accident when she was eight so she didn't like driving. When she grew up this was a problem, because she got a job with a car company. Then six years ago she met Julian Swayland, a racing driver, and she told him she was afraid of cars. He wanted to help, so he took her to Brands Hatch, a Grand Prix racing circuit. He drove her round corners at 100 mph and she loved it. Then she heard about a special motor racing course. She did the course with five men and was amazed when she got top marks. She says:

'I think I did well because I listened to everything the teacher said. I needed to because I was so afraid. The men often didn't listen. The best moment was my first championship race. I didn't win but I came fourth. I beat 20 men. I love the excitement of motor racing but it's a dangerous sport and I'm always very frightened. In fact I stopped doing it a year ago, because I got so nervous before each race, I felt really sick. I'm not going to race again, I'm going to teach other people to drive. I'm going to open a driving school next year.'

## VOCABULARY AND SPEAKING
### The weather

1 Match the words and symbols.

   sunny   rainy   windy   snowy   cloudy   foggy

   Which symbols can the following adjectives go with?

   hot   warm   cold   cool   wet   dry

2 **T 12.6** Listen and complete the answers.

   'What's the weather like today?'   'It's _____ and _____ .'
   'What was it like yesterday?'   'Oh, it was _____ and _____ .'
   'What's it going to be like tomorrow?'   'I think it's going to be _____ .'

   > ! The question *What . . . like?* asks for a description.
   >    *What's the weather like?* = Tell me about the weather.

   Practise the questions and answers. Ask and answer about the weather where *you* are today, yesterday, and tomorrow.

3 Work with a partner. Find out about the weather round the world yesterday.

   **Student A** Look at the information on this page.
   **Student B** Look at the information from your teacher.

   Ask and answer questions to complete the information.

   *What was the weather like in Athens?*

   *It was sunny and warm. 18 degrees.*

   ### WORLD WEATHER: NOON YESTERDAY

   |  |  | °C |
   |---|---|---|
   | Athens | S | 18 |
   | Berlin | R | 7 |
   | Bombay | ___ | ___ |
   | Edinburgh | C | 5 |
   | Geneva | ___ | ___ |
   | Hong Kong | S | 29 |
   | Lisbon | ___ | ___ |
   | London | R | 10 |
   | Los Angeles | ___ | ___ |
   | Luxor | S | 40 |
   | Milan | ___ | ___ |
   | Moscow | Sn | –1 |
   | Oslo | ___ | ___ |

   S = sunny
   C = cloudy
   Fg = foggy
   R = rainy
   Sn = snowy

4 Which city was the hottest? Which was the coldest? Which month do you think it is?

## EVERYDAY ENGLISH

### Making suggestions

1. Make a list of things you can do in good weather and things you can do in bad weather. Compare your list with a partner.

| Good weather | Bad weather |
|---|---|
| go to the beach | watch TV |
|  |  |
|  |  |
|  |  |

2. **T 12.7** Read and listen to the beginning of two conversations. Complete B's suggestions.

   1  **A** It's a lovely day! What shall we do?
      **B** Let's _____ !

   2  **A** It's raining again! What shall we do?
      **B** Let's _____ and _____ .

   > 1  We use *shall* to ask for and make suggestions.
   >    What shall we do?
   >    Shall we go swimming? = I suggest that we go swimming.
   > 2  We use *Let's* to make a suggestion for everyone.
   >    Let's go! = I suggest that we all go. (Let's = Let us)
   >    Let's have a pizza!

3. Match these lines with the two conversations in exercise 2. Put them in the correct order to complete the conversations.

   Well, let's go to the beach.          Oh no! We watched a video last night.
   OK. Which film do you want to see?    OK. I'll get my swimming costume.
   Oh no! It's too hot to play tennis.   Well, let's go to the cinema.

   **T 12.8** Listen and check. Practise the conversations with your partner.

4. Have more conversations suggesting what to do when the weather is good or bad. Use your lists of activities in exercise 1 to help you.

Unit 12 • Life's an adventure!  97

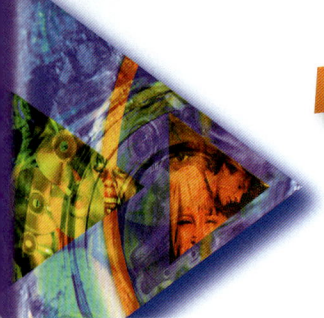

# 13 How terribly clever!

Question forms • Adverbs and adjectives • Describing feelings • Catching a train

**STARTER**

1 Match a question word with an answer.
2 Look at the answers. What do you think the story is?

| | |
|---|---|
| When . . . ? | Six. |
| Where . . . ? | 1991. |
| What . . . ? | Paris. |
| Who . . . ? | Because I love him. |
| Why . . . ? | John. |
| Which . . . ? | Some roses. |
| How . . . ? | £25. |
| How much . . . ? | The red ones. |
| How many . . . ? | By plane. |

## A QUIZ
### Question words

1 Work in groups and answer the quiz.
2 **T 13.1** Listen and check your answers. Listen carefully to the intonation of the questions.

> **GRAMMAR SPOT**
>
> 1 Underline all the question words in the quiz.
> 2 Make *two* questions for each of these statements, one with a question word and one without.
>
>   I live in London. (where)
>   'Where do you live?' 'In London.'
>   'Do you live in London?' 'Yes, I do.'
>   1 She's wearing jeans. (what)
>   2 She works in the bank. (where)
>   3 He's leaving tomorrow. (when)
>   4 I visited my aunt. (who)
>   5 We came by taxi. (how)
>   6 They're going to have a party. (why)
> 3 What are the short answers to the questions?
>
> ▶▶ Grammar Reference 13.1 p133

3 In groups, write some general knowledge questions. Ask the class!

## GENERAL KN

1 When did the first man walk on the moon?
  a 1961   b 1965   c 1969

2 Where are the Andes mountains?

3 Who did Mother Teresa look after?

4 Who won the last World Cup?

5 How many American states are there?

6 How much does an African elephant weigh?
  a 3–5 tonnes   b 5–7 tonnes   c 7–9 tonnes

7 How far is it from London to New York?

  a 6,000 kilometres

  b 9,000 kilometres

  c 12,000 kilometres

# PRACTICE

## Questions and answers

1 Look at the question words in **A** and the answers in **C**. Choose the correct question from **B**.

| A | B | C |
|---|---|---|
| Where<br>What<br>When<br>Who<br>Why<br>Which one<br>How<br>How much<br>How many | did you buy?<br>did you go?<br>did you go with?<br>did you pay? | To the shops.<br>A new jacket.<br>This morning.<br>A friend from work.<br>To buy some new clothes.<br>The black, leather one.<br>We drove.<br>£120.99.<br>Only one. |

## KNOWLEDGE QUIZ

8 How old was Princess Diana when she died?
   **a** 33   **b** 36   **c** 39

9 What languages do Swiss people speak?

10 What did Marconi invent in 1901?

11 What sort of music did Louis Armstrong play?
   **a** Jazz   **b** Blues   **c** Rock 'n' roll

12 What happens at the end of *Romeo and Juliet*?

13 What happened in Europe in 1939?

14 Why do birds migrate?

15 Which was the first country to have TV?
   **a** Britain   **b** the USA   **c** Russia

16 Which language has the most words?
   **a** French   **b** Chinese   **c** English

## Listening and pronunciation

2 **T 13.2** Tick (✓) the sentence you hear.
   1 ☐ Where do you want to go?
     ☐ Why do you want to go?
   2 ☐ How is she?
     ☐ Who is she?
   3 ☐ Where's he staying?
     ☐ Where's she staying?
   4 ☐ Why did they come?
     ☐ Why didn't they come?
   5 ☐ How old was she?
     ☐ How old is she?
   6 ☐ Does he play the guitar?
     ☐ Did he play the guitar?
   7 ☐ Where did you go at the weekend?
     ☐ Where do you go at the weekend?

## Asking about you

3 Put the words in the correct order to make questions.

   1 like learning do English you?
   _____
   2 do you night what did last?
   _____
   3 languages mother many does how your speak?
   _____
   4 last go you shopping did when?
   _____
   5 football which you do team support?
   _____
   6 come car today school by you to did?
   _____
   7 much do weigh you how?
   _____
   8 usually who sit you do next class in to?
   _____
   9 English want learn to you do why?
   _____

4 Work with a partner. Ask and answer the questions.

# DO IT CAREFULLY!
## Adverbs and adjectives

1 Are the words in *italics* adjectives or adverbs?
   1 Smoking is a *bad* habit.
     The team played *badly* and lost the match.
   2 Please listen *carefully*.
     Jane's a *careful* driver.
   3 The homework was *easy*.
     Peter's very good at tennis. He won the game *easily*.
   4 I know the Prime Minister *well*.
     My husband's a *good* cook.
   5 It's a *hard* life.
     Teachers work *hard* and don't earn much money.

> ### GRAMMAR SPOT
> 1 Look at these sentences.
>    Lunch is a quick meal for many people.
>    (*quick* = adjective. It describes a noun.)
>    I ate my lunch quickly.
>    (*quickly* = adverb. It describes a verb.)
> 2 How do we make regular adverbs? What happens when the adjective ends in *-y*?
> 3 There are two irregular adverbs in exercise 1. Find them.
>
> ▶▶ Grammar Reference 13.2 p133

2 Match the verbs or phrases with an adverb. Usually more than one answer is possible. Which are the irregular adverbs?

| | |
|---|---|
| get up | slowly |
| walk | quietly |
| work | early |
| run | fluently |
| speak | carefully |
| speak English | easily |
| pass the exam | hard |
| do your homework | fast/quickly |

# PRACTICE
## Order of adjectives/adverbs

1 Put the adjective in brackets in the correct place in the sentence. Where necessary, change the adjective to an adverb.
   1 We had a holiday in Spain, but unfortunately we had weather. (terrible)
   2 Maria dances. (good)
   3 When I saw the accident, I phoned the police. (immediate)
   4 Don't worry. Justin is a driver. (careful)
   5 Jean-Pierre is a Frenchman. He loves food, wine, and rugby. (typical)
   6 Please speak. I can't understand you. (slow)
   7 We had a test today. (easy)
   8 We all passed. (easy)
   9 You speak English. (good)

## Telling a story

2 Complete these sentences in a suitable way.
   1 It started to rain. **Fortunately** …
   2 Peter invited me to his party. **Unfortunately** …
   3 I was fast asleep when **suddenly** …
   4 I saw a man with a gun outside the bank. **Immediately** …

3 **T 13.3** Look at the picture and listen to a man describing what happened to him in the middle of the night. Number the adverbs in the order you hear them.

☐ quickly
☐ quietly
☐ slowly
☐ immediately
☐ carefully
☐ suddenly
☐ fortunately
☐ really

4 Work with a partner and tell the story again. Use the order of the adverbs to help you.

## Check it

5 Each sentence has a mistake. Find it and correct it.
   1 Where does live Anna's sister?
   2 The children came into the classroom noisyly.
   3 What means *whistle*?
   4 I always work hardly.
   5 Do you can help me, please?
   6 When is going Peter on holiday?

# VOCABULARY
## Describing feelings

**1** Match the feelings to the pictures.

| bored   tired   worried   excited   annoyed   interested |

**2** Match the feelings and reasons to make sentences.

| | Feelings | | Reasons |
|---|---|---|---|
| I am | bored<br>tired<br>worried<br>excited<br>annoyed<br>interested | because | I'm going on holiday tomorrow.<br>we have a good teacher.<br>I worked very hard today.<br>I can't find my keys.<br>I have nothing to do.<br>I want to go to the party but I can't. |

> ❗ Some adjectives can end in both *-ed* and *-ing*.
> The book was <u>interesting</u>.
> I was <u>interested</u> in the book.
> The lesson was <u>boring</u>.
> The students were <u>bored</u>.

**3** Complete each sentence with the correct adjective.

1 **excited, exciting**
   Life in New York is very …
   The football fans were very …

2 **tired, tiring**
   The marathon runners were very …
   That game of tennis was very …

3 **annoyed, annoying**
   The child's behaviour was really …
   The teacher was … when nobody did the homework.

4 **worried, worrying**
   The news is very …
   Everybody was very … when they heard the news.

**4** Answer your teacher's questions using adjectives from exercises 1 and 2.

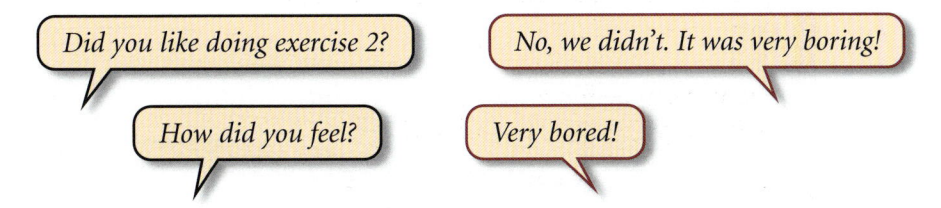

*Did you like doing exercise 2?*   *No, we didn't. It was very boring!*

*How did you feel?*   *Very bored!*

Unit 13 • How terribly clever!   101

## READING AND LISTENING
### A story in a story

1. Think about when you were a small child. Did your parents tell you stories? Which was your favourite story? Tell the class.

2. Look at the first picture. Who do you think the people on the train are? Do they know each other?

3. **T 13.4** Read and listen to part one of the story.

4. Answer the questions.
   1. Who are the people on the train?
   2. What does Cyril ask questions about?
   3. Why does the aunt tell the children a story?
   4. What is the story about?
   5. Do the children like the story?
   6. Why does the young man start speaking?
   7. Which of these adjectives best describe the people? Write them in the correct column.

   | quiet noisy badly-behaved tired worried bored boring annoyed annoying |
   |---|

   | The aunt |
   |---|
   |  |

   | The children |
   |---|
   |  |

   | The young man |
   |---|
   |  |

# A TRAIN JOURNEY

The people on the train were hot and tired. A tall young man sat next to three small children and their aunt. The aunt and the children talked. When the aunt spoke she always began with 'Don't … '. When the children spoke they always began with 'Why … ?' The young man said nothing.

The small boy whistled loudly. 'Don't do that, Cyril,' said his aunt. Cyril stood up and looked out of the window at the countryside.
'Why is that man taking those sheep out of that field?' he asked.
'Perhaps he's taking them to another field where there's more grass,' said the aunt.
'But there's lots of grass in that field. Why can't the sheep stay there?'

102 Unit 13 • How terribly clever!

73

'Perhaps the grass in the other field is better.'
'Why is it better?'
The young man looked annoyed.
'Oh dear,' thought the aunt, 'he doesn't like children.'
'Sit down quietly, Cyril. Now, listen, I'm going to tell you all a story.'

The children looked bored but they listened. The story was very boring indeed. It was about a very beautiful little girl, who worked hard and behaved beautifully. Everybody loved her. One day she fell into a lake and everyone in the village ran to save her.

'Why did they save her?' asked the bigger girl.
'Because she was so good,' said the aunt.
'But that's stupid,' said the girl. 'When people fall into lakes, it doesn't matter if they're good or bad, you run to save them.'
'You're right,' said the young man, speaking for the first time. 'That's a ridiculous story.'
'Well, perhaps *you* would like to tell a story,' said the aunt coldly.
'OK,' said the man. The children looked interested and he began.

**5** The young man tells the story of a little girl called Bertha. Look at the pictures. What do you think happened to Bertha?

Unit 13 · How terribly clever!

**6** **T 13.5** Read and listen to part two.

## 74

### The tale of horribly good Bertha

'Once upon a time, a long time ago there was a little girl called Bertha. She was always well behaved and worked hard at school to please her parents and her teachers. She was never late, never dirty or untidy, never rude, and she never told lies.'

The children on the train began to look bored. 'Was she pretty?' asked the smaller girl.
'No,' said the young man. 'She wasn't pretty at all. She was just *horribly* good. Bertha was so good that she won three gold medals. One said *Never late*, one said *Always polite*, and the third said *Best Child in the World*.'

'Yuk!' said the three children.

'Anyway,' said the young man, 'Bertha was so good that the king invited her to his palace. So she put on her best clean white dress and she pinned her three medals to the

## 75

front and she walked through the woods to the king's palace. But in the woods there lived a big hungry wolf. He saw Bertha's lovely white dress through the trees and he heard the medals clinking together as she walked.

'Aha!' thought the wolf. 'Lunch!' And he started to move quickly but quietly through the trees towards Bertha.'

'Oh, no!' cried the children. 'Is he going to eat Bertha?'

'Yes, of course,' answered the young man. 'Bertha tried to run away but she couldn't run fast because the medals were so heavy. The wolf caught her easily and he ate everything, every bit of Bertha, except her three medals.'

'That's a terrible story,' said the aunt.
'No it isn't,' shouted the children. 'It's the best story ever!'
'Ah,' said the young man, 'the train's stopping. It's my station.'

**7** Answer the questions.
1 What is the same and what is different in the aunt's story and the young man's story?
2 Does the aunt like the young man's story? Why/Why not?
3 Do the children like the story? Why/Why not?
4 Which of these do you think is the moral of Bertha's story?

> It pays to be good.
> It never pays to be good.
> It doesn't always pay to be good.

**8** Tell the story of Bertha. Use the pictures in exercise 5 on p103 to help you.

### Language work

**1** Put some adjectives and adverbs from the story of Bertha into the correct box.

| Adjectives | Adverbs |
|---|---|
|  |  |
|  |  |
|  |  |

**2** Write questions about Bertha's story using these question words. Ask and answer the questions across the class.

| ~~when~~  how many  what  why  where  how |

*When did the story take place?*   *A long time ago.*

## EVERYDAY ENGLISH
### Catching a train

1 Ann is phoning to find out the times of trains to Bristol.

**T 13.6** Listen and write in the arrival times.

> ! Notice we often use the twenty-four hour clock for timetables.
> 7.00 in the morning = 0700 (oh seven hundred hours)

| DEPARTURE TIME from OXFORD | ARRIVAL TIME at Bristol Temple Meads |
|---|---|
| 0816 | |
| 0945 | |
| 1040 | |

2 **T 13.7** Ann is at Oxford Station. Listen and complete the conversation. Then practise with a partner.

A Good morning. (1) _____ the times of trains (2) _____ Bristol (3) _____ Oxford, please?
B Afternoon, evening? When (4) _____ ?
A About five o'clock this afternoon.
B About (5) _____ . Right. Let's have a look. There's a train that (6) _____ 5.28, then there isn't (7) _____ until 6.50.
A And (8) _____ get in?
B The 5.28 gets into Oxford at 6.54 and the 6.50 (9) _____ .
A Thanks a lot.

3 Ann goes to the ticket office. Put the lines of the conversation in the correct order.

- [1] A Hello. A return to Bristol, please.
- [ ] A A day return.
- [ ] C How do you want to pay?
- [11] A OK, thanks very much. Goodbye.
- [ ] C Here's your change and your ticket.
- [ ] C You want platform 1 over there.
- [ ] A Here's a twenty-pound note.
- [ ] C Day return or period return?
- [ ] A Cash, please.
- [ ] C That's eighteen pounds.
- [ ] A Thank you. Which platform is it?

**T 13.8** Listen and check. Practise the conversation with a partner.

4 Make more conversations with your partner. Look at the information from your teacher. Decide where you want to go. Find out about times, then buy your ticket.

Unit 13 · How terribly clever! 105

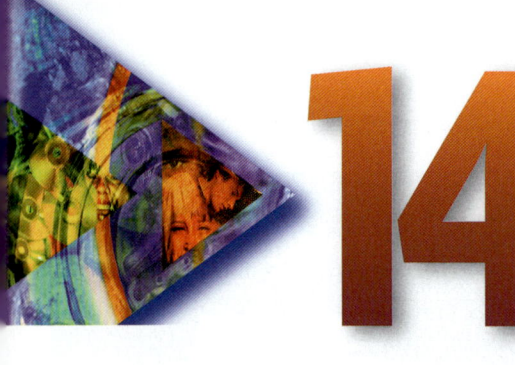

# 14 Have you ever?

Present Perfect + *ever, never, yet,* and *just* • At the airport

## STARTER

**1** Match the countries and flags.

Australia   Brazil   France   Germany   Great Britain   Greece
Hungary   Italy   Japan   Canada   Spain   the USA

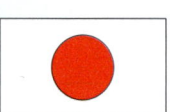

1 _____   2 _____   3 _____   4 _____   5 _____   6 _____

7 _____   8 _____   9 _____   10 _____   11 _____   12 _____

**2** Tick (✓) the countries that you have visited.

## IN MY LIFE
### Present Perfect + *ever* and *never*

**1** **T 14.1** Read and listen to the sentences. Then listen and repeat.

I've been to Germany.  (I've = I have)
I haven't been to France.
I've been to the USA.
I've never been to Australia.
I haven't been to any of the countries!

Work in groups. Tell each other which of the countries above you have or haven't been to. Have you been to any other countries?

**2** **T 14.2** Read and listen to the conversation. Practise with a partner.

A Have you ever been to Paris?
B No, I haven't.
A Have you ever been to Berlin?
B Yes, I have.
A When did you go?
B Two years ago.

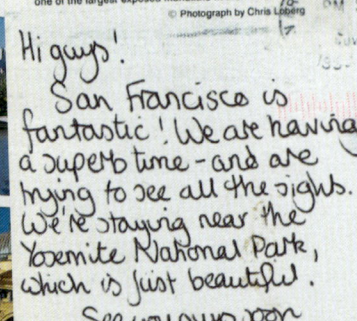

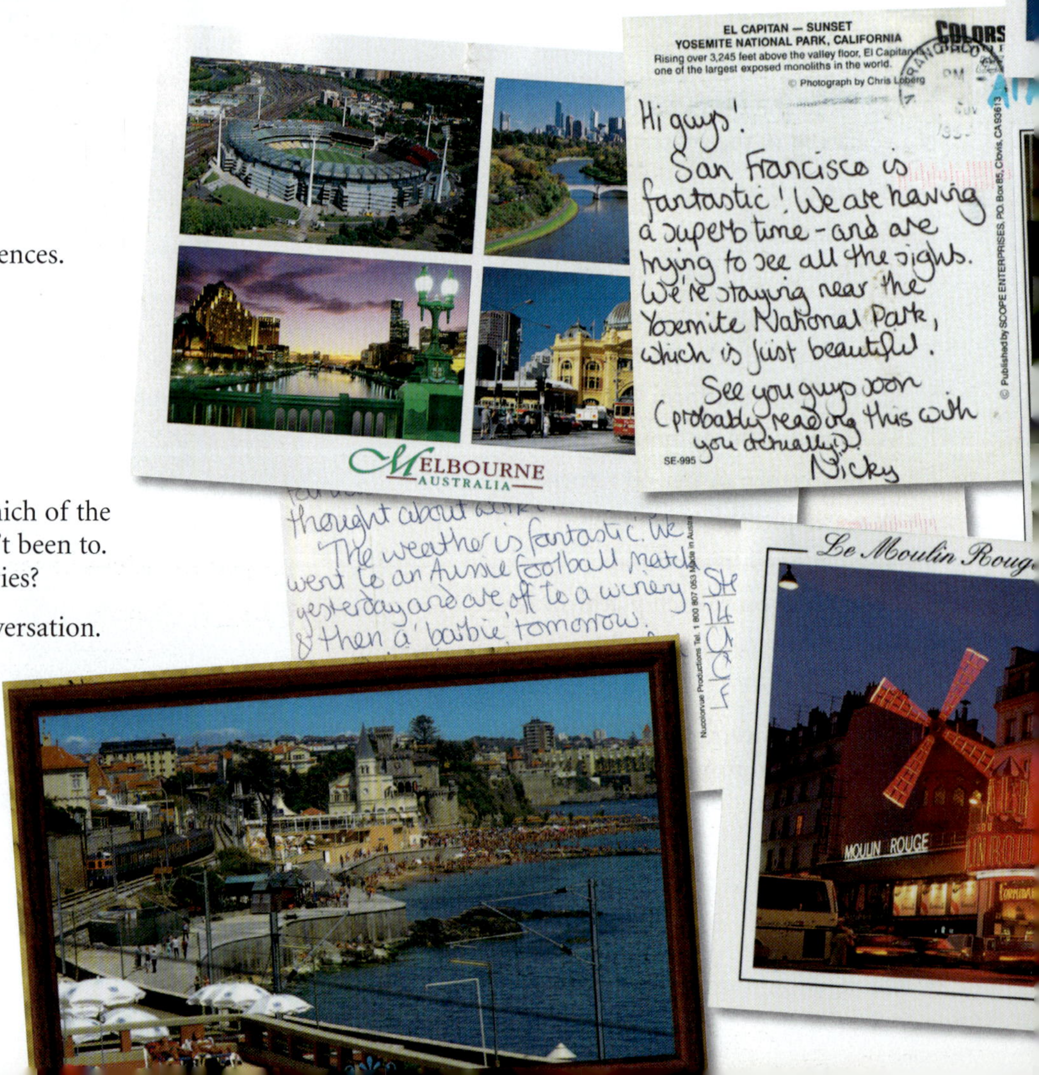

106  Unit 14 • Have you ever?

3 Write down the names of four cities in your country or another country that you have been to. Have similar conversations with your partner.

4 Tell the class about your partner.

> Maria's been to Berlin.

(Maria's = Maria has)

> She went there two years ago.

> But she hasn't been to Paris. / She's never been to Paris.

(She's = She has)

### GRAMMAR SPOT

1 We use the Present Perfect to talk about experiences in our lives.
   Have you ever (at any time in your life) been to Paris?

2 We use the Past Simple to say exactly *when* something happened.
   When did you go to Paris?
   I went there | last year.
   | two years ago.
   | in 1998.

3 We make the Present Perfect tense with *has/have* + the past participle. Complete the table.

|  | Positive | Negative |  |
|---|---|---|---|
| I/You/We/They | _____ | _____ | been to Paris. |
| He/She/It | _____ | _____ |  |

4 Write *ever* and *never* in the right place in these sentences.
   Has he _____ been to London?
   He's _____ been to London.

▶▶ Grammar Reference 14.1 p134

## PRACTICE

### Past participles

1 Here are the past participles of some verbs. Write the infinitive.

| eaten | *eat* | made | _____ | given | _____ |
| seen | _____ | taken | _____ | won | _____ |
| met | _____ | driven | _____ | had | _____ |
| drunk | _____ | cooked | _____ | stayed | _____ |
| flown | _____ | bought | _____ | done | _____ |

2 Which are the two regular verbs?

3 What are the Past Simple forms of the verbs?

4 Look at the list of irregular verbs on p142 and check your answers.

## The life of Ryan

**1** **T 14.3** Listen to Ryan talking about his life and tick (✓) the things he has done.

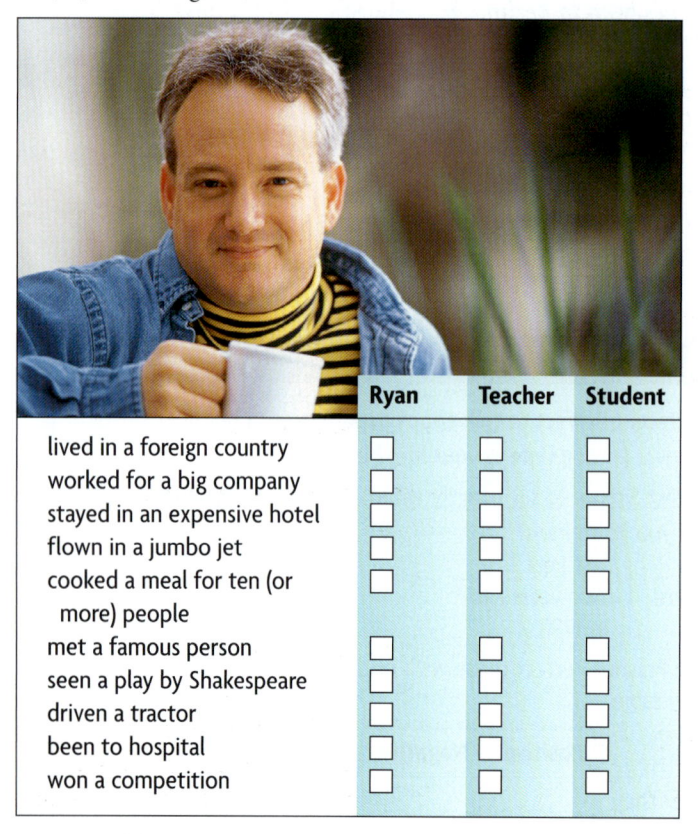

|  | Ryan | Teacher | Student |
|---|---|---|---|
| lived in a foreign country | ☐ | ☐ | ☐ |
| worked for a big company | ☐ | ☐ | ☐ |
| stayed in an expensive hotel | ☐ | ☐ | ☐ |
| flown in a jumbo jet | ☐ | ☐ | ☐ |
| cooked a meal for ten (or more) people | ☐ | ☐ | ☐ |
| met a famous person | ☐ | ☐ | ☐ |
| seen a play by Shakespeare | ☐ | ☐ | ☐ |
| driven a tractor | ☐ | ☐ | ☐ |
| been to hospital | ☐ | ☐ | ☐ |
| won a competition | ☐ | ☐ | ☐ |

**2** Tell your teacher about Ryan and answer your teacher's questions.

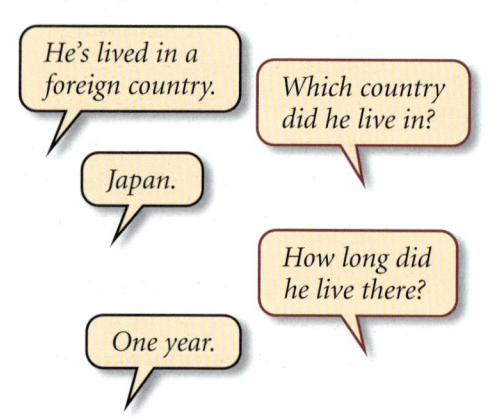

*He's lived in a foreign country.*

*Which country did he live in?*

*Japan.*

*How long did he live there?*

*One year.*

**3** Ask your teacher the questions and complete the chart.

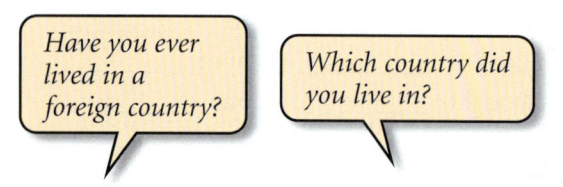

*Have you ever lived in a foreign country?*

*Which country did you live in?*

**4** Ask a partner the questions. Tell the class about your partner.

## A HONEYMOON IN LONDON
### Present Perfect + *yet* and *just*

**1** Rod and Marilyn come from Christchurch, New Zealand. They are on honeymoon in London. Before they went, they made a list of things they wanted to do there. Read the list below.

**2** **T 14.4** Marilyn is phoning her sister Judy, back home in New Zealand. Listen to their conversation. Tick (✓) the things she and Rod have done.

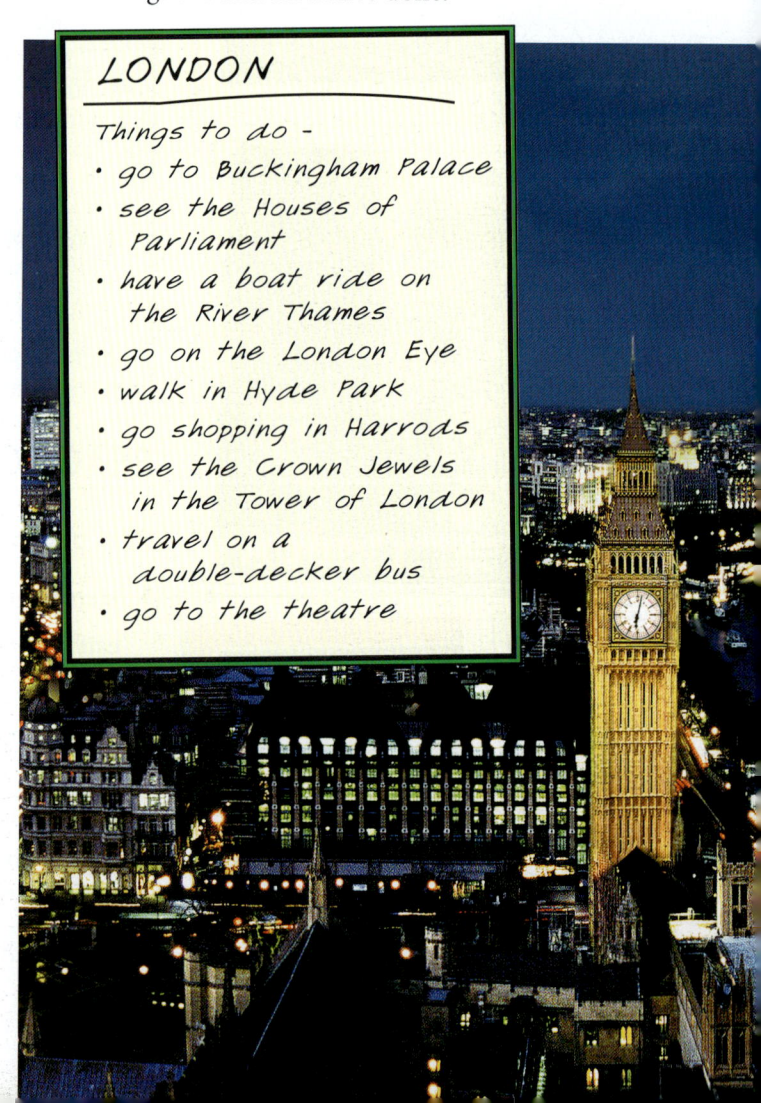

**LONDON**

Things to do –
- go to Buckingham Palace
- see the Houses of Parliament
- have a boat ride on the River Thames
- go on the London Eye
- walk in Hyde Park
- go shopping in Harrods
- see the Crown Jewels in the Tower of London
- travel on a double-decker bus
- go to the theatre

## GRAMMAR SPOT

1. Complete the sentences.
   1. Have you _____ the Crown Jewels **yet**?
   2. We _____ been to the theatre **yet**.
   3. We've **just** _____ a boat ride on the Thames.
2. Where do we put *yet* in a sentence? Where do we put *just* in a sentence?
3. We can only use *yet* with **two** of the following. Which two?
   - [ ] Positive sentences
   - [ ] Questions
   - [ ] Negative sentences

▶▶ **Grammar Reference 14.2 p134**

3 Look at the list with a partner. Say what Rod and Marilyn have done and what they haven't done yet.

*They've travelled on a double-decker bus.*

*They haven't seen the Crown Jewels yet.*

**T 14.4** Listen again and check.

# PRACTICE

## I've just done it

1 Work with a partner. Make questions with *yet* and answers with *just*.

*Have you done the washing-up yet?*

*Yes, I've just done it.*

1. do the washing-up
2. do the shopping
3. wash your hair
4. clean the car
5. make the dinner
6. meet the new student
7. have a coffee
8. give your homework to the teacher
9. finish the exercise

## Check it

2 Tick (✓) the correct sentence.
1. ☐ I saw John yesterday.
   ☐ I've seen John yesterday.
2. ☐ Did you ever eat Chinese food?
   ☐ Have you ever eaten Chinese food?
3. ☐ Donna won £5,000 last month.
   ☐ Donna has won £5,000 last month.
4. ☐ I've never drank champagne.
   ☐ I've never drunk champagne.
5. ☐ Tom has ever been to America.
   ☐ Tom has never been to America.
6. ☐ Has your sister yet had the baby?
   ☐ Has your sister had the baby yet?
7. ☐ I haven't finished my homework yet.
   ☐ I've finished my homework yet.
8. ☐ Did she just bought a new car?
   ☐ Has she just bought a new car?

## READING AND SPEAKING
### How to live to be 100

1. Who is the oldest person you know? How old is he/she? What do you know about their lives? Why do you think they have lived so long? Tell the class.

2. These words are in the texts. Write them in the correct column.

   pneumonia  ambulance driver  engineer  heart attack
   lung cancer  rheumatic fever  secretary  dressmaker

   | Jobs | Illnesses |
   |------|-----------|
   |      |           |
   |      |           |
   |      |           |

3. Read the introduction. Are similar facts true for your country?

### How to live to be 100

More and more people are living to be 100 years old. There are now 4,400 centenarians in Britain – 10 times more than there were 40 years ago. Professor Grimley Evans of Oxford University believes that future generations will live even longer, to 115 years and more. Here are the stories of three people who have lived to be 100.

4. Work in groups of three. Each choose a different person and read about her/him. Answer the questions.
   1. What jobs has she/he had in her/his life?
   2. Where does he/she live now?
   3. Which countries has she/he been to?
   4. Did he/she marry and have children?
   5. Is her husband/his wife still alive?
   6. When and why did she/he give up smoking cigarettes?
   7. What do you learn about other people in his/her family?
   8. Has she/he ever been very ill?
   9. What food does he/she like?
   10. What exercise does she/he like doing?

5. Work with your group. Compare the three people, using your answers.

### What do you think?

- Why do you think these people have lived so long? How many reasons can you find?
- Would you like to live to be 100? Why/why not?

## Joyce Bews

Joyce Bews was 100 last year. She was born and grew up in Portsmouth on the south coast of England, where she still lives. For many years she was a dressmaker, and she didn't marry until she was 65. Her husband died of lung cancer only 10 weeks after they married. It was then that she gave up smoking. Joyce has had only one serious illness in her life – she had pneumonia when she was 20. She has lived in Australia and America. She lived in Australia after her husband died, and she went to America when she was 75. She has just returned from a holiday in Spain with her niece, aged 75. She says: 'I'm not sure why I've lived so long. I've never exercised but I've always eaten well, lots of fruit. My youngest brother has just died, aged 90.'

110  Unit 14 • Have you ever?

# Alice Patterson-Smythe

Alice Patterson-Smythe was born just over 100 years ago in Edinburgh. She now lives in Norfolk. She drove ambulances in the First World War, and worked as a school secretary until she retired. She has been a widow for 25 years and has three children, six grandchildren, and 11 great-grandchildren. She smoked quite a lot when she was a young girl but she gave up when she was 68 because she had a heart attack. Her nineties were the best years of her life because her millionaire grandson took her on his aeroplane to visit Tokyo, Los Angeles, and Miami. She says: 'I love life. I play golf once a week and do Latin American dancing, and I eat lots of fruit and vegetables. We are a long-lived family – my mother was 95 when she died.'

# Tommy Harrison

Tommy Harrison is exactly 100 years old. He's a retired engineer. His wife, Maude, died 14 years ago. They had no children and now he lives alone in his flat in Bristol. Tommy has smoked all his life. First he smoked cigarettes, about 10 a day, but 40 years ago he changed to a pipe. He has only been ill once in his life, and that was just before the First World War, when he had rheumatic fever. The only time he visits his doctor is to get a certificate to say that he can still drive his car. Every day he has a full English breakfast – bacon, eggs, toast and marmalade. He has only been abroad once, to France during the war. He says: 'I still go dancing and swimming but I don't want to live for ever, perhaps 12 more months. My father lived until he was 99.'

## LISTENING
### Leaving on a jet plane

1 **T 14.5** Close your books and your eyes and listen to a song. What is it about?

2 Read the words of the song. Choose the word on the right which best completes the line.

# Leaving on a jet plane

All my (1)_____ are packed, I'm ready to go,
I'm standing here outside your (2)_____,
I (3)_____ to wake you up to say goodbye,
But the dawn is breaking,
It's early morn',
The taxi's (4)_____,
He's blowing his (5)_____,
Already I'm so lonesome
I could (6)_____ .

*Chorus*  So kiss me and (7)_____ for me,
(8)_____ me that you'll wait for me,
(9)_____ me like you'll never let me go,
'Cos I'm leaving on a jet plane,
I don't know when I'll be back again.
Oh babe, I hate to go.

There's so (10)_____ times I've let you down,
So many times I've (11)_____ around,
I tell you now
They don't mean a thing.
Every (12)_____ I go, I'll think of you
Every song I sing, I'll sing for you
When I (13)_____ back
I'll wear your wedding (14)_____ .

1  bags     suitcases
2  window   door
3  hate     want

4  here     waiting
5  horn     trumpet

6  cry      die

7  laugh    smile
8  tell     say
9  love     hold

10 much     many
11 played   walked

12 time     place

13 come     go
14 ring     dress

3 Listen again and check the words. Sing along!

# EVERYDAY ENGLISH
## At the airport

**1** What do you do at an airport? Read the sentences and put them in the correct order.

- ☐ You wait in the departure lounge.
- ☐ You board the plane.
- ☐ You get a trolley for your luggage.
- ☑ You arrive at the airport.
- ☐ You check in your luggage and get a boarding pass.
- ☐ You go through passport control.
- ☐ You check the departures board for your gate number.

**2** **T 14.6** Listen to the airport announcements and complete the chart.

| FLIGHT NUMBER | DESTINATION | GATE NUMBER | REMARK |
|---|---|---|---|
| BA516 | GENEVA | 4 | LAST CALL |
| SK | | | DELAYED |
| AF | | | NOW BOARDING GATE |
| LH | | | NOW BOARDING GATE |
| VS | | | WAIT IN LOUNGE |

**3** **T 14.7** Listen to the conversations. Who are the people? Where are they? Choose from these places.

- in the arrival hall
- in the departure lounge
- at the departure gate
- at the check-in desk

**4** Complete each conversation with the correct question.

> When can we see each other again?
> Did you have a good honeymoon?
> Did the announcement say gate 4 or 14?
> have you got much hand luggage?

1 **A** Listen! … BA 516 to Geneva. That's our flight.
  **B** _____ ?
  **A** I couldn't hear. I think it said 4.
  **B** Look! There it is on the departure board. It *is* gate 4.
  **A** OK. Come on! Let's go.

2 **A** Can I have your ticket, please?
  **B** Yes, of course.
  **A** Thank you. How many suitcases have you got?
  **B** Just one.
  **A** And _____ ?
  **B** Just this bag.
  **A** That's fine.
  **B** Oh … can I have a seat next to the window?
  **A** Yes, that's OK. Here's your boarding pass. Have a nice flight!

3 **A** Rod! Marilyn! Over here!
  **B** Hi! Judy! Great to see you!
  **A** It's great to see you too. You look terrific! _____ ?
  **B** Fantastic. Everything was fantastic.
  **A** Well, you haven't missed anything here. Nothing much has happened at all!

4 **A** There's my flight. It's time to go.
  **B** Oh no! It's been a wonderful two weeks. I can't believe it's over.
  **A** I know. _____ ?
  **B** Soon, I hope. I'll write every day.
  **A** I'll phone too. Goodbye.
  **B** Goodbye. Give my love to your family.

**T 14.7** Listen and check. Practise the conversations with a partner.

**5** Work with a partner. Make more conversations at each of the places.

# Tapescripts

## Unit 1

**T 1.1** see p6

**T 1.2**
- A Hello. My name's Richard. What's your name?
- B Kurt.
- A Where are you from, Kurt?
- B I'm from Hamburg. Where are you from?
- A I'm from London.

**T 1.3** see p7

**T 1.4** Listen carefully!
1. He's from Spain.
2. What's her name?
3. They're from Brazil.
4. Where's she from?
5. He's a teacher in Italy.

**T 1.5** see p9

**T 1.6** Yasmina

My name's Yasmina Kamal and I'm a student. I'm 19. I'm not married. I have one sister and two brothers. I live in a flat in Cairo, Egypt. I want to learn English because it's an international language.

**T 1.7** The alphabet song

A B C D E F G
H I J K L M N O P
L M N O P Q R S T
L M N O P Q R S T
U V W X Y Z

That is the English alphabet!

**T 1.8** see p10

**T 1.9** Telephone numbers

682 947
8944 5033
020 7399 7050

**T 1.10** What are the numbers?
1. Hello. 01913 786 499.
2. My brother has four children.
3. I have 10 stamps in my bag.
4. Hello, extension 4177.
5. I live at number 19.
6. Goodbye. See you at five.

**T 1.11** Everyday conversations
1. Hello, extension 3442.
   Hello, Mary. This is Edward. How are you?
   I'm fine, thank you. And you?
   I'm OK, thanks.
2. Goodbye, Marcus.
   Goodbye, Bianca. Have a nice day.
   Thanks, Marcus. See you this evening!
   Yes, at seven in the cinema.
3. Hello, 270899.
   Hi, Flora! It's me, Leo. How are you?
   Not bad, thanks. And you?
   Very well. How are the children?
   They're fine.

## Unit 2

**T 2.1** Keesha Anderson
1. A What's her surname?
   B Anderson.
2. A What's her first name?
   B Keesha.
3. A Where's she from?
   B London, England.
4. A What's her job?
   B She's a journalist.
5. A What's her address?
   B 42, Muswell Hill Road, London N10 3JD.
6. A What's her phone number?
   B 020 8863 5741.
7. A How old is she?
   B Twenty-eight.
8. A Is she married?
   B No, she isn't.

**T 2.2** see p13

**T 2.3** see p14

**T 2.4** Adjectives
1. He's old. She's young.
2. It's easy. It's difficult.
3. It's new. It's old.
4. It's fast. It's slow.
5. It's lovely. It's horrible.
6. They're hot. They're cold.
7. They're cheap. They're expensive.
8. It's small. It's big.

**T 2.5** see p17

**T 2.6** Dorita in New York

D = Dorita   O = Orlando
1. D Hello. My name's Dorita.
   O Hello, Dorita. I'm Orlando.
   D Where are you from, Orlando?
   O I'm from Italy, from Rome. And you? Where are you from?
   D I'm from Argentina.
   O From Buenos Aires?
   D Yes, that's right.

I = Isabel   C = class   D = Dorita
2. I Good morning everybody.
   C Good morning, Isabel.
   I How are you all?
   C Fine.
   Good.
   OK.
   I How are you Dorita?
   D I'm fine thank you. And you?
   I Very well. Now listen everybody ...

M = Marnie   D = Dorita   A = Annie
3. M Bye, Dorita. Have a nice day.
   D Pardon?
   A Have a good day at the school of English.
   D Oh, yes. Thank you. Same to you.
   M What's your teacher called?
   D My teacher called?
   A Your teacher's name – what is it?
   D Ah, yes. Her name's Isabel.
   M And is she good?
   D My teacher good?
   A Yeah. Isabel, your teacher, is she a good teacher?
   D Oh yes, yes. Very good, very nice.

**T 2.7** see p18

**T 2.8**
1. That's five pounds fifty, please.
2. Look, it's only twelve pounds.
3. Here you are. Twenty p change.
4. Pizza is three pounds seventy-five.
5. One hundred pounds for that is very expensive.
6. Nine pounds fif**teen**, not nine pounds fifty.

**T 2.9** see p19

**T 2.10** In a snack bar
1. A Good morning.
   B Good morning. Can I have an orange juice, please?
   A Here you are. Anything else?
   B No, thanks.
   A Ninety p, please.
   B Thanks.
   A Thank you.
2. A Hi. Can I help?
   B Yes. Can I have a tuna and egg salad, please?
   A Anything to drink?
   B Yeah. A mineral water, please.
   A OK. Here you are.
   B How much is that?
   A Four pounds ninety-five, please.
   B Thanks.

# Unit 3

**T 3.1**  see p20

**T 3.2**
1  She's a scientist. He's a doctor.
2  Alison comes from England. Bob comes from England, too.
3  She lives in a big city, but he lives in a small town.
4  She works three days a week. He works 16 hours a day non-stop.
5  He speaks to sick people on his radio. She speaks three languages.
6  She loves her job and he loves his job, too.
7  She has a daughter. He isn't married.
8  She likes skiing and going for walks in her free time. He never has free time.

**T 3.3  Questions and answers**
Where does Alison come from?  Cambridge, in England.
What does she do?  She's a scientist.
Does she speak French?  Yes, she does.
Does she speak Spanish?  No, she doesn't.

**T 3.4**
1  Where does Bob come from?  England.
2  What does he do?  He's a doctor.
3  Does he fly to help people?  Yes, he does.
4  Does he speak French and German?  No, he doesn't.

**T 3.5  Is it true or false?**
1  Philippe comes from Paris.
2  Philippe lives in London.
3  He works in the centre of Paris.
4  He speaks English very well.
5  He's married.
6  Keiko lives and works in New York.
7  She speaks French and German.
8  She plays tennis in her free time.
9  She isn't married.
10  Mark works in an office in Moscow.
11  He has three sons.
12  He likes playing football in his free time.

**T 3.6  Listen carefully!**
1  She likes her job.
2  She loves walking.
3  He isn't married.
4  Does he have three children?
5  What does he do?

**T 3.7  Mr McSporran's day**
1  A  Good afternoon. Can I have two ice-creams, please?
   B  Chocolate or vanilla?
   A  One chocolate, one vanilla please.
   B  That's £1.80. Anything else?
   A  No, thank you.

2  A  Only two letters for you this morning, Mrs Craig.
   B  Thank you very much, Mr McSporran. And how's Mrs McSporran this morning?
   A  Oh, she's very well, thank you. She's busy in the shop.

3  A  A glass of wine before bed, my dear?
   B  Oh, yes please.
   A  Here you are.
   B  Thank you, my dear. I'm very tired this evening.

4  A  Hello Mr McSporran!
   B  Good morning, boys and girls. Hurry up, we're late.
   A  Can I sit here, Mr McSporran?
   C  No, no, I want to sit there.
   B  Be quiet all of you, and SIT DOWN!

**T 3.8  What time is it?**
It's five o'clock.           It's eight o'clock.
It's half past five.         It's half past eleven.
It's quarter past five.      It's quarter past two.
It's quarter to six.         It's quarter to nine.
It's five past five.         It's ten past five.
It's twenty past five.       It's twenty-five past five.
It's twenty-five to six.     It's twenty to six.
It's ten to six.             It's five to six.

**T 3.9**  see p27

# Unit 4

**T 4.1  Bobbi Brown's weekdays**
My weekends are fast and exciting. My weekdays are fast and domestic! I have two sons, Dylan 7, and Dakota 5. Every morning I get up one hour before them, at 6.00, and I go to the gym. I come home and I make breakfast, then I take them to school. On Mondays I always go shopping. I buy all the food for the week. I often cook dinner in the evenings, but not every day because I don't like cooking. Fortunately, my husband, Don, loves cooking. On Tuesdays and Thursdays I visit my father. He lives on the next block. Every afternoon I pick up the kids from school. In the evenings Don and I usually relax, but sometimes we visit friends. We never go out on Friday evenings because I start work so early on Saturdays.

**T 4.2  Questions and answers**
B = Bobbi
A  Where do you work?
B  In New York.
A  Do you like your work?
B  Yes, I do.
A  Do you relax at weekends?
B  No, I don't.
A  Why don't you relax at weekends?
B  Because I work.

**T 4.3**
1  What time do you go to bed?
   At 11 o'clock.
2  Where do you go on holiday?
   To Spain or Portugal.
3  What do you do on Sundays?
   I always relax.
4  When do you do your homework?
   After dinner.
5  Who do you live with?
   My mother and sisters.
6  Why do you like your job?
   Because it's interesting.
7  How do you travel to school?
   By bus.
8  Do you go out on Friday evenings?
   Yes, I do sometimes.

**T 4.4  Listen carefully!**
1  What does she do on Sundays?
2  Do you stay home on Thursday evenings?
3  He lives here.
4  What do you do on Saturday evenings?
5  I read a lot.
6  Why don't you like your job?

**T 4.5  Favourite seasons**
1  **Al Wheeler from Canada**
We have long, cold winters and short, hot summers. We have a holiday home near a lake, so in summer I go sailing a lot and I play baseball, but in winter I often play ice hockey and go ice-skating. My favourite season is autumn, or fall, as we say in North America. I love the colours of the trees – red, gold, orange, yellow, and brown.

2  **Manuela da Silva from Portugal**
People think it's always warm and sunny in Portugal, but January and February are often cold, wet, and grey. I don't like winter. I usually meet friends in restaurant and bars and we chat. Sometimes we go to a Brazilian bar. I love Brazilian music. But then suddenly it's summer and at weekends we drive to the beach, sunbathe, and go swimming. I love summer.

3  **Toshi Suzuki from Japan**
I work for Pentax cameras, in the export department. I don't have a lot of free time, but I have one special hobby – taking photographs, of course! I like taking photographs of flowers, especially in spring. Sometimes, after work, I relax in a bar near my office with friends. My friend, Shigeru, likes singing pop songs in the bar. This has a special name, *karaoke*. I don't sing – I'm too shy!

### T 4.6 Who's who?

M = Manuela   J = Jane
F = Manuela's friends

1 M Hello, everybody! This is my friend Jane from England.
   F Hi!
     Hello!
     Hello Jane!
   J Hello. Pleased to meet you.
   M Sit down here, Jane.
   J Thanks.
   F Do you like the music, Jane?
   J Yes, I do. Is it American?
   F No, it's Brazilian jazz!
   M Come and have a drink, Jane.

T = Toshi   J = Ann Jones

2 T Mrs Jones! How do you do?
   J How do you do?
   T Please come in. You're from our office in London, aren't you?
   J Yes, that's right.
   T Welcome to Tokyo! Do you like our headquarters here?
   J Yes. It's very big. How many people work here?
   T About six thousand people. Do you want to see our offices?

A = Al   M = Mick

3 A What do you want to do today, Mick?
   M Ooh, I don't know. What do you …
   A Ah! Do you like sailing?
   M Yes, very much. I sometimes go sailing in Scotland but not very often.
   A OK – so today it's sailing and fishing on the lake.
   M Fantastic. I love fishing too – we go fishing a lot in Scotland.

### T 4.7 Everyday conversations

1 A I'm sorry I'm late. The traffic is bad today.
   B Don't worry. Come and sit down. We're on page 25.

2 A Excuse me.
   B Yes?
   A Do you have a dictionary?
   B I'm sorry, I don't. It's at home.
   A That's OK.

3 A It's very hot in here. Can I open the window?
   B Really? I'm quite cold.
   A OK. It doesn't matter.

4 A Excuse me!
   B Can I help you?
   A Can I have a film for my camera?
   B How many exposures?
   A Pardon?
   B How many *exposures*?
   A What does 'exposures' mean?
   B How many pictures? 24? 36? 40?
   A Ah! Now I understand! 40, please.

## Unit 5

### T 5.1 Questions and answers

A Is there a television?
B Yes, there is.
A Is there a radio?
B No, there isn't.
A Are there any books?
B Yes, there are.
A How many books are there?
B There are a lot.
A Are there any photographs?
B No, there aren't.

### T 5.2 Description of a living room

There are three people in the living room. A man and a woman on the sofa and a little girl in the armchair. There's a radio on the coffee table and a rug under it. There's a cat on the rug in front of the fire. There are a lot of pictures on the walls but there aren't any photographs. There are two plants on the floor next to the television and some flowers on the small table next to the sofa.

### T 5.3 Helen's kitchen

H = Helen   B = Bob

H And this is the kitchen.
B Mmm, it's very nice.
H Well, it's not very big, but there are a lot of cupboards. And there's a new fridge, and a cooker. That's new, too.
B But what's *in* all these cupboards?
H Well, not a lot. There are some cups, but there aren't any plates. And I have some knives and forks, but I don't have any spoons!
B Do you have any glasses?
H No. Sorry.
B Never mind. We can drink this champagne from those cups! Cheers!

### T 5.4 What's in Pierre's briefcase?

What's in my briefcase? Well, there's a newspaper – a French newspaper – and there's a dictionary – my French/English dictionary. I have some pens, three I think. Also I have a notebook for vocabulary, I write words in that every day. And of course I have my keys, my car keys and my house keys. Oh yes, very important, there are some photos of my family, my wife and my daughter and there's my mobile phone. I ring my home in Paris every night. That's all I think. I don't have any stamps and my address book is in my hotel.

### T 5.5 Homes around the world

1 Manola from Lisbon
I live in the old town near the sea. It is called the Alfama. I have a very beautiful flat. There's just *one* room in my flat, one very big room with one very big window. My bed's next to the window so I see the sea and all the lights of the city when I go to sleep. I live alone, but I have a cat and I'm near the shops and lots of friends come to visit me. I love my flat.

2 Ray and Elsie from Toronto
Elsie Our house is quite old, about fifty years old. It's quite near to the city centre. We have a living room, quite a big kitchen and three bedrooms, but the room we all love is our family room.
Ray Yes, there's a TV and a stereo and a large comfortable sofa in there, and some big, old armchairs. We love sitting there in winter with the snow outside.
Elsie Our children aren't at home now, they both have jobs in the USA, so most of the time it's just Ray and me.

3 Brad from Malibu
My house is fantastic. It's right next to the sea. My neighbours are very rich. Some of them are famous film stars. In my house there are ten rooms, five are bedrooms, and everything is white, the floors, the walls, the sofas, everything. I also have a swimming pool, a cinema and an exercise room. I live here alone. I'm not married at the moment. My ex-wife is French. She lives in Paris now with our three sons.

4 Alise from Samoa
I live with my family in a house near the sea. We have an open house, … er … that is … er … our house doesn't have any walls. Houses in Samoa don't have walls because it is very, very hot, but we have blinds to stop the rain and sun. Our house is in the old style. We have only *one* room for living and sleeping, so it is both a bedroom and a living room. We have rugs and we sit and sleep on the floor.

### T 5.6 Asking for directions

1 A Excuse me! Is there a chemist near here?
   B Yes. It's over there.
   A Thanks.

2 A Excuse me! Is there a newsagent near here?
   B Yes. It's in Church Street. Take the first street on the right. It's next to the music shop.
   A Oh yes. Thanks.

3 A Excuse me! Is there a restaurant near here?
   B There's a Chinese one in Park Lane next to the bank, and there's an Italian one in Church Street next to the travel agent.
   A Is that one far?
   B No. Just two minutes, that's all.

4 A Is there a post office near here?
   B Go straight ahead, and it's on the left, next to the pub.
   A Thanks a lot.

# Unit 6

### T 6.1 What can you do?
a She can use a computer.
b We can't understand the question.
c 'Can dogs swim?' 'Yes, they can.'
d He can ski really well.
e I can't spell your name.
f 'Can you speak Japanese?' 'No, I can't.'

### T 6.2 Listen and repeat
I can speak French.
Can you speak French?
Yes, I can.
No, I can't.

### T 6.3 Listen and complete the sentences
1 I can speak French, but I can't speak German.
2 He can't dance, but he can sing.
3 'Can you cook?' 'Yes, I can.'
4 They can ski, but they can't swim.
5 We can dance and we can sing.
6 'Can she drive?' 'No, she can't.'

### T 6.4 Tina can't cook. Can you?
Well, there are a lot of things I can't do. I can't drive a car, but I want to have lessons soon. I can't speak French but I can speak Italian, my mother's Italian, and we often go to Italy. My mother's a really good cook, she can cook really well, not just Italian food, all kinds of food, but I can't cook at all. I just love eating! What about sports? Er … I think I'm good at quite a lot of sports. I can play tennis, and ski, sometimes we go skiing in the Italian Alps, and of course I can swim. But musical instruments – no – I can't play any at all – no I'm not very musical, but I love dancing! Of course I can use a computer – all my friends can.

### T 6.5 Listen and repeat
It was Monday yesterday. We were at school.
'Was it hot?' 'Yes, it was.'
'Were you tired?' 'Yes, we were.'

### T 6.6 Charlotte's party
K = Kim   M = Max
K Were you at Charlotte's party last Saturday?
M Yes, I was.
K Was it good?
M Well, it was OK.
K Were there many people?
M Yes, there were.
K Was Henry there?
M No, he wasn't. And where were you? Why weren't you there?
K Oh … I couldn't go because I was at Mark's party! It was brilliant!

### T 6.7 Directory Enquiries
**Operator** International Directory Enquiries. Which country, please?
**Operator** And which town?
**Operator** Can I have the last name, please?
**Operator** And the initial?
**Operator** What's the address?
**Recorded message** The number you require is 006198 4681133.

### T 6.8 On the phone
1 A Hello.
  B Hello. Can I speak to Jo, please?
  A This is Jo.
  B Oh! Hi, Jo. This is Pat. Is Sunday still OK for tennis?
  A Yes. That's fine.
  B Great! See you on Sunday at ten, then. Bye!
  A Bye!
2 A Hello.
  B Hello. Is that Liz?
  A No it isn't. I'll just get her.
  C Hello, Liz here.
  B Hi, Liz. It's Tom. Listen! There's a party at my house on Saturday. Can you come?
  C Oh sorry, Tom. I can't. It's my sister's wedding.
  B Oh, never mind. Perhaps next time. Bye!
  C Bye!
3 A Good morning. Barclays Bank, Watford. How can I help you?
  B Good morning. Can I speak to the manager, please?
  A I'm afraid Mr Smith isn't in his office at the moment. Can I take a message?
  B Don't worry. I'll ring back later.
  A All right. Goodbye.
  B Goodbye.

# Unit 7

### T 7.1 Mattie Smith
Mattie Smith is 91 years old. She lives alone in Atlanta, Georgia. She starts her day at 7.30. First she has a bath, next she cleans the house, and then she sits outside on her verandah and thinks about her past life. Then she writes poems about it.

### T 7.2 see p52

### T 7.3 Listen and repeat
looked
worked
loved
learned
earned
married
died
hated
wanted

### T 7.4 Listen to Mattie
I worked from 6.00 in the morning until 10.00 at night. Sixteen hours in the cotton fields and I only earned $2 a day. I sure hated that job but I loved the poems in my head. I really wanted to learn to read and write. When I was sixteen I married Hubert, and soon there were six children, five sons, then a daughter, Lily. Hubert died just before she was born. That was sixty-five years ago. So I looked after my family alone. There was no time for learning, but my children, they all learned to read and write – that was important to me. And when did I learn to read and write? I didn't learn until I was 86, and now I have three books of poems.

### T 7.5 Questions and answers
1 A When did she start work?
  B When she was eight years old.
2 A Where did she work?
  B In the cotton fields.
3 A Who did she live with?
  B Her mother and sisters.
4 A How many hours did she work?
  B Sixteen hours a day.
5 A How much did she earn?
  B $2 a day.
6 A Who did she marry?
  B Hubert.
7 A When did Hubert die?
  B Sixty-five years ago.
8 A When did she learn to read?
  B She didn't learn until she was 86.

### T 7.6 Listen carefully!
worked
lived
started
married
loved
hated
finished
looked
died
visited
cleaned
liked

### T 7.7 Listen and repeat
had
began
came
went
did
left
got
studied
became
won
lost
bought
met

### T 7.8 Simon's 1990s

What do I remember of the nineties ... er ... well, I left school in 1994 and I went to university. I studied graphic design – it was really good. I had a good time. Then after university, in 1997, I was really lucky. I got a job immediately. A job with Saatchi and Saatchi, they're an advertising agency in London. Soon after that, 1998 it was, I met Zoë, she's my girlfriend. She has a good job, too, and we bought a flat together in 1999.

The only sport I like is football, so I remember when France won the World Cup in 1998. Brazil lost in '98 but they won in '94.

I remember when Tony Blair became Prime Minister in 1997, that was just after I started at Saatchi and Saatchi. Oh, and I remember Bill Clinton and all the problems he had in his last years in the White House. And the Euro – eleven countries in Europe began to use the Euro in 1999, but Britain didn't.

Oh yes – and of course I remember Princess Diana – she died in a car crash in Paris in '97 and millions of people came to London for her funeral. I was there. I can remember it really well.

### T 7.9 Listen and repeat

1. walk
2. listen
3. know
4. write
5. eight
6. farm
7. work
8. war
9. island
10. build
11. resign
12. daughter

### T 7.10 Listen and repeat

1. born
2. bought
3. world
4. answer
5. knives
6. wrong
7. cupboard
8. Christmas

### T 7.11 Special days

1. A Ugh! Work again! I hate Monday mornings!
   B Me, too. Did you have a nice weekend?
   A Yes. It was brilliant.
2. Happy birthday to you.
   Happy birthday to you.
   Happy birthday, dear Tommy,
   Happy birthday to you.
3. A Did you get any Valentine cards?
   B Yes, I did. Listen to this.
   *Roses are red. Violets are blue*
   *You are my Valentine*
   *And I love you.*
   A Oooh-er! Do you know who it's from?
   B No idea!
4. A Congratulations!
   B Oh ... thank you very much.
   A When's the happy day?
   B Pardon?
   A Your wedding day. When is it?
   B Oh! We're not sure. Perhaps some time in June.
5. A It's midnight! Happy New Year everybody!
   B Happy New Year!
   C Happy New Year!
6. A Thank goodness! It's Friday!
   B Yeah. Have a nice weekend!
   A Same to you.

### T 7.12 Listen and answer

1. Did you have a nice weekend?
2. Did you get any Valentine cards?
3. Congratulations!
4. Happy New Year!
5. Have a nice weekend!

## Unit 8

### T 8.1 Inventions

**JEANS**
Two Americans, Jacob Davis and Levi Strauss, made the first jeans in 1873. Davis bought cloth from Levi's shop. He told Levi that he had a special way to make strong trousers for workmen. The first jeans were blue. In 1935 jeans became fashionable for women after they saw them in *Vogue* magazine. In the 1970s, Calvin Klein earned $12.5 million a week from jeans.

**TELEVISION**
A Scotsman, John Logie Baird, transmitted the first television picture on 25 October, 1925. The first thing on television was a boy who worked in the office next to Baird's workroom in London. In 1927 Baird sent pictures from London to Glasgow. In 1928 he sent pictures to New York, and also produced the first colour TV pictures.

**ASPIRIN**
Felix Hofman a 29-year-old chemist who worked for the German company Bayer, invented the drug Aspirin in March 1899. He gave the first aspirin to his father for his arthritis. By 1950 it was the best-selling painkiller in the world, and in 1969 the Apollo astronauts took it to the moon. The Spanish philosopher, José Ortega y Gasset, called the 20th century 'The Age of Aspirin'.

### T 8.2 Negatives and positives

1. Two Germans didn't make the first jeans. Two Americans made them.
2. Davis didn't sell cloth in Levi's shop. He bought cloth from Levi's shop.
3. Women didn't see pictures of jeans in *She* magazine. They saw them in *Vogue*.
4. Baird didn't send pictures from London to Paris. He sent pictures from London to Glasgow.
5. Felix Hofman didn't give the first aspirin to his mother. He gave it to his father.
6. A Spanish philosopher didn't call the 19th century, 'the Age of Aspirin'. He called the 20th century, 'the Age of Aspirin'.

### T 8.3 see p62

### T 8.4 Listen and repeat

1. recipe
2. chat
3. shy
4. funny
5. face
6. worried
7. delicious
8. sandwich
9. machine
10. century

### T 8.5 Everyday conversations

1. A Why didn't you laugh at my joke?
   B Because it wasn't very funny. That's why!
2. A Hello. Hello. I can't hear you. Who is it?
   B It's me, Jonathon ... JONATHON! I'm on my mobile phone.
   A Oh, Jonathon! Hi! Sorry, I can't chat now. I'm in a hurry.
3. A Good luck in your exams!
   B Oh, thank you. I always get so nervous before exams.
4. A Mmmmm! Did you make this chocolate cake?
   B I did. Do you like it?
   A Like it? I *love* it. It's delicious. Can I have the recipe?
5. A Come on, Tommy. Say hello to Auntie Mavis. Don't be shy.
   B Hello, Auntie Mavis.

### T 8.6

**Love on the Internet – Debbie and Per**

Debbie  I'm really quite shy. I find it difficult to talk to people face to face. But I find it easy to chat on the Internet. I met Per there about a year ago. It was on a chatline called 'the Chat Room'. He was so funny.

Per  But I'm only funny on the Internet! Anyway, we chatted on the Internet for a year, we exchanged hundreds of e-mails and some photographs. I wanted to phone Debbie but ...

Debbie  I said no. I was worried. I didn't want it to end.

Per  She didn't even give me her address. But finally she said OK, I could phone, so I did, and we spoke for an hour. It was very expensive! That was six months ago. Then she sent me her address and ...

Debbie  ... that was three months ago and one week later, there was a knock at the door and I knew before I opened it. Somehow I wasn't worried any more. I opened the door and ...

Per  ... and I stood there with some flowers ...

Debbie  ... lots of flowers. Red roses. Beautiful ... and ...

Per  ... and well, we fell in love and ...

Both  ... and we got married last Saturday.

**Love in a bottle – Rosa and Vincent**

**Rosa** I love the sea. I like walking on the beach. One day, it was five years ago now, I was on the beach and I stood on something, it was a bottle, a green bottle. I could see something inside. Some paper, so I broke the bottle, it was a letter but …

**Vincent** … but you couldn't read it …

**Rosa** No, I couldn't. You see it was in English and I couldn't speak English then.

**Vincent** You can speak it well now …

**Rosa** No, not really, but anyway. I asked a friend to translate the letter for me. We couldn't believe it. A man in America – he wanted a wife, but the letter was ten years old.

**Vincent** And I still wasn't married!

**Rosa** But I didn't know that. Anyway for a joke I wrote and sent a photo …

**Vincent** And now, I couldn't believe it. I got this letter and a photo. She looked beautiful. I wrote back immediately and we wrote every week for six months … and we spoke on the phone and …

**Rosa** … and finally I flew to America and we met face to face. I was very shy but it was good, very good and now …

**Vincent** … now, we have three children. We have a house by the sea …

**Rosa** We're very happy. You see, we both love the sea!

### T 8.7 Ordinals

first
second
third
fourth
fifth
sixth
tenth
twelfth
thirteenth
sixteenth
seventeenth
twentieth
twenty-first
thirtieth
thirty-first

### T 8.8 Dates

1 The first of April
   April the first
2 The second of March
   March the second
3 The seventeenth of September
   September the seventeenth
4 The nineteenth of November
   November the nineteenth
5 The twenty-third of June
   June the twenty-third
6 The twenty-ninth of February, nineteen seventy-six
7 The nineteenth of December, nineteen eighty-three
8 The third of October, nineteen ninety-nine
9 The thirty-first of May, two thousand
10 The fifteenth of July, two thousand and four

### T 8.9 What's the date?

1 The fourth of January
2 May the seventh, 1997
3 The fifteenth of August, 2001
4 A It was a Friday.
   B No, it wasn't. It was a Thursday.
   A No, I remember. It was Friday the thirteenth. The thirteenth of July.
5 A Oh no! I forgot your birthday.
   B It doesn't matter, really.
   A It was last Sunday, wasn't it? The thirtieth. November the thirtieth.
6 A Hey! Did you know that Shakespeare was born and died on the same day?
   B That's not possible!
   A Yes, it is. He was born on April the twenty-third, fifteen sixty-four and he died on April the twenty-third, sixteen sixteen.

## Unit 9

### T 9.1 Food you like

D = Daisy   T = Tom

**D** I don't like tea.
**T** Oh, I do. Well, sometimes, with sugar. But coffee's horrible!
**D** Yeah. Disgusting. I don't like wine or beer either.
**T** Well – I don't like wine but I like beer. My dad has beer every day after work and sometimes I have a bit.
**D** Beer! Yuk! But apple juice is nice. I really like apple juice. It's delicious.
**T** Mmmm! Yeah, it's delicious and it's good for you. Apples are too! I love all fruit – apples, oranges, bananas, strawberries.
**D** Yeah. OK. I like fruit, but I hate all vegetables, 'specially carrots.
**T** Yeah, vegetables are disgusting. Er – but not all of them, – I quite like peas. Hamburgers, chips, and peas. Mmm! That's one of my favourite meals.
**D** Yeah – hamburgers, I like. Chips, I like. But peas – yuk!
**T** My very favourite meal is spaghetti. Spaghetti, then ice-cream after. Yummy! … Or yoghurt. I love strawberry yoghurt.
**D** Ice-cream – OK, yes. Yoghurt, no! Spaghetti – yes. I like all pasta and pizza! But I don't like it with tomatoes or cheese. I don't like tomatoes very much and I hate cheese.
**T** Mmmm! Pizza. The best. But … you can't have pizza without tomatoes and cheese.
**D** You can.
**T** You can't!
**D** Can!
**T** Can't!
**D** Well, I can. I don't like cheese at all!
**T** What do you like then?
**D** Well, I like … er … I like chocolate and chocolate biscuits …
**T** Yeah! I really like chocolate. Everybody likes chocolate.
**D** Yeah!

### T 9.2 see p67

### T 9.3 Questions and answers

1 Would you like a cigarette?
   No, thanks. I don't smoke.
2 Do you like your teacher?
   Yes. She's very nice.
3 Would you like a drink?
   Yes, please. Some Coke, please.
4 Can I help you?
   Yes. I'd like a book of stamps, please.
5 What sports do you do?
   Well, I like swimming very much.
6 Excuse me, are you ready to order?
   Yes. I'd like a steak, please.

### T 9.4 Listen carefully!

1 Good afternoon. Can I help you?
2 Who's your favourite writer?
3 What would you like for your birthday?
4 Do you like animals?
5 Here's the wine list, sir.
6 Have some ice-cream with your strawberries.

### T 9.5

1 A Good afternoon. Can I help you?
   B Yes. I'd like some fruit, please.
2 A Who's your favourite writer?
   B I like books by John Grisham.
3 A What would you like for your birthday?
   B I'd like a new bike.
4 A Do you like animals?
   B I like cats, but I don't like dogs.
5 A Here's the wine list, sir.
   B We'd like a bottle of French red wine.
6 A Have some ice-cream with your strawberries.
   B No, thanks. I don't like ice-cream.

### T 9.6 Going shopping

B = Barry   MP = Miss Potts

**MP** Good morning. Can I help you?
**B** Yes. I'd like some orange juice, please.
**MP** Er … sorry. There's apple juice but no orange juice.
**B** What's that then? Isn't that orange juice?
**MP** Oh, yes. So it is! My eyes! Here you are.
**B** Thank you, and some milk, please.
**MP** Sorry. I sold the last bottle two minutes ago.
**B** Oh, dear! What about some coffee?
**MP** Yes. Here you are.
**B** Thanks. That's orange juice, coffee … er … and … er … a kilo of apples, please.
**MP** I don't sell apples.
**B** You don't sell apples! That's strange. What about cheese. Can I have some cheese?
**MP** I don't sell cheese, either.

**B** You don't sell cheese! That's amazing. Now, I want some pizza, but I'm sure you don't sell pizza, do you?
**MP** Oh, yes I do. What would you like? Pizza with mushrooms, pizza with cheese and ham, pizza with sausage, or pizza with tomatoes?
**B** Wow! Can I have … er … some pizza with cheese and tomatoes, please?
**MP** Oh, sorry. I forgot. Usually, I have pizza but not on Thursdays. Today's Thursday, isn't it?
**B** Yes, it is. Mmm … OK, … er … OK, forget the pizza. What about bread? I don't suppose you have any bread?
**MP** Yes, you're right.
**B** Pardon?
**MP** You're right. There isn't any bread.
**B** Tell me. Do you do a lot of business?
**MP** Oh, yes sir. This shop is open 24 hours.
**B** Really! What do people buy?
**MP** All the things you see.
**B** Mmmm. OK. That's all for me. How much?
**MP** That's £5.60, please.
**B** Thank you. Goodbye.
**MP** Goodbye sir. See you again soon.
**B** I don't think so.

### T 9.7 My favourite food

**Marian**
Well, I love vegetables, all vegetables – I eat meat too – but not much. I think this is why I like Chinese food so much. There are lots of vegetables in Chinese food. Yes, Chinese is my very favourite food, I like the noodles too. Can you eat with chopsticks? I can!

**Graham**
Now in my job, I travel the world, and I like all kinds of food … but my favourite, my favourite is … er … I always have it as soon as I come home … is a full English breakfast. Bacon, eggs, sausage, mushrooms, tomatoes, and of course toast. I love it, not every day but when I'm at home we have it every Sunday. Mmmm! I'd like it right now – delicious.

**Lucy**
Oh, no question, no problem. I know exactly what my favourite food is. Pasta. All pasta. Especially spaghetti. Pasta with tomato sauce – and I like it best when I'm in Italy. I went on holiday to the Italian lakes last year. The food was wonderful.

**Gavin**
… er … I'm not sure. No, I know what it is. My … favourite … food is Indian food. Friday night I like to go to the pub with friends from work and … have a few beers, … er … no, not too many, … and after we always go to an Indian restaurant and I have a chicken curry with rice. It's the best! I like it more than chips!

**Sally**
Well, shhh! But my very, very favourite food is chocolate. Chocolate anything, I love it. Chocolate ice-cream, chocolate biscuits, chocolate cake, but especially just a big bar of chocolate. Mmmm! Terrible, isn't it? Go on! Have some of this! My friend brought it back from Switzerland for me!

### T 9.8 Polite requests

1 Would you like some more carrots?
Yes, please. They're delicious.
2 Could you pass the salt, please?
Yes, of course. Here you are.
3 Could I have a glass of water, please?
Do you want fizzy or still?
4 Does anybody want more dessert?
Yes, please. I'd love some. It's delicious.
5 How would you like your coffee?
Black, no sugar, please.
6 This is delicious! Can you give me the recipe?
Yes, of course. I'm glad you like it.
7 Do you want help with the washing-up?
No, of course not. We have a dishwasher.

### T 9.9

1 Can I have a cheese sandwich, please?
Yes, of course. That's £1.75.
2 Could you tell me the time, please?
It's just after ten.
3 Can you take me to school?
Jump in.
4 Can I see the menu, please?
Here you are. And would you like a drink to start?
5 Could you lend me some money, please?
Not again! How much would you like this time?
6 Can you help me with my homework, please?
What is it? French? I can't speak a word of French.
7 Can I borrow your dictionary, please?
Yes, if I can find it. I think it's in my bag.

# Unit 10

### T 10.1 Listen and repeat

The country is cheaper and safer than the city.
The city is noisier and dirtier than the country.
The city is more expensive than the country.
The city is more exciting than the country.

### T 10.2 Much more than …

1 **A** Life in the country is slower than city life.
   **B** Yes, the city's much faster.
2 **A** New York is safer than London.
   **B** No, it isn't. New York is much more dangerous.
3 **A** Paris is bigger than Madrid.
   **B** No, it isn't! It's much smaller.
4 **A** Madrid is more expensive than Rome.
   **B** No, it isn't. Madrid is much cheaper.
5 **A** The buildings in Rome are more modern than the buildings in New York.
   **B** No, they aren't. They're much older.
6 **A** The Underground in London is better than the Metro in Paris.
   **B** No! The Underground is much worse.

### T 10.3 Mel's got a better job

**Tara** Why did you leave London? You had a good job.
**Mel** Yes, but I've got a better job here.
**Tara** And you had a big flat in London.
**Mel** Well, I've got a bigger flat here.
**Tara** Really? How many bedrooms has it got?
**Mel** Three. And it's got a garden. It's nicer than my flat in London and it's cheaper.
**Tara** But you haven't got any friends!
**Mel** I've got a lot of friends here. People are much friendlier than in London.
**Tara** But the country's so boring.
**Mel** No, it isn't. It's much more exciting than London. Seacombe has got shops, a cinema, a theatre, and a park. And the air is cleaner and the streets are safer.
**Tara** OK. Everything is wonderful! So when can I visit you?

### T 10.4 The biggest and best!

1 That house is very big.
Yes, it's the biggest house in the village.
2 Claridge's is a very expensive hotel.
Yes, it's the most expensive hotel in London.
3 Castle Combe is a very pretty village.
Yes, it's the prettiest village in England.
4 New York is a very cosmopolitan city.
Yes, it's the most cosmopolitan city in the world.
5 Tom Hanks is a very popular film star.
Yes, he's the most popular film star in America.
6 Miss Smith is a very funny teacher.
Yes, she's the funniest teacher in our school.
7 Anna is a very intelligent student.
Yes, she's the most intelligent student in the class.
8 This is a very easy exercise.
Yes, it's the easiest exercise in the book.

### T 10.5 Listen and respond

1 That house is very big.
2 Claridge's is a very expensive hotel.
3 Castle Combe is a very pretty village.
4 New York is a very cosmopolitan city.
5 Tom Hanks is a very popular film star.
6 Miss Smith is a very funny teacher.
7 Anna is a very intelligent student.
8 This is a very easy exercise.

### T 10.6 A musical interlude

(three music excerpts)

### T 10.7 Listen and repeat
wood
theatre
farm
village
factory
cottage
field
church

### T 10.8 To the lake
Drive along Park Road and turn right. Go under the bridge and past the pub. Turn left up the hill, then drive down the hill to the river. Turn right after the farm and the lake is on the right. It takes twenty minutes.

### T 10.9 A drive in the country
Well, I drove out of the garage, along the road, and under the bridge. Then I drove past the pub, up the hill, and down the hill. But then I drove over the river, and then – it was terrible – I went through the hedge, and into the lake!

## Unit 11

### T 11.1 Who's at the party?
**O = Oliver   M = Monica**
O  Oh dear! Monica, I don't know any of these people. Who are they?
M  Don't worry Oliver. They're all very nice. Can you see that man over there? He's sitting down. That's Harry. He's a musician. He works in LA.
O  Sorry, where?
M  You know, LA. Los Angeles.
O  Oh yeah.
M  And he's talking to Mandy. She's wearing a red dress. She's very nice and very rich! She lives in a beautiful old house in the country.
O  Rich, eh?
M  Yes. Rich and married! Next to her is Fiona. She's drinking a glass of red wine. Fiona's my oldest friend, she and I were at school together.
O  And what does Fiona do?
M  She's a writer. She writes children's stories – they're not very good but … anyway, she's talking to George. He's laughing and smoking a cigar. He's a pilot. He travels the world, thousands of miles every week.
O  And who are those two over there? They're dancing. Mmmm. They know each other very well.
M  Oh, that's Roz and Sam. They're married. They live in the flat upstairs.
O  So … er … that's Harry and Mandy and … er … it's no good, I can't remember all those names.

### T 11.2 Listen to the questions
1  Whose is the baseball cap?
2  Whose are the roller blades?
3  Whose is the dog?

### T 11.3 who's or whose?
1  Who's on the phone?
2  I'm going to the pub. Who's coming?
3  Wow! Look at that sports car. Whose is it?
4  Whose dictionary is this? It's not mine.
5  There are books all over the floor. Whose are they?
6  Who's the most intelligent in our class?
7  Who's got my book?
8  Do you know whose jacket this is?

### T 11.4 What a mess!
A  Whose is this tennis racket?
B  It's mine.
A  What's it doing here?
B  I'm playing tennis this afternoon.

### T 11.5 What a wonderful world
I see trees of green
Red roses too
I see them bloom for me and you
And I think to myself
what a wonderful world.
I see skies of blue
and clouds of white
the bright sunny day
and the dark starry night
and I think to myself
what a wonderful world
The colours of the rainbow
so pretty in the sky
are also on the faces
of the people going by.
I see friends shaking hands
saying 'How do you do?'
They're really saying
'I love you.'
I hear babies cry
I watch them grow.
They'll learn much more
than you'll ever know
and I think to myself
what a wonderful world.
Yes, I think to myself
what a wonderful world.

### T 11.6 Vowels and diphthongs
**Vowels**
1  red       said
2  hat       that
3  kissed    list
4  green     mean
5  laugh     half
6  whose     shoes
7  short     bought

**Diphthongs**
1  white     night
2  near      beer
3  they      pay
4  hair      wear
5  rose      knows
6  ours      flowers

### T 11.7 Tongue twisters
1  Four fine fresh fish for you.
2  Six silly sisters selling shiny shoes.
3  If a dog chews shoes, whose shoes does he choose?
4  I'm looking back,
   To see if she's looking back,
   To see if I'm looking back,
   To see if she's looking back at me!

### T 11.8 In a clothes shop
**SA = shop assistant   C = customer**
SA  Can I help you?
C   Yes, please. I'm looking for a shirt to go with my new suit.
SA  What colour are you looking for?
C   Blue.
SA  What about this one? Do you like this?
C   No, it isn't the right blue.
SA  Well, what about this one? It's a bit darker blue.
C   Oh yes. I like that one much better. Can I try it on?
SA  Yes, of course. The changing rooms are over there.
    Is the size OK?
C   No, it's a bit too big. Have you got a smaller size?
SA  That's the last blue one we've got, I'm afraid. But we've got it in white.
C   OK. I'll take the white. How much is it?
SA  £39.99. How do you want to pay?
C   Can I pay by credit card?
SA  Credit card's fine. Thank you very much.

## Unit 12

### T 12.1
**Rosie**
When I grow up I'm going to be a ballet dancer. I love dancing. I go dancing three times a week. I'm going to travel all over the world and I'm going to learn French and Russian because I want to dance in Paris and Moscow. I'm not going to marry until I'm thirty-five and then I'm going to have two children. First I'd like a girl and then a boy – but maybe I can't plan that! I'm going to work until I'm 75. I'm going to teach dancing and I'm going to open a dance school. It's all very exciting.

**Miss Bishop**
When I retire … ? … er … well … er … two things. First, I'm going to learn Russian – I can already speak French and German, and I want to learn another language. And second, I'm going to learn to drive. It's terrible that I'm 59 and I can't drive – no time to learn. Then I'm going to buy a car and travel all over the world. Also I'm not going to wear boring clothes any more, I hate the skirts and blouses I wear every day for school. I'm going to wear jeans and T-shirts all the time. And when I return from my travels I'm going to write a book and go on TV to talk about it. I'm going to become a TV star!

**T 12.2** Listen and repeat
A Is she going to be a ballet dancer?
B Yes, she is.
A What's she going to do?
B Travel all over the world.

**T 12.3** Questions about Rosie
1 A Why is she going to learn French and Russian?
  B Because she wants to dance in Paris and Moscow.
2 A When is she going to marry?
  B Not until she's thirty-five.
3 A How many children is she going to have?
  B Two.
4 A How long is she going to work?
  B Until she's seventy-five.
5 A What is she going to teach?
  B Dancing.

**T 12.4** It's going to rain
1 Take an umbrella. It's going to rain.
2 Look at the time! You're going to be late for the meeting.
3 Anna's running very fast. She's going to win the race.
4 Look! Jack's on the wall. He's going to fall.
5 Look at that man! He's going to jump.
6 They're going to have a baby. It's due next month.
7 There's my sister and her boyfriend! Yuk! They're going to kiss.
8 'Oh dear. I'm going to sneeze. Aaattishooo!'
  'Bless you!'

**T 12.5** Why are you going?
MB = Miss Bishop   H = Harold
MB First I'm going to Holland.
H Why?
MB To see the tulips, of course!
H Oh yes! How wonderful! Where are you going after that?
MB Well, then I'm going to Spain to watch flamenco dancing.

**T 12.6** The weather
A What's the weather like today?
B It's snowy and it's very cold.
A What was it like yesterday?
B Oh, it was cold and cloudy.
A What's it going to be like tomorrow?
B I think it's going to be warmer.

**T 12.7** Conversations about the weather
1 A It's a lovely day! What shall we do?
  B Let's play tennis!
2 A It's raining again! What shall we do?
  B Let's stay at home and watch a video.

**T 12.8**
1 A It's a lovely day! What shall we do?
  B Let's play tennis!
  A Oh no! It's too hot to play tennis.
  B Well, let's go to the beach.
  A OK. I'll get my swimming costume.
2 A It's raining again! What shall we do?
  B Let's stay at home and watch a video.
  A Oh no! We watched a video last night.
  B Well, let's go to the cinema.
  A OK. Which film do you want to see?

## Unit 13

**T 13.1** A general knowledge quiz
1 When did the first man walk on the moon?
  In 1969.
2 Where are the Andes mountains?
  In South America.
3 Who did Mother Teresa look after?
  Poor people in Calcutta.
4 Who won the last World Cup?
  France in 1998.
5 How many American states are there?
  50.
6 How much does an African elephant weigh?
  5–7 tonnes.
7 How far is it from London to New York?
  6,000 kilometres.
8 How old was Princess Diana when she died?
  36.
9 What languages do Swiss people speak?
  German, French, Italian, and Romansch.
10 What did Marconi invent in 1901?
  The radio.
11 What sort of music did Louis Armstrong play?
  Jazz.
12 What happens at the end of *Romeo and Juliet*?
  Romeo and Juliet kill themselves.
13 What happened in Europe in 1939?
  The Second World War started.
14 Why do birds migrate?
  Because the winter is cold.
15 Which was the first country to have TV?
  Britain.
16 Which language has the most words?
  English.

**T 13.2** Listen carefully!
1 Why do you want to go?
2 Who is she?
3 Where's he staying?
4 Why didn't they come?
5 How old was she?
6 Does he play the guitar?
7 Where did you go at the weekend?

**T 13.3** Noises in the night
It was about 2 o'clock in the morning, and … suddenly I woke up. I heard a noise. I got out of bed and went slowly downstairs. There was a light on in the living room. I listened carefully. I could hear two men speaking very quietly. 'Burglars!' I thought. 'Two burglars!' Immediately I ran back upstairs and phoned the police. I was really frightened. Fortunately the police arrived quickly. They opened the front door and went into the living room. Then they came upstairs to find me. 'It's all right now, sir,' they explained. 'We turned the television off for you!'

**T 13.4** see p102

**T 13.5** see p104

**T 13.6** Catching a train
Trains from Oxford to Bristol Temple Meads. Monday to Friday.
Here are the departure times from Oxford and arrival times in Bristol.
0816 arriving 0946
0945 arriving 1114
1040 arriving 1208
11…

**T 13.7** The information bureau
A = Ann   B = clerk
A Good morning. Can you tell me the times of trains from Bristol back to Oxford, please?
B Afternoon, evening? When do you want to come back?
A About five o'clock this afternoon.
B About five o'clock. Right. Let's have a look. There's a train that leaves at 5.28, then there isn't another one until 6.50.
A And what time do they get in?
B The 5.28 gets into Oxford at 6.54 and the 6.50 gets in at 8.10.
A Thanks a lot.

**T 13.8** At the ticket office
A Hello. A return to Bristol, please.
C Day return or period return?
A A day return.
C How do you want to pay?
A Cash, please.
C That's eighteen pounds.
A Here's a twenty-pound note.
C Here's your change and your ticket.
A Thank you. Which platform is it?
C You want platform 1 over there.
A OK, thanks very much. Goodbye.

## Unit 14

**T 14.1** see p106

**T 14.2** see p106

**T 14.3** The life of Ryan
Yes, I've lived in a foreign country. In Japan, actually. I lived in Osaka for a year. I enjoyed it very much. I loved the food. And, yes, I have worked for a big company. I worked for Nissan, the car company, that's why I was in Japan. That was two years ago, then I got another job.
  Have I stayed in an expensive hotel? No, never – only cheap hotels for me, I'm afraid, but I have flown in a jumbo jet – four or five times, actually. Oh, I've never cooked a meal

for a lot of people. I love food but I don't like cooking, sometimes I cook for me and my girlfriend but she likes it better if we go out for a meal! And I've never met a famous person – oh, just a minute, well not met but I've seen … er… I saw a famous politician at the airport once – Oh, who was it? I can't remember his name. Er … I've only seen one Shakespeare play, when I was at school, we saw *Romeo and Juliet*. It was OK. I've driven a tractor though, I had a holiday job on a farm when I was 17. I enjoyed that. Good news – I've never been to hospital. I was born in hospital, of course, but that's different. Bad news – I've never won a competition. I do the lottery every week but I've never, ever won a thing!

### T 14.4  A honeymoon in London

M = Marilyn    J = Judy

M  We're having a great time!
J  Tell me about it! What have you done so far?
M  Well, we've been to Buckingham Palace. That was the first thing we did. It's right in the centre of London! We went inside and looked around.
J  Have you seen the Houses of Parliament yet?
M  Yeah, we have. We've just had a boat ride on the River Thames and we went right past the Houses of Parliament. We saw Big Ben! Then we went on the London Eye. That's the big wheel near Big Ben. That was this morning. This afternoon we're going to take a taxi to Hyde Park and then go shopping in Harrods. Tomorrow morning we're going to see the Crown Jewels in the Tower of London.
J  Wow! You're busy! And what about those big red buses? Have you travelled on a double-decker bus yet?
M  Oh, yeah we took one when we went to Buckingham Palace. We sat upstairs. You get a great view of the city.
J  Tomorrow's your last night. What are you going to do on your last night?
M  Well, we're going to the theatre, but we haven't decided what to see yet.
J  Oh, you're so lucky! Give my love to Rod!
M  Yeah. Bye, Judy. See you soon!

### T 14.5  Leaving on a jet plane

My bags are packed, I'm ready to go
I'm standing here outside your door,
I hate to wake you up to say goodbye
But the dawn is breaking,
It's early morn'
The taxi's waiting,
He's blowing his horn.
Already I'm so lonesome
I could die.

So kiss me and smile for me,
Tell me that you'll wait for me,
Hold me like you'll never let me go,
'Cos I'm leaving on a jet plane,
I don't know when I'll be back again.
Oh babe, I hate to go.

There's so many times I've let you down,
So many times I've played around,
I tell you now
They don't mean a thing.
Every place I go, I'll think of you
Every song I sing, I'll sing for you
When I come back
I'll wear your wedding ring.

### T 14.6  Flight information

British Airways flight BA 516 to Geneva boarding at gate 4, last call. Flight BA 516 to Geneva, last call. Scandinavian Airlines flight SK 832 to Frankfurt is delayed one hour. Flight SK 832 to Frankfurt, delayed one hour. Air France flight 472 to Amsterdam is now boarding at gate 17. Flight AF 472 to Amsterdam, now boarding, gate 17. Lufthansa flight 309 to Miami is now boarding at gate 32. Flight LH 309 to Miami, now boarding, gate 32. Virgin Airlines flight to New York, VS 876 to New York. Please wait in the departure lounge until a further announcement. Thank you. Passengers are reminded to keep their hand luggage with them at all times.

### T 14.7  Conversations at the airport

1  A  Listen! … BA 516 to Geneva. That's our flight.
   B  Did the announcement say gate 4 or 14?
   A  I couldn't hear. I think it said 4.
   B  Look! There it is on the departure board. It *is* gate 4.
   A  OK. Come on! Let's go.

2  A  Can I have your ticket, please?
   B  Yes, of course.
   A  Thank you. How many suitcases have you got?
   B  Just one.
   A  And have you got much hand luggage?
   B  Just this bag.
   A  That's fine.
   B  Oh … can I have a seat next to the window?
   A  Yes, that's OK. Here's your boarding pass. Have a nice flight!

3  A  Rod! Marilyn! Over here!
   B  Hi! Judy! Great to see you!
   A  It's great to see you too. You look terrific! Did you have a good honeymoon?
   B  Fantastic. Everything was fantastic.
   A  Well, you haven't missed anything here. Nothing much has happened at all!

4  A  There's my flight. It's time to go.
   B  Oh no! It's been a wonderful two weeks. I can't believe it's over.
   A  I know. When can we see each other again?
   B  Soon, I hope. I'll write every day.
   A  I'll phone too. Goodbye.
   B  Goodbye. Give my love to your family.

# Grammar Reference

## Unit 1

### 1.1 Verb *to be*

**Positive**

| I | am | | I'm = I am |
|---|---|---|---|
| He<br>She<br>It | is | from the USA. | He's = He is<br>She's = She is<br>It's = It is |
| We<br>You<br>They | are | | We're = We are<br>You're = You are<br>They're = They are |

**Question**

| | am | I | |
|---|---|---|---|
| Where | is | he<br>she<br>it | from? |
| | are | we<br>you<br>they | |

*I'm 20*

I'm 20.                NOT    ~~I'm 20 years.~~
I'm 20 years old.            ~~I have 20 years.~~

### 1.2 Possessive adjectives

| What's | my<br>your<br>his<br>her | name? |
|---|---|---|
| This is | its<br>our<br>your<br>their | house. |

What's = What is

### 1.3 Question words

**What** is your phone number?
**Where** are you from?
**How** are you?

### 1.4 *a/an*

| It's a | ticket.<br>newspaper.<br>magazine. |
|---|---|

We use *an* before a vowel.

| It's an | apple.<br>envelope.<br>English dictionary. |
|---|---|

I'm a doctor.         NOT    ~~I'm doctor.~~
I'm a student.                ~~I'm student.~~

### 1.5 Plural nouns

1. Most nouns add *-s* in the plural.
   stamp**s**
   key**s**
   camera**s**

2. If the noun ends in *-s*, *-ss*, *-sh*, or *-ch*, add *-es*.
   bus        bus**es**
   class      class**es**
   wish       wish**es**
   match      match**es**

3. If the noun ends in a consonant + *-y*, the y changes to *-ies*.
   country    countr**ies**
   party      part**ies**
   But if the noun ends in a vowel + *-y*, the *-y* doesn't change.
   key        key**s**
   day        da**ys**

4. Some nouns are irregular. Dictionaries show this.
   child      children
   person     people
   woman      women
   man        men

### 1.6 Numbers 1–20

1  one
2  two
3  three
4  four
5  five
6  six
7  seven
8  eight
9  nine
10 ten
11 eleven
12 twelve
13 thirteen
14 fourteen
15 fifteen
16 sixteen
17 seventeen
18 eighteen
19 nineteen
20 twenty

### 1.7 Prepositions

Where are you **from**?
I live **in** a house **in** Toluca.
What's this **in** English?

# Unit 2

## 2.1 Verb *to be*

**Questions with question words**

| | | | Answers |
|---|---|---|---|
| What | is her surname? | | Anderson. |
| | is his job? | | He's a policeman. |
| | is her address? | | 34, Church Street. |
| Where | is she | from? | Mexico. |
| | are you | | |
| | are they | | |
| Who | is Lara? | | She's Patrick's daughter. |
| | is she? | | |
| How old | is he? | | Twenty-two. |
| | are you? | | |
| How much | is an ice-cream? | | One pound 50p. |

*Yes/No* **questions**

| | | | Short answers |
|---|---|---|---|
| Is | he | hot? | Yes, he is. |
| | she | | No, she isn't. |
| | it | | Yes, it is. |
| Are | you | married? | No, I'm not./No, we aren't. |
| | they | | Yes, they are./No, they aren't. |

**Negative**

| | | |
|---|---|---|
| I | 'm not | |
| He | isn't | |
| She | | from the States. |
| It | | |
| We | aren't | |
| You | | |
| They | | |

I'm not = I am not (~~I amn't~~)

He isn't = He is not
She isn't = She is not
It isn't = It is not

We aren't = We are not
You aren't = You are not
They aren't = They are not

## 2.2 Possessive *'s*

My wife**'s** name is Judy.
That's Andrea**'s** dictionary.

## 2.3 Numbers 21–100

21 twenty-one
22 twenty-two
23 twenty-three
24 twenty-four
25 twenty-five
26 twenty-six
27 twenty-seven
28 twenty-eight
29 twenty-nine
30 thirty
31 thirty-one
40 forty
50 fifty
60 sixty
70 seventy
80 eighty
90 ninety
100 one hundred

## 2.4 Prepositions

This is a photo **of** my family.
It's good practice **for** you.

I'm **at** home. My mother and father are **at** work.
I'm **at** La Guardia Community College.

I'm **in** New York. I'm **in** a class **with** eight other students.
I live **in** an apartment **with** two American girls.
Central Park is lovely **in** the snow.

# Unit 3

## 3.1 Present Simple *he, she, it*

1 The Present Simple expresses a fact which is always true, or true for a long time.
   He **comes** from Switzerland.
   She **works** in a bank.
2 It also expresses a habit.
   She **goes** skiing in winter.
   He never **has** a holiday.

**Positive**

| He / She / It | lives | in Australia. |
|---|---|---|

*Have* is irregular.   She **has** a dog.   NOT   she ~~haves~~

**Negative**

| He / She / It | doesn't live | in France. | doesn't = does not |
|---|---|---|---|

**Question**

| Where does | he / she / it | live? |
|---|---|---|

*Yes/No* questions

| Does | he / she / it | live | in Australia? |
|---|---|---|---|
|  |  |  | in France? |

**Short answers**

Yes, he does.
No, she doesn't.
Yes, it does.

## 3.2 Spelling of the third person singular

1 Most verbs add *-s* in the third person singular.
   wear      wear**s**
   speak     speak**s**
   live      live**s**
   But *go* and *do* are different. They add *-es*.
   go        go**es**
   do        do**es**
2 If the verb ends in *-s*, *-sh*, or *-ch*, add *-es*.
   finish    finish**es**
   watch     watch**es**
3 If the verb ends in a consonant + *-y*, the *y* changes to *-ies*.
   fly       fl**ies**
   study     stud**ies**
   But if the verb ends in a vowel + *-y* the *y* does not change.
   play      play**s**
4 *Have* is irregular.
   have      has

## 3.3 Prepositions

She lives **in** Switzerland.
She goes skiing **in** her free time.
**In** the evening we have supper.
A nurse looks **after** people **in** hospital.
She likes going **for** walks **in** summer.

Get **on** the bus.
He lives **on** an island **in** the west of Scotland.

He collects the post **from** the boat.
He delivers the beer **to** the pub.
He drives the children **to** school.
At ten we go **to** bed.
He likes listening **to** music.
He speaks **to** people **on** his radio.
She's married **to** an American.

There's a letter **for** you.
He makes breakfast **for** the guests.
He writes **for** a newspaper.

He works **as** an undertaker.
Tourists come **by** boat.
It's **about** 6.30.

# Unit 4

## 4.1 Present Simple

**Positive**

| I You We They | start | |
|---|---|---|
| He She It | starts | at 6.30. |

**Negative**

| I You We They | don't | | |
|---|---|---|---|
| He She It | doesn't | start | at 6.30. |

**Question**

| When | do | I you we they | start? |
|---|---|---|---|
| | does | he she it | |

**Yes/No questions**

| Do | you they | have | a camera? |
|---|---|---|---|
| Does | he she it | like | Chinese food? |

**Short answers**

No, I don't./No, we don't.
Yes, they do.

Yes, he does.
No, she doesn't.
Yes, it does.

## 4.2 Adverbs of frequency

| 0% | | 50% | | 100% |
|---|---|---|---|---|
| never | sometimes | often | usually | always |

1 These adverbs usually come before the main verb.
   I **usually** go to bed at about 11.00.
   I don't **often** go swimming.
   She **never** eats meat.
   We **always** have wine in the evenings.
   I **sometimes** play tennis on Saturdays.

2 *Sometimes* and *usually* can also come at the beginning or the end of a sentence.
   **Sometimes** we play cards.    We play cards **sometimes**.
   **Usually** I walk to school.    I walk to school **usually**.

3 *Never* and *always* can't come at the beginning or the end of a sentence.
   NOT ~~Never I go to the theatre.~~
   ~~Always I have tea in the morning.~~

## 4.3 *like/love* + verb + *-ing*

When *like* and *love* are followed by a verb, it is usually verb + *-ing*.
   I **like** cook**ing**.
   She **loves** listen**ing** to music.
   They **like** sail**ing** very much.

## 4.4 Prepositions

She gets up early **on** weekdays.
He plays football **on** Friday mornings.
They never go out **on** Friday evenings.
Where do you go **on** holiday?
He lives **on** the next block.
He hates watching football **on** television.

Do you relax **at** weekends?
She gets up **at** six o'clock.

She gets up early **in** the morning.
We go out **in** the evening.
He takes photos **in** (the) spring.

# Unit 5

## 5.1 *There is/are*

**Positive**

| There | is | a sofa. | (singular) |
|---|---|---|---|
| | are | two books. | (plural) |

**Negative**

| There | isn't | an armchair. | (singular) |
|---|---|---|---|
| | aren't | any flowers. | (plural) |

**Yes/No questions**

| Is | there | a table? |
|---|---|---|
| Are | | any photos? |

**Short answers**

Yes, there is.
No, there isn't.

Yes, there are.
No, there aren't.

## 5.2 *How many . . . ?*

**How many** books do you have?

## 5.3 *some/any*

**Positive**
There are **some** flowers.    *some* + plural noun

**Negative**
There aren't **any** cups.    *any* + plural noun

**Question**
Are there **any** books?    *any* + plural noun

## 5.4 this, that, these, those

We use *this* and *these* to talk about people/things that are near to us.
  I like **this** ice-cream.
  I want **these** shoes.

We use *that* and *those* to talk about people/things that aren't near to us.
  Do you like **that** picture on the wall?
  Who are **those** children outside?

## 5.5 Prepositions

It's the best home **in** the world.
The front door is **at** the top of the steps.
There are magazines **under** the table.

There is a photo **on** the television.
There are two pictures **on** the wall.
The cinema is **on** the left, **opposite** the flower shop.

The bank is **next to** the supermarket.
The bus stop is **near** the park.
There is a post box **in front of** the chemist's.

# Unit 6

## 6.1 can/can't

*Can* and *can't* have the same form in all persons.
There is no *do* or *does*.
*Can* is followed by the infinitive (without *to*).

### could/couldn't

*Could* is the past of *can*. *Could* and *couldn't* have the same form in all persons.
*Could* is followed by the infinitive (without *to*).

**Positive**

| I<br>He/She/It<br>We<br>You<br>They | can<br>could | swim. |
|---|---|---|

**Negative**

| I<br>He/She/It<br>We<br>You<br>They | can't<br>couldn't | dance. |
|---|---|---|

NOT  He ~~doesn't can~~ dance.

**Question**

| What | can<br>could | I<br>you<br>he/she/it<br>we<br>they | do? |
|---|---|---|---|

**Yes/No questions**

| Can<br>Could | you<br>she<br>they | drive?<br>cook? |
|---|---|---|

**Short answers**
No, I can't./No, we couldn't.
Yes, she can/could.
Yes, they can/could.

NOT  ~~Do you can~~ drive?

## 6.2 was/were

*Was/were* is the past of *am/is/are*.

**Positive**

| I<br>He/She/It | was | in Paris yesterday.<br>in England last year. |
|---|---|---|
| We<br>You<br>They | were | |

**Negative**

| I<br>He/She/It | wasn't | at school yesterday.<br>at the party last night. |
|---|---|---|
| We<br>You<br>They | weren't | |

**Question**

| Where | was | I?<br>he/she/it? |
|---|---|---|
| | were | we?<br>you?<br>they? |

**Yes/No questions**

| Was | he<br>she | at work?<br>at home? |
|---|---|---|
| Were | you<br>they | |

**Short answers**
No, he wasn't.
Yes, she was.
Yes, I was./Yes, we were.
No, they weren't.

### was born

| Where | was | she<br>he | born? |
|---|---|---|---|
| | were | you<br>they | |

I **was born** in Manchester in 1980.   NOT  ~~I am born~~ in 1980.

## 6.3 Prepositions

They were **in** England in 1998.
I was **at** a party.
Yesterday there was a party **at** my house.
Can I speak **to** you?
She sells pictures **for** $10,000.
She paints **for** two hours **until** bedtime.

# Unit 7

## 7.1 Past Simple – spelling of regular verbs

1. The normal rule is to add *-ed*.
   work**ed**    start**ed**
   If the verb ends in *-e*, add *-d*.
   live**d**    love**d**

2. If the verb has only one syllable and one vowel and one consonant, double the consonant.
   sto**pp**ed    pla**nn**ed

3. Verbs that end in a consonant + *-y* change to *-ied*.
   stud**ied**    carr**ied**

## 7.2 Past Simple

The Past Simple expresses a past action that is finished.
   I **lived** in Rome when I was 6.
   She **started** work when she was 8.
The form of the Past Simple is the same in all persons.

**Positive**

| I He/She/It We You They | moved went | to London in 1985. |
|---|---|---|

**Negative**
We use *didn't* + infinitive (without *to*) in all persons.

| I He/She/It We You They | didn't | move go | to London. |
|---|---|---|---|

**Question**
We use *did* + infinitive (without *to*) in all persons.

| When Where | did | I you he/she/it we they | go? |
|---|---|---|---|

**Yes/No questions**

| Did | you she they etc. | like enjoy | the film? the party? |
|---|---|---|---|

**Short answers**
No, I didn't./No, we didn't.
Yes, she did.
No, they didn't.

There is list of irregular verbs on p142.

## 7.3 Time expressions

| last | night Saturday week month year |
|---|---|
| yesterday | morning afternoon evening |

## 7.4 Prepositions

She thinks **about** her past life.
She died **in** a car crash.
He was tired **of** politics.
People were afraid **of** her.
Politics was the love **of** her life.
Who is the card **from**?
She worked **from** 6.00 **until** 10.00.

# Unit 8

## 8.1 Past Simple

**Negative**
Negatives in the Past Simple are the same in all persons.

| I He/She We You They | didn't | go out see Tom watch TV | last night. |
|---|---|---|---|

*ago*

| I went to the USA | ten years two weeks a month | ago. |
|---|---|---|

## 8.2 Time expressions

| in | the twentieth century 1924 the 1990s winter/summer the evening/the morning September |
|---|---|
| on | 10 October Christmas Day Saturday Sunday evening |
| at | seven o'clock weekends night |

## 8.3 Prepositions

What's **on** television this evening?
I'm **on** a mobile phone.
We spoke for an hour **on** the phone.
Some people try to find love **on** the internet.
We didn't laugh **at** his joke.
There was a knock **at** the door.
Today's the third **of** April.

# Unit 9

## 9.1 Count and uncount nouns

Some nouns are countable.
    a book   two books
    an egg   six eggs
Some nouns are uncountable.
    bread   rice
Some nouns are both!
    Do you like ice-cream?
    We'd like three ice-creams, please.

## 9.2 would like

*Would* is the same in all persons. We use *would like* in offers and requests.

**Positive**

| I<br>You<br>He/She/It<br>We<br>They | 'd like | a drink. |

'd = would

**Yes/No questions**

| Would | you<br>he/she/it<br>they | like a biscuit? |

**Short answers**

Yes, please.
No, thank you.

## 9.3 some and any

We use *some* in positive sentences with uncountable nouns and plural nouns.

| There is | some | bread | on the table. |
| There are | | oranges | |

We use *some* in questions when we ask for things and offer things.

| Can I have | some | coffee, please? | (I know there is some coffee.) |
| Would you like | | grapes? | (I know there are some grapes.) |

We use *any* in questions and negative sentences with uncountable nouns and plural nouns.

| Is there | any | water? | (I don't know if there is any water.) |
| Does she have | | children? | (I don't know if she has any children.) |
| I can't see | | rice. | |
| There aren't | | people. | |

## 9.4 How much . . . ? and How many . . . ?

We use *How much . . . ?* with uncount nouns.
    **How much** rice is there?
    There isn't much rice.
We use *How many . . . ?* with count nouns.
    **How many** apples are there?
    There aren't many apples.

## 9.5 Prepositions

I've got a book **by** John Grisham.
Help me **with** my homework.

# Unit 10

## 10.1 Comparative and superlative adjectives

|  | Adjective | Comparative | Superlative |
|---|---|---|---|
| One-syllable adjectives | old<br>safe<br>big<br>hot | old**er**<br>saf**er**<br>big**ger**<br>hot**ter** | the old**est**<br>the saf**est**<br>the big**gest**\*<br>the hot**test**\* |
| Adjectives ending in -y | noisy<br>dirty | nois**ier**<br>dirt**ier** | the nois**iest**<br>the dirt**iest** |
| Adjectives with two or more syllables | boring<br>beautiful | **more** boring<br>**more** beautiful | the **most** boring<br>the **most** beautiful |
| Irregular adjectives | good<br>bad<br>far | **better**<br>**worse**<br>**further** | the **best**<br>the **worst**<br>the **furthest** |

\* Adjectives which end in one vowel and one consonant double the consonant.

You're **older than** me.
New York is **dirtier than** Paris.
Prague is one of **the most beautiful** cities in Europe.

## 10.2 *have got* and *have*

*Have got* means the same as *have* to talk about possession, but the form is very different. We often use *have got* in spoken English.

### have got

**Positive**

| I<br>You<br>We<br>They | have | got | a cat.<br>a garden. |
|---|---|---|---|
| He<br>She<br>It | has | | |

**Negative**

| I<br>You<br>We<br>They | haven't | got | a dog.<br>a garage. |
|---|---|---|---|
| He<br>She<br>It | hasn't | | |

**Questions**

| Have | I<br>you<br>we<br>they | got | any money?<br>a sister? |
|---|---|---|---|
| Has | he<br>she<br>it | | |

How many children **have they got**?

**Short answers**
Yes, I have./No, I haven't.
Yes, she has./No, she hasn't.

### have

**Positive**

| I<br>You<br>We<br>They | have | | a cat.<br>a garden. |
|---|---|---|---|
| He<br>She<br>It | has | | |

**Negative**

| I<br>You<br>We<br>They | don't | have | a dog.<br>a garage. |
|---|---|---|---|
| He<br>She<br>It | doesn't | | |

**Questions**

| Do | I<br>you<br>we<br>they | have | any money?<br>a sister? |
|---|---|---|---|
| Does | he<br>she<br>it | | |

How many children **do they have**?

**Short answers**
Yes, I do./No, I don't.
Yes, she does./No, she doesn't.

The past of both *have* and *have got* is *had*.

## 10.3 Prepositions

The country is quieter **than** the city.
The house is 50 metres **from** the sea.
Everest is the highest mountain **in** the world.
He spends his time **on** the banks of the river.
She came **out of** the garage.
He drove **along** the road.
They ran **over** the bridge.
I walked **past** the pub.
He walked **up** the hill.
He ran **down** the hill.
The boat went **across** the river.
The cat ran **through** the hedge.
He jumped **into** the lake.

# Unit 11

## 11.1 Present Continuous

1 The Present Continuous describes an activity happening now.
   She**'s wearing** jeans.
   **I'm studying** English.

2 It also describes an activity in the near future.
   **I'm playing** tennis this afternoon.
   Jane**'s seeing** her boyfriend tonight.

**Positive and Negative**

| I | am | | |
|---|---|---|---|
| He She It | is | (not) going | outside. |
| We You They | are | | |

**Question**

| | am | I | |
|---|---|---|---|
| Where | is | he/she/it | going? |
| | are | we you they | |

*Yes/No* questions          Short answers
Are you having a good time?   Yes, we are.
Is my English getting better?  Yes, it is.
Are they having a party?      No, they aren't.

## Spelling of verb + -ing

1 Most verbs just add *-ing*.
   wear    wea**ring**
   go      go**ing**
   cook    coo**king**
   hold    hold**ing**

2 If the infinitive ends in *-e*, drop the *-e*.
   write   wri**ting**
   smile   smi**ling**
   take    ta**king**

3 When a one-syllable verb has one vowel and ends in a consonant, double the consonant.
   sit     si**tt**ing
   get     ge**tt**ing
   run     ru**nn**ing

## 11.2 Present Simple and Present Continuous

1 The Present Simple describes things that are always true, or true for a long time.
   I **come** from Switzerland.
   He **works** in a bank.

2 The Present Continuous describes activities happening now, and temporary activities.
   Why **are you wearing** a suit? You usually wear jeans.

## 11.3 *Whose* + possessive pronouns

*Whose …?* asks about possession.

| Subject | Object | Adjective | Pronoun |
|---------|--------|-----------|---------|
| I | me | my | mine |
| You | you | your | yours |
| He | him | his | his |
| She | her | her | hers |
| We | us | our | ours |
| They | them | their | theirs |

| | | |
|---|---|---|
| Whose is this book? Whose book is this? Whose is it? | It's | mine. yours. hers. his. ours. theirs. |

## 11.4 Prepositions

I read **in** bed.
We've got this jumper **in** red.
He's talking **to** Mandy.
There's a girl **with** fair hair.
I'm looking **for** a jumper.
I always pay **by** credit card.

# Unit 12

## 12.1 going to

1. *Going to* expresses a person's plans and intentions.
   She's **going to** be a ballet dancer when she grows up.
   We're **going to** stay in a villa in France this summer.

2. Often there is no difference between *going to* and the Present Continuous to refer to a future intention.
   **I'm seeing** Peter tonight.
   **I'm going to see** Peter tonight.

3. We also use *going to* when we can see now that something is sure to happen in the future.
   Careful! That glass is **going to** fall!

**Positive and negative**

| I | am | | |
|---|---|---|---|
| He/She/It | is | (not) going to | have a break. stay at home. |
| We You They | are | | |

**Question**

| | am | I | | |
|---|---|---|---|---|
| When | is | he/she/it | going to | have a break? stay at home? |
| | are | we you they | | |

With the verbs *to go* and *to come*, we usually use the Present Continuous for future plans.
   We're **going** to Paris next week.
   Joe and Tim **are coming** for lunch tomorrow.

## 12.2 Infinitive of purpose

The infinitive can express why a person does something.
   I'm saving my money **to buy** a CD player.
   ( = because I want to buy a CD player)

   We're going to Paris **to have** a holiday.
   ( = because we want to have a holiday)

   NOT
   I'm saving my money ~~for to buy~~ a CD player.
   I'm saving my money ~~for buy~~ a CD player.

## 12.3 Prepositions

I'm going to Florida **in** a year's time.
He's interested **in** flying.
She's good **at** singing.
She was afraid **of** cars.
What's the weather **like**?
What's **on** TV tonight?
There's a film **on** Channel 4.
What's **on at** the cinema?

# Unit 13

## 13.1 Question forms

**When** did Columbus discover America?
**Where** are the Andes?
**Who** did she marry?
**Who** was Mother Teresa?
**How** do you get to school?
**What** do you have for breakfast?
**What** happens at the end of the story?
**Why** do you want to learn English?

**How many** people are there in the class?
**How much** does she earn?
**How far** is it to the centre?
**What sort of** car do you have?
**Which newspaper** do you read?

## 13.2 Adjectives and adverbs

Adjectives describe nouns.
   a **big** dog
   a **careful** driver

Adverbs describe verbs.
   She ran **quickly**.
   He drives too **fast**.

To form regular adverbs, add *-ly* to the adjective.
Words ending in *-y* change to *-ily*.

| Adjective | Adverb |
|---|---|
| quick | quickly |
| bad | badly |
| careful | carefully |
| immediate | immediately |
| easy | easily |

Some adverbs are irregular.

| Adjective | Adverb |
|---|---|
| good | well |
| hard | hard |
| early | early |
| fast | fast |

## 13.3 Prepositions

What's the story **about**?
What happens **at** the end of the story?
The train leaves **from** platform 9.

# Unit 14

## 14.1 Present Perfect

1 The Present Perfect refers to an action that happened some time before now.
   She's **travelled** to most parts of the world.
   **Have you** ever **been** in a car accident?

2 If we want to say *when* these actions happened, we must use the Past Simple.
   She **went** to Russia two years ago.
   I **was** in a crash when I was 10.

3 Notice the time expressions used with the Past Simple.

| I left | last night. yesterday. in 1990. at three o'clock. on Monday. |
|---|---|

**Positive and negative**

| I You We They | have | (not) been | to the States. |
|---|---|---|---|
| He She It | has | | |

I've been = I have been
You've been = You have been
We've been = We have been
They've been = They have been

He's been = He has been
She's been = She has been
It's been = It has been

**Question**

| Where | have | I you we they | been? |
|---|---|---|---|
| | has | she he it | |

*Yes/No* questions
Have you been to Russia?

**Short answers**
Yes, I have.
No, I haven't.

### *ever* and *never*

We use *ever* in questions and *never* in negative sentences.
   Have you **ever** been to Russia?
   I've **never** been to Russia.

## 14.2 *yet* and *just*

We use *just* in positive sentences. We use *yet* in negative sentences and questions.
   Have you done your homework **yet**?
   I haven't done it **yet** (but I'm going to).
   I have **just** done it (a short time before now).

## 14.3 *been* and *gone*

She's **gone** to Portugal (and she's there now).
She's **been** to Portugal (sometime in her life, but now she has returned).

## 14.4 Prepositions

She works **for** a big company.
Hamlet is a play **by** Shakespeare.
Brad and Marilyn are **on** honeymoon
Wait **for** me!

# Word list

Here is a list of most of the new words in the units of New Headway Elementary.

adj = adjective
adv = adverb
conj = conjunction
opp = opposite
pl = plural
prep = preposition
pron = pronoun
pp = past participle
n = noun
v = verb
infml = informal
US – American English

## Unit 1

apple n /'æpl/
bag n /bæg/
because conj /bɪ'kɒz/
Brazil n /brə'zɪl/
brother n /'brʌðə/
camera n /'kæmərə/
children n pl /'tʃɪldrən/
cinema n /'sɪnəmə/
country n /'kʌntri/
day n /deɪ/
dictionary n /'dɪkʃənri/
doctor n /'dɒktə/
Egypt n /'iːdʒɪpt/
England n /'ɪŋglənd/
evening n /'iːvnɪŋ/
extension n /ɪk'stenʃən/
fine adj /faɪn/
flat n /flæt/
France n /frɑːns/
from prep /frɒm/
Germany n /'dʒɜːməni/
goodbye /gʊd'baɪ/
have v /hæv/
hello /hə'ləʊ/
her pron /hɜː/
house n /haʊs/
Hungary n /'hʌŋgəri/
international adj /ˌɪntə'næʃnəl/
Italy n /'ɪtəli/
Japan n /dʒə'pæn/
job n /dʒɒb/
key n /kiː/
language n /'læŋgwɪdʒ/
learn v /lɜːn/
letter n /'letə/
live v /lɪv/
magazine n /mægə'ziːn/
married adj /'mærɪd/
me pron /miː/
Mexico n /'meksɪkəʊ/
my pron /maɪ/
name n /neɪm/
newspaper n /'njuːspeɪpə/
nice adj /naɪs/
not bad adj infml /ˌnɒt 'bæd/
orange n /'ɒrɪndʒ/
postcard n /'pəʊskɑːd/
Russia n /'rʌʃə/
see you v infml /ˌsiː 'juː/
sister n /'sɪstə/
Spain n /speɪn/
stamp n /stæmp/
student n /'stjuːdənt/
teacher n /'tiːtʃə/
telephone number n /'telɪfəʊn ˌnʌmbə/
thank you /'θæŋk juː/
thanks /θæŋks/
the USA n /ðə ˌjuːes'eɪ/
this (book) /ðɪs/
ticket n /'tɪkɪt/
want v /wɒnt/
where adv /weə/
your pron /jɔː/

## Unit 2

accountant n /ə'kaʊntənt/
address n /ə'dres/
age n /eɪdʒ/
American adj /ə'merɪkən/
anything else /'enɪθɪŋ 'els/
apartment n /ə'pɑːtmənt/
Argentina n /ˌɑːdʒən'tiːnə/
at home /ət 'həʊm/
aunt n /ɑːnt/
big adj /bɪg/
boyfriend n /'bɔɪfrend/
brother n /'brʌðə/
cake n /keɪk/
Can I have … ? /ˌkæn aɪ 'hæv/
Can I help? /ˌkæn aɪ 'help/
cheap adj /tʃiːp/
chicken n /'tʃɪkɪn/
chips n pl /tʃɪps/
chocolate n /'tʃɒklət/
coffee n /'kɒfi/
coffee bar n /'kɒfi ˌbɑː/
cold adj /kəʊld/
college n /'kɒlɪdʒ/
dancer n /'dɑːnsə/
daughter n /'dɔːtə/
different adj /'dɪfrənt/
difficult adj /'dɪfɪkəlt/
drink v /drɪŋk/
easy adj /'iːzi/
egg n /eg/
exciting adj /ɪk'saɪtɪŋ/
expensive adj /ɪk'spensɪv/
fast adj /fɑːst/
father n /'fɑːðə/
first name n /'fɜːst neɪm/
French adj /frentʃ/
friendly adj /'frendli/
girl n /gɜːl/
girlfriend n /'gɜːlfrend/
good adj /gʊd/
grandfather n /'grænfɑːðə/
grandmother n /'grænmʌðə/
hamburger n /'hæmbɜːgə/
happy adj /'hæpi/
here adv /hɪə/
here you are /'hɪə juː ˌɑː/
hi /haɪ/
holiday n /'hɒlɪdeɪ/
horrible adj /'hɒrəbl/
hot adj /hɒt/
how much? adv /ˌhaʊ 'mʌtʃ/
how old? adv /ˌhaʊ 'əʊld/
husband n /'hʌzbənd/
ice-cream n /'aɪskriːm/
identity card n /aɪ'dentɪti ˌkɑːd/
Ireland n /'aɪələnd/
journalist n /'dʒɜːnəlɪst/
love n /lʌv/
lovely adj /'lʌvli/
menu n /'menjuː/
mineral water n /'mɪnərəl ˌwɔːtə/
morning n /'mɔːnɪŋ/
mother n /'mʌðə/
new adj /njuː/
now adv /naʊ/
nurse n /nɜːs/
old adj /əʊld/
orange juice n /'ɒrɪndʒ ˌdʒuːs/
pardon? /'pɑːdn/
photo n /'fəʊtəʊ/
pizza n /'piːtsə/
please /pliːz/
Poland n /'pəʊlənd/
policeman n /pə'liːsmən/
pound n /paʊnd/
practice n /'præktɪs/
price n /praɪs/
salad n /'sæləd/
slow adj /sləʊ/
small adj /smɔːl/
snack bar n /'snæk ˌbɑː/
snow n, v /snəʊ/
son n /sʌn/
soon adv /suːn/
speak v /spiːk/
subway n US /'sʌbweɪ/
surname n /'sɜːneɪm/
Switzerland n /'swɪtsələnd/
tea n /tiː/
tuna n /'tjuːnə/
uncle n /'ʌŋkl/
understand v /ʌndə'stænd/
use v /juːz/
who? pron /huː/
wife n /waɪf/
write v /raɪt/
young adj /jʌŋ/

# Unit 3

a little *adj* /ə 'lɪtl/
afternoon *n* /ˌɑːftə'nuːn/
ambulance *n* /'æmbjuːləns/
architect *n* /'ɑːkɪtekt/
Australia *n* /ɒ'streɪliə/
barman *n* /'bɑːmən/
be quiet *v* /ˌbiː 'kwaɪət/
beer *n* /bɪə/
before *prep* /bɪ'fɔː/
biology *n* /baɪ'ɒlədʒi/
boat *n* /bəʊt/
breakfast *n* /'brekfəst/
busy *adj* /'bɪzi/
but *conj* /bʌt/, /bət/
centre *n* /'sentə/
city *n* /'sɪti/
clock *n* /klɒk/
collect *v* /kə'lekt/
come *v* /kʌm/
day *n* /deɪ/
deliver *v* /dɪ'lɪvə/
design *v* /dɪ'zaɪn/
do the accounts *v*
  /ˌduː ði ə'kaʊnts/
dog *n* /dɒg/
drive *n* /draɪv/
end *n* /end/
every day *adv* /ˌevri 'deɪ/
Excuse me /ɪk'skjuːz 'miː/
fireman *n* /'faɪəmən/
fly *v* /flaɪ/
flying doctor *n* /ˌflaɪɪŋ 'dɒktə/
football *n* /'fʊtbɔːl/
free time *n* /ˌfriː 'taɪm/
German *adj* /'dʒɜːmən/
get up *v* /ˌget 'ʌp/
glass *n* /glɑːs/
go *v* /gəʊ/
go to bed *v* /ˌgəʊ tə 'bed/
guest *n* /gest/
help *v* /help/
hospital *n* /'hɒspɪtl/
house *n* /haʊs/
How's (Ann)? *adv* /haʊz/
hurry up *v* /ˌhʌri 'ʌp/
interpreter *n* /ɪn'tɜːprɪtə/
island *n* /'aɪlənd/
language *n* /'læŋgwɪdʒ/
late *adj* /leɪt/
like *v* /laɪk/
listen *v* /'lɪsən/
look after *v* /ˌlʊk 'ɑːftə/
love *v* /lʌv/
make *v* /meɪk/
man *n* /mæn/
money *n* /'mʌni/
music *n* /'mjuːzɪk/
never *adv* /'nevə/
non-stop *adv* /ˌnɒn 'stɒp/
north *n* /nɔːθ/
office *n* /'ɒfɪs/
only *adj* /'əʊnli/
ordinary *adj* /'ɔːdənri/
people *n pl* /'piːpl/
perhaps *adv* /pə'hæps/
petrol *n* /'petrəl/
pilot *n* /'paɪlət/
plane *n* /pleɪn/
play *v* /pleɪ/
post *n* /pəʊst/
postman *n* /'pəʊsmən/
pub *n* /pʌb/
radio *n* /'reɪdiəʊ/
school *n* /skuːl/
scientist *n* /'saɪəntɪst/
sell *v* /sel/
serve *v* /sɜːv/
shop *n* /ʃɒp/
shopkeeper *n* /'ʃɒpkiːpə/
sick *adj* /sɪk/
sit down *v* /ˌsɪt 'daʊn/
skiing *n* /'skiːɪŋ/
small *adj* /smɔːl/
speak *v* /spiːk/
summer *n* /'sʌmə/
supper *n* /'sʌpə/
taxi driver *n* /'tæksi ˌdraɪvə/
television *n* /'telɪvɪʒn/
tennis *n* /'tenɪs/
that's right /ˌðæts 'raɪt/
there *adv* /ðeə/
thing *n* /θɪŋ/
tired *adj* /taɪəd/
too *adv* /tuː/
tourist *n* /'tʊərɪst/
town *n* /taʊn/
translate *v* /trænz'leɪt/
undertaker *n* /'ʌndəteɪkə/
vanilla *adj* /və'nɪlə/
walk *n, v* /wɔːk/
watch *n, v* /wɒtʃ/
week *n* /wiːk/
weekday *n* /'wiːkdeɪ/
wine *n* /waɪn/
winter *n* /'wɪntə/
work *v* /wɜːk/
world *n* /wɜːld/

# Unit 4

a lot *pron* /ə 'lɒt/
after *adv* /'ɑːftə/
always *adv* /'ɔːlweɪz/
Autumn *n* /'ɔːtəm/
bad *adj* /bæd/
bar *n* /bɑː/
baseball *n* /'beɪsbɔːl/
beach *n* /biːtʃ/
block *n* /blɒk/
boring *adj* /'bɔːrɪŋ/
brown *adj* /braʊn/
bus *n* /bʌs/
buy *v* /baɪ/
called *pp* /kɔːld/
car *n* /kɑː/
chat *v* /tʃæt/
Chinese *adj* /tʃaɪ'niːz/
colour *n* /'kʌlə/
come *v* /kʌm/
computer *n* /kəm'pjuːtə/
computer game *n*
  /kəm'pjuːtə geɪm/
cook *v* /kʊk/
dance *v* /dɑːns/
different *adj* /'dɪfrənt/
dinner *n* /'dɪnə/
do *v* /duː/
domestic *adj* /də'mestɪk/
don't worry *v* /ˌdəʊnt 'wʌri/
early *adj* /'ɜːli/
especially *adv* /ɪ'speʃəli/
every day *adv* /ˌevri 'deɪ/
Excuse me /ɪk'skjuːz 'miː/
export department *n*
  /'ekspɔːt dɪˌpɑːtmənt/
exposure *n* /ɪk'spəʊʒə/
fall (= autumn) *n US* /fɔːl/
family *n* /'fæməli/
famous *adj* /'feɪməs/
fantastic *adj* /fæn'tæstɪk/
favourite *adj* /'feɪvrɪt/
film *n* /fɪlm/
flower *n* /'flaʊə/
food *n* /fuːd/
fortunately *adv* /'fɔːtʃənətli/
friend *n* /frend/
go out *v* /ˌgəʊ 'aʊt/
gold *adj* /gəʊld/
grey *adj* /greɪ/
gym *n* /dʒɪm/
headquarters *n pl* /ˌhed'kwɔːtəz/
here *adv* /hɪə/
hobby *n* /'hɒbi/
hour *n* /aʊə/
how? *adv* /haʊ/
I'm sorry /ˌaɪm 'sɒri/
ice hockey *n* /'aɪs ˌhɒki/
ice-skating *n* /'aɪs ˌskeɪtɪŋ/
interesting *adj* /'ɪntrəstɪŋ/
interview *n* /'ɪntəvjuː/
it doesn't matter /ɪt 'dʌznt 'mætə/
jogging *n* /'dʒɒgɪŋ/
kid *n* /kɪd/
lake *n* /leɪk/
learn *v* /lɜːn/
leisure activity *n*
  /'leʒə(r) æk'tɪvəti/
long *adj* /lɒŋ/
make *v* /meɪk/
meet *v* /miːt/
near *adv* /nɪə/
never *adv* /'nevə/
news programme *n*
  /'njuːz ˌprəʊgræm/
next *adj* /nekst/
of course /əv 'kɔːs/
often *adv* /'ɒfən/, /'ɒftən/
only *adj* /'əʊnli/
open *v* /'əʊpən/
pardon? /'pɑːdn/
parents *n pl* /'peərənts/
pop song *n* /'pɒp sɒŋ/
Portugal *n* /'pɔːtʃʊgl/
reading *n* /'riːdɪŋ/
really? /'rɪəli/
red *adj* /red/
relax *v* /rɪ'læks/
sailing *n* /'seɪlɪŋ/
say *v* /seɪ/
season *n* /'siːzn/
short *adj* /ʃɔːt/
shy *adj* /ʃaɪ/
smoke *v* /sməʊk/
sometimes *adv* /'sʌmtaɪmz/
special *adj* /'speʃl/
Spring *n* /sprɪŋ/
start *v* /stɑːt/
suddenly *adv* /'sʌdnli/
sunbathing *n* /'sʌnbeɪðɪŋ/
sunny *adj* /'sʌni/
swimming *n* /'swɪmɪŋ/
take *v* /teɪk/
take photos *v* /'teɪk 'fəʊtəʊz/
That's OK /'ðæts əʊˌkeɪ/
then *adv* /ðen/
traffic *n* /'træfɪk/
tree *n* /triː/
usually *adj* /'juːʒəli/
visit *v* /'vɪzɪt/
warm *adj* /wɔːm/
weekend *n* /'wiːkend/
wet *adj* /wet/
What does ... mean?
  /wɒt dʌz ... miːn/
what time? /wɒt 'taɪm/
what? /wɒt/
when? /wen/
where? /weə/
why? /waɪ/
window *n* /'wɪndəʊ/
year *n* /jɪə/
yellow *adj* /'jeləʊ/

# Unit 5

address book n /ə'dres ˌbʊk/
air conditioning n /'eə kənˌdɪʃnɪŋ/
alone adj /ə'ləʊn/
armchair n /'ɑːmtʃeə/
at the moment adv /ˌæt ðə 'məʊmənt/
bank n /bæŋk/
bathroom n /'bɑːθrʊm/
beautiful adj /'bjuːtɪfl/
bedroom n /'bedrʊm/
best adj /best/
blinds n pl /blaɪndz/
bookshelf n /'bʊkʃelf/
both /bəʊθ/
briefcase n /'briːfkeɪs/
bus ticket n /'bʌs ˌtɪkɪt/
cat n /kæt/
CD n /ˌsiː 'diː/
champagne n /ʃæm'peɪn/
Cheers! /tʃɪəz/
chemist('s) n /'kemɪst(s)/
clock n /klɒk/
cockpit n /'kɒkpɪt/
coffee table n /'kɒfi ˌteɪbl/
comfortable adj /'kʌmftəbl/
cooker n /'kʊkə/
cup n /kʌp/
cupboard n /'kʌbəd/
dishwasher n /'dɪʃwɒʃə/
door n /dɔː/
downstairs adv /ˌdaʊn'steəz/
emergency exit n /ɪ'mɜːdʒənsi ˌeksɪt/
everything pron /'evrɪθɪŋ/
exactly adv /ɪg'zæktli/
ex-wife n /ˌeks'waɪf/
famous adj /'feɪməs/
fantastic adj /fæn'tæstɪk/
far adv /fɑː/
film star n /'fɪlm ˌstɑː/
fire n /faɪə/
first /fɜːst/
first class adj /'fɜːst 'klɑːs/
flat n /flæt/
flight attendant n /'flaɪt əˌtendənt/
floor n /flɔː/
fork n /fɔːk/
fridge n /frɪdʒ/
front door n /ˌfrʌnt 'dɔː/
garden n /'gɑːdn/
grandma n /'grænmɑː/
how many? /'haʊ 'meni/
just (= only) adv /dʒʌst/
key n /kiː/
kitchen n /'kɪtʃɪn/
knife n /naɪf/
lady n /'leɪdi/
lamp n /læmp/
left adv (opp right) /left/
living room n /'lɪvɪŋ ˌrʊm/
lots (of books) /lɒts/
luxury n /'lʌkʃəri/
mirror n /'mɪrə/
mobile phone n /'məʊbaɪl 'fəʊn/
modern adj /'mɒdən/
most of the time /'məʊst əv ðə ˌtaɪm/
neighbour n /'neɪbə/
newsagent('s) n /'njuːzeɪdʒənt(s)/
notebook n /'nəʊtbʊk/
open v /'əʊpən/
over there /ˌəʊvə 'ðeə/
park n /pɑːk/
party n /'pɑːti/
passport n /'pɑːspɔːt/
pen n /pen/
picture n /'pɪktʃə/
plane n /pleɪn/
plant n /plɑːnt/
plate n /pleɪt/
quite (big) adv /kwaɪt/
rain v /reɪn/
rich adj /rɪtʃ/
right adv (opp left) /raɪt/
room n /rʊm/, /ruːm/
rug n /rʌg/
sandwich n /'sænwɪdʒ/
second /'sekənd/
section n /'sekʃn/
shelf n /ʃelf/
shop n /ʃɒp/
sofa n /'səʊfə/
spoon n /spuːn/
stop (bus) n /stɒp/
steps n /steps/
stereo n /'steriəʊ/
supermarket n /'suːpəˌmɑːkɪt/
swimming pool n /'swɪmɪŋ ˌpuːl/
thanks a lot /'θæŋks ə ˌlɒt/
toilet n /'tɔɪlət/
top n /tɒp/
upstairs adv /ˌʌp'steəz/
wall n /wɔːl/
washing machine n /'wɒʃɪŋ məˌʃiːn/

# Unit 6

bedtime n /'bedtaɪm/
between prep /bɪ'twiːn/
bike n /baɪk/
brilliant adj /'brɪliənt/
can't stop v /'kɑːnt 'stɒp/
Canada n /'kænədə/
check v /tʃek/
chess n /tʃes/
concert n /'kɒnsət/
conversation n /kɒnvə'seɪʃn/
do homework v /ˌduː 'həʊmwɜːk/
eye n /aɪ/
fall in love v /ˌfɔːl ɪn 'lʌv/
family n /'fæməli/
feel v /fiːl/
football n /'fʊtbɔːl/
genius n /'dʒiːniəs/
hear v /hɪə/
her pron /hɜː/
his pron /hɪz/
hour n /aʊə/
house n /haʊs/
initial n /ɪ'nɪʃl/
Italian adj /ɪ'tæliən/
Japanese adj /dʒæpə'niːz/
know v /nəʊ/
large adj /lɑːdʒ/
last month adv /ˌlɑːst 'mʌnθ/
laugh v /lɑːf/
little adj /'lɪtl/
manager n /'mænɪdʒə/
message n /'mesɪdʒ/
now adv /naʊ/
our pron /aʊə/
paint v /peɪnt/
pianist n /'pɪənɪst/
piano n /pi'ænəʊ/
poetry n /'pəʊtri/
Portuguese adj /ˌpɔːtʃʊ'giːz/
poor adj /pɔː/
practise v /'præktɪs/
question n /'kwestʃən/
really adv /'riːəli/
require v /rɪ'kwaɪə/
sad adj /sæd/
save v /seɪv/
sea n /siː/
see v /siː/
sell v /sel/
Spanish adj /'spænɪʃ/
spell v /spel/
spelling n /'spelɪŋ/
spend v /spend/
style n /staɪl/
sun n /sʌn/
swim v /swɪm/
their pron /ðeə/
think v /θɪŋk/
today adv /tə'deɪ/
travel v /'trævl/
until conj /ʌn'tɪl/
use v /juːz/
very adv /'veri/
very well adv /ˌveri 'wel/
was born v /wəz 'bɔːn/
wear v /weə/
wedding n /'wedɪŋ/
well adv /wel/
yesterday adv /'jestədeɪ/
yesterday evening adv /ˌjestədeɪ 'iːvnɪŋ/

## Unit 7

advertising agency n /ˈædvətaɪzɪŋ ˌeɪdʒənsi/
afraid adj /əˈfreɪd/
after that adv /ˌɑːftə ˈðæt/
agree v /əˈgriː/
army n /ˈɑːmi/
at night adv /ət ˈnaɪt/
bath n /bɑːθ/
become v /bɪˈkʌm/
begin v /bɪˈgɪn/
birthday n /ˈbɜːθdeɪ/
bomb v /bɒm/
build v /bɪld/
businessman n /ˈbɪznɪsmæn/
buy v /baɪ/
capital adj /ˈkæpɪtl/
car crash n /ˈkɑː ˌkræʃ/
century n /ˈsentʃəri/
chemistry n /ˈkemɪstri/
child n /tʃaɪld/
Christmas n /ˈkrɪsməs/
congratulations /kənˌgrætʃʊˈleɪʃnz/
cotton field n /ˈkɒtn ˌfiːld/
create v /kriˈeɪt/
die v /daɪ/
dinner n /ˈdɪnə/
earn v /ɜːn/
Easter Day n /ˈiːstə ˌdeɪ/
education n /ˌedʒʊˈkeɪʃn/
end v /end/
Euro n /ˈjʊərəʊ/
event n /ɪˈvent/
everybody pron /ˈevrɪbɒdi/
farm n /fɑːm/
farmer n /ˈfɑːmə/
fight v /faɪt/
finally adv /ˈfaɪnəli/
first (... next) adv /fɜːst/
funeral n /ˈfjuːnərəl/
great grandparents n pl /ˌgreɪt ˈgrænpeərənts/
grocer n /ˈgrəʊsə/
grow v /grəʊ/
Hallowe'en n /ˌhæləʊˈiːn/
happen v /ˈhæpn/
hate v /heɪt/
have a holiday v /ˌhæv ə ˈhɒlədeɪ/
horse n /hɔːs/
immediately adv /ɪˈmiːdɪətli/
important adj /ɪmˈpɔːtənt/
independence n /ˌɪndɪˈpendəns/
iron adj /ˈaɪən/
kiss v /kɪs/
later adv /ˈleɪtə/
leader n /ˈliːdə/
leave v /liːv/
life n /laɪf/
listen v /ˈlɪsn/
little (money) /ˈlɪtl/
look v /lʊk/
lose v /luːz/
lucky adj /ˈlʌki/
marry v /ˈmæri/
midnight n /ˈmɪdnaɪt/
million n /ˈmɪljən/
moon n /muːn/
Mother's Day n /ˈmʌðəz ˌdeɪ/
need v /niːd/
New Year's Eve /ˌnjuː ˌjɪəz ˈiːv/
nineties n pl /ˈnaɪntiz/
own v /əʊn/
pardon? /ˈpɑːdn/
personality n /ˌpɜːsəˈnæləti/
poem n /ˈpəʊɪm/
politician n /ˌpɒləˈtɪʃn/
politics n /ˈpɒlətɪks/
present (= birthday) n /ˈpreznt/
president n /ˈprezɪdənt/
prime minister n /ˌpraɪm ˈmɪnɪstə/
problem n /ˈprɒbləm/
read v /riːd/
remember v /rɪˈmembə/
resign v /rɪˈzaɪn/
same to you /ˈseɪm tə ˈjuː/
sit v /sɪt/
slave n /sleɪv/
sleep v /sliːp/
soldier n /ˈsəʊldʒə/
soon adv /suːn/
start v /stɑːt/
strong adj /strɒŋ/
study v /ˈstʌdi/
subject (school) n /ˈsʌbdʒekt/
sure adj /ʃʊə/, /ʃɔː/
survive v /səˈvaɪv/
tear (+ cry) n /tɪə/
terrorist n /ˈterərɪst/
thank goodness /ˈθæŋk ˈgʊdnes/
Thanksgiving n /θæŋksˈgɪvɪŋ/
theatre n /ˈθɪətə/
think v /θɪŋk/
tobacco n /təˈbækəʊ/
together adv /təˈgeðə/
tomorrow adv /təˈmɒrəʊ/
twin n /twɪn/
university n /ˌjuːnɪˈvɜːsəti/
Valentine's Day n /ˈvæləntaɪnz ˌdeɪ/
video n /ˈvɪdiəʊ/
war n /wɔː/
wedding day n /ˈwedɪŋ ˌdeɪ/
widow n /ˈwɪdəʊ/
win v /wɪn/
work hard v /ˌwɜːk ˈhɑːd/
wrong adj /rɒŋ/

## Unit 8

(3 years) ago adv /əˈgəʊ/
(coffee) break n /breɪk/
arthritis n /ɑːˈθraɪtɪs/
aspirin n /ˈæsprɪn/
astronaut n /ˈæstrənɔːt/
banana n /bəˈnɑːnə/
beach n /biːtʃ/
bestselling adj /ˈbestˈselɪŋ/
blue adj /bluː/
bottle n /ˈbɒtl/
boy n /bɔɪ/
chat v /tʃæt/
chatline n /ˈtʃætlaɪn/
chicken n /ˈtʃɪkɪn/
clock n /klɒk/
cloth n /klɒθ/
company n /ˈkʌmpəni/
couple n pl /ˈkʌpl/
date n /deɪt/
delicious adj /dɪˈlɪʃəs/
drug n /drʌg/
e-mail n /ˈiːmeɪl/
exam n /ɪgˈzæm/
face n /feɪs/
face to face /ˈfeɪs tə ˈfeɪs/
fashionable adj /ˈfæʃnəbl/
fax n /fæks/
fisherman n /ˈfɪʃəmən/
funny adj /ˈfʌni/
get engaged v /ˌget ɪnˈgeɪdʒd/
get married v /ˌget ˈmærɪd/
go to a party v /ˌgəʊ tuː ə ˈpɑːti/
good luck! /ˌgʊd ˈlʌk/
green adj /griːn/
in a hurry /ˌɪn ə ˈhʌri/
incredible adj /ɪnˈkredəbl/
internet n /ˈɪntənet/
invention n /ɪnˈvenʃn/
jeans n pl /dʒiːnz/
joke n /dʒəʊk/
leg n /leg/
mobile phone n /ˈməʊbaɪl ˈfəʊn/
moon n /muːn/
mouth n /maʊθ/
nervous adj /ˈnɜːvəs/
nowadays adv /ˈnaʊədeɪz/
painkiller n /ˈpeɪnkɪlə/
philosopher n /fɪˈlɒsəfə/
phone call n /ˈfəʊn ˌkɔːl/
produce v /prəˈdjuːs/
public holiday n /ˈpʌblɪk ˈhɒlədeɪ/
recipe n /ˈresəpi/
record (for music) n /ˈrekɔːd/
ride v /raɪd/
rose n /rəʊz/
send v /send/
take v /teɪk/
term n /tɜːm/
them pron /ðem/
throw v /θrəʊ/
transmit v /trænzˈmɪt/
trousers n pl /ˈtraʊzəz/
true adj /truː/
true love n /ˌtruː ˈlʌv/
vacuum cleaner n /ˈvækjuːm ˌkliːnə/
watch v /wɒtʃ/
way n /weɪ/
women n pl /ˈwɪmɪn/
workmen n pl /ˈwɜːkmen/, /ˈwɜːkmən/
workroom n /ˈwɜːkrʊm/
worried adj /ˈwʌrid/

# Unit 9

a bit *n* /ə ˈbɪt/
all sorts *n pl* /ˈɔːl ˈsɔːts/
anybody *pron* /ˈenibɒdi/
anyway *adv* /ˈeniweɪ/
apple juice *n* /ˈæpl ˌdʒuːs/
away from *adv* /əˈweɪ frəm/
bacon *n* /ˈbeɪkən/
bag *n* /bæg/
bar of chocolate *n* /ˈbɑː(r) əv ˈtʃɒklət/
beer *n* /bɪə/
birthday *n* /ˈbɜːθdeɪ/
biscuit *n* /ˈbɪskɪt/
black (coffee) *adj* /blæk/
borrow *v* /ˈbɒrəʊ/
bottle *n* /ˈbɒtl/
bread *n* /bred/
carrot *n* /ˈkærət/
central *adj* /ˈsentrəl/
cheese *n* /tʃiːz/
China *n* /ˈtʃaɪnə/
Chinese *adj* /tʃaɪˈniːz/
chopsticks *n pl* /ˈtʃɒpstɪks/
cigarette *n* /sɪgəˈret/
control *v* /kənˈtrəʊl/
course (of a meal) *n* /kɔːs/
curry *n* /ˈkʌri/
dangerous *adj* /ˈdeɪndʒərəs/
depend *v* /dɪˈpend/
dessert *n* /dɪˈzɜːt/
disgusting *adj* /dɪsˈgʌstɪŋ/
easily *adv* /ˈiːzəli/
egg *n* /eg/
either *adv* /ˈaɪðə/
environment *n* /ɪnˈvaɪrənmənt/
especially /ɪˈspeʃəli/
farm *v* /fɑːm/
finger *n* /ˈfɪŋgə/
fish *n* /fɪʃ/
fizzy water *n* /ˈfɪzi ˈwɔːtə/
for example /fɔː(r) ɪgˈzɑːmpl/
foreign *adj* /ˈfɒrɪn/
fruit *n* /fruːt/
full *adj* /fʊl/
glad *adj* /glæd/
ham *n* /hæm/
herring *n* /ˈherɪŋ/
history *n* /ˈhɪstəri/
horrible *adj* /ˈhɒrəbl/
human *adj* /ˈhjuːmən/
hungry *adj* /ˈhʌŋgri/
land *n* /lænd/
main (meal) *adj* /meɪn/
meal *n* /miːl/
meat *n* /miːt/
milk *n* /mɪlk/
money *n* /ˈmʌni/
mushroom *n* /ˈmʌʃrʊm/
noodles *n pl* /ˈnuːdlz/
north *n* /nɔːθ/
part (of the world) *n* /pɑːt/
pass (= give) *v* /pɑːs/
pasta *n* /ˈpæstə/
pea *n* /piː/
petrol *n* /ˈpetrəl/
pick up *v* /ˌpɪk ˈʌp/
pocket *n* /ˈpɒkɪt/
poor *adj* /pʊə/, /pɔː/
possible *adj* /ˈpɒsəbl/
potatoes *n pl* /pəˈteɪtəʊz/
rice *n* /raɪs/
right now *adv* /ˌraɪt ˈnaʊ/
salt *n* /sɔːlt/, /sɒlt/
sardine *n* /sɑːˈdiːn/
sauce *n* /sɔːs/
sausages *n pl* /ˈsɒsɪdʒɪz/
shopping list *n* /ˈʃɒpɪŋ ˌlɪst/
south *n* /saʊθ/
still water *n* /ˈstɪl ˈwɔːtə/
strawberry *n* /ˈstrɔːbəri/
sugar *n* /ˈʃʊgə/
table *n* /ˈteɪbl/
terrible *adj* /ˈterəbl/
toast *n* /təʊst/
together *adv* /təˈgeðə/
tomato *n* /təˈmɑːtəʊ/
transport *v* /trænˈspɔːt/
typical *adj* /ˈtɪpɪkl/
vegetable *n* /ˈvedʒtəbl/
washing-up *n* /ˌwɒʃɪŋ ˈʌp/
wonderful *adj* /ˈwʌndəfʊl/
yoghurt *n* /ˈjɒgət/

# Unit 10

art *n* /ɑːt/
blues (music) *n pl* /bluːz/
bridge *n* /brɪdʒ/
building *n* /ˈbɪldɪŋ/
busy *adj* /ˈbɪzi/
car park *n* /ˈkɑː ˌpɑːk/
carnival *n* /ˈkɑːnɪvl/
castle *n* /ˈkɑːsl/
cathedral *n* /kəˈθiːdrəl/
church *n* /tʃɜːtʃ/
clean *adj* /kliːn/
cosmopolitan *adj* /ˌkɒzməˈpɒlɪtən/
cottage *n* /ˈkɒtɪdʒ/
country (not the city) *n* /ˈkʌntri/
cousin *n* /ˈkʌzən/
cultural centre *n* /ˈkʌltʃərəl ˌsentə/
dangerous *adj* /ˈdeɪndʒərəs/
dirty *adj* /ˈdɜːti/
empire *n* /ˈempaɪə/
expensive *adj* /ɪkˈspensɪv/
factory *n* /ˈfæktri/
field *n* /fiːld/
found (a university) *v* /faʊnd/
garage *n* /ˈgærɪdʒ/, /ˈgærɑːʒ/
garden *n* /ˈgɑːdn/
gateway *n* /ˈgeɪtweɪ/
group *n* /gruːp/
hedge *n* /hedʒ/
hill *n* /hɪl/
hotel *n* /həʊˈtel/
hymn *n* /hɪm/
immigrants *n pl* /ˈɪmɪgrənts/
intelligent *adj* /ɪnˈtelɪdʒənt/
library *n* /ˈlaɪbrəri/
mixture *n* /ˈmɪkstʃə/
mountain *n* /ˈmaʊntɪn/
museum *n* /mjuːˈzɪəm/
night club *n* /ˈnaɪt ˌklʌb/
noisy *adj* /ˈnɔɪzi/
orchestra *n* /ˈɔːkɪstrə/
passenger *n* /ˈpæsɪndʒə/
popular *adj* /ˈpɒpjʊlə/
port *n* /pɔːt/
pretty *adj* /ˈprɪti/
quiet *adj* /ˈkwaɪət/
restaurant *n* /ˈrestrɒnt/
river bank *n* /ˈrɪvə ˌbæŋk/
rock group *n* /ˈrɒk ˌgruːp/
safe *adj* /seɪf/
ship *n* /ʃɪp/
small *adj* /smɔːl/
song *n* /sɒŋ/
spices *n pl* /ˈspaɪsɪz/
stand *v* /stænd/
street *n* /striːt/
tall *adj* /tɔːl/
the Underground *n* /ði ˈʌndəgraʊnd/
top ten (music) *n* /ˌtɒp ˈten/
travel *n* /ˈtrævl/
unfriendly *adj* /ʌnˈfrendli/
village *n* /ˈvɪlɪdʒ/
wood *n* /wʊd/

# Unit 11

baby *n* /ˈbeɪbi/
baseball cap *n* /ˈbeɪsbɔːl ˌkæp/
beautiful *adj* /ˈbjuːtɪfl/
bloom *v* /bluːm/
boot *n* /buːt/
bright *adj* /braɪt/
changing rooms *n pl* /ˈtʃeɪndʒɪŋ ˌruːmz/
chewing gum *n* /ˈtʃuːɪŋ ˌɡʌm/
choose *v* /tʃuːz/
cigar *n* /sɪˈɡɑː/
cloud *n* /klaʊd/
coat *n* /kəʊt/
credit card *n* /ˈkredɪt ˌkɑːd/
cry *v* /kraɪ/
dark *adj* /dɑːk/
dress *n* /dres/
eat *v* /iːt/
fair (hair) *adj* /feə/
fresh *adj* /freʃ/
good-looking *adj* /ˌɡʊdˈlʊkɪŋ/
grey *adj* /ɡreɪ/
guest *n* /ɡest/
hair *n* /heə/
half *n* /hɑːf/
handsome *adj* /ˈhænsəm/
hat *n* /hæt/
hill *n* /hɪl/
jacket *n* /ˈdʒækɪt/
jumper *n* /ˈdʒʌmpə/
laugh *v* /lɑːf/
long *adj* /lɒŋ/
musician *n* /mjuːˈzɪʃn/
pay *v* /peɪ/
pram *n* /præm/
rainbow *n* /ˈreɪnbəʊ/
roller skates *n pl* /ˈrəʊlə ˌskeɪts/
run *v* /rʌn/
shake *v* /ʃeɪk/
shiny *adj* /ˈʃaɪni/
shirt *n* /ʃɜːt/
shoe *n* /ʃuː/
short *adj* /ʃɔːt/
shorts *n pl* /ʃɔːts/
silly *adj* /ˈsɪli/
size *n* /saɪz/
skateboard *n* /ˈskeɪtbɔːd/
skirt *n* /skɜːt/
sky *n* /skaɪ/
smile *v* /smaɪl/
smoke *v* /sməʊk/
sports car *n* /ˈspɔːts ˌkɑː/
starry *adj* /ˈstɑːri/
suit *n* /suːt/
sunglasses *n pl* /ˈsʌŋɡlɑːsɪz/
T-shirt *n* /ˈtiːʃɜːt/
talk *v* /tɔːk/
trainers *n pl* /ˈtreɪnəz/
try on *v* /ˌtraɪ ˈɒn/
umbrella *n* /ʌmˈbrelə/
whose? *pron* /huːz/

# Unit 12

accident *n* /ˈæksɪdənt/
adventure *n* /ədˈventʃə/
amazed *adj* /əˈmeɪzd/
blouse *n* /blaʊz/
championship *n* /ˈtʃæmpiənʃɪp/
cloudy *adj* /ˈklaʊdi/
coast *n* /kəʊst/
cool *adj* /kuːl/
corner *n* /ˈkɔːnə/
degrees *n pl* /dɪˈɡriːz/
driving school *n* /ˈdraɪvɪŋ ˌskuːl/
dry *adj* /draɪ/
excitement *n* /ɪkˈsaɪtmənt/
feel sick *v* /ˌfiːl ˈsɪk/
float *v* /fləʊt/
foggy *adj* /ˈfɒɡi/
forever *adv* /fɔːˈrevə/
forget *v* /fəˈɡet/
fresh air *n* /ˌfreʃ ˈeə/
full-time *adj* /ˌfʊlˈtaɪm/
garden shed *n* /ˌɡɑːdn ˈʃed/
golf *n* /ɡɒlf/
grow up *v* /ˌɡrəʊ ˈʌp/
lion *n* /ˈlaɪən/
motor racing *n* /ˈməʊtə ˌreɪsɪŋ/
nervous *adj* /ˈnɜːvəs/
parachute *n* /ˈpærəʃuːt/
pyramid *n* /ˈpɪrəmɪd/
race *v* /reɪs/
racing circuit *n* /ˈreɪsɪŋ ˌsɜːkɪt/
racing driver *n* /ˈreɪsɪŋ ˌdraɪvə/
record *n* /ˈrekɔːd/
retire *v* /rɪˈtaɪə/
safe *adj* /seɪf/
sky diving *n* /ˈskaɪ ˌdaɪvɪŋ/
sneeze *v* /sniːz/
star (TV) *n* /stɑː/
sunbathe *v* /ˈsʌnbeɪð/
swimming costume *n* /ˈswɪmɪŋ ˌkɒstjuːm/
top marks *n pl* /ˌtɒp ˈmɑːks/
trouble *n* /ˈtrʌbl/
tulip *n* /ˈtjuːlɪp/
view *n* /vjuː/
weather *n* /ˈweðə/
windsurfing *n* /ˈwɪndsɜːfɪŋ/
windy *adj* /ˈwɪndi/

# Unit 13

annoyed  adj  /əˈnɔɪd/
arrive  v  /əˈraɪv/
badly  adv  /ˈbædli/
behave  v  /bɪˈheɪv/
behaviour  n  /bɪˈheɪvɪə/
burglar  n  /ˈbɜːglə/
carefully  adv  /ˈkeəfəli/
change (= money)  n  /tʃeɪndʒ/
depart  v  /dɪˈpɑːt/
elephant  n  /ˈelɪfənt/
explain  v  /ɪkˈspleɪn/
fast  adv  /fɑːst/
fluently  adv  /ˈfluːəntli/
fortunately  adv  /ˈfɔːtʃənətli/
generation  n  /ˌdʒenəˈreɪʃn/
gold medal  n  /ˈgəʊld ˈmedl/
grass  n  /grɑːs/
guitar  n  /gɪˈtɑː/
leather  n  /ˈleðə/
marathon  n  /ˈmærəθən/
migrate  v  /maɪˈgreɪt/
moon  n  /muːn/
pin  v  /pɪn/
platform  n  /ˈplætfɔːm/
please  v  /pliːz/
quietly  adv  /ˈkwaɪətli/
return ticket  n  /rɪˈtɜːn ˈtɪkɪt/
ridiculous  adj  /rɪˈdɪkjələs/
rude  adj  /ruːd/
sheep  n  /ʃiːp/
shout  v  /ʃaʊt/
slowly  adv  /ˈsləʊli/
station  n  /ˈsteɪʃn/
support (a team)  v  /səˈpɔːt/
tell a lie  v  /ˌtel ə ˈlaɪ/
timetable  n  /ˈtaɪmteɪbl/
typical  adj  /ˈtɪpɪkl/
untidy  adj  /ʌnˈtaɪdi/
weigh  v  /weɪ/
well-behaved  adj  /ˌwel bɪˈheɪvd/
whistle  v  /ˈwɪsl/
wolf  n  /wʊlf/
worrying  adj  /ˈwʌriɪŋ/

# Unit 14

abroad  adv  /əˈbrɔːd/
airport  n  /ˈeəpɔːt/
ambulance driver  n  /ˈæmbjələns ˌdraɪvə/
announcement  n  /əˈnaʊnsmənt/
arrival hall  n  /əˈraɪvl ˌhɔːl/
board  v  /bɔːd/
boarding pass  n  /ˈbɔːdɪŋ ˌpɑːs/
boat ride  n  /ˈbəʊt ˌraɪd/
business class  n  /ˈbɪznəs ˌklɑːs/
call  n  /kɔːl/
certificate  n  /səˈtɪfɪkət/
check in  v  /ˌtʃek ˈɪn/
check-in desk  n  /ˈtʃek ɪn ˌdesk/
competition  n  /kɒmpəˈtɪʃn/
crown  n  /kraʊn/
dawn  n  /dɔːn/
delay  v  /dɪˈleɪ/
delayed  pp  /dɪˈleɪd/
departures board  n  /dɪˈpɑːtʃəz ˌbɔːd/
departure lounge  n  /dɪˈpɑːtʃə ˌlaʊndʒ/
double-decker bus  n  /ˌdʌbl ˌdekə ˈbʌs/
dressmaker  n  /ˈdresmeɪkə/
engineer  n  /ˌendʒɪˈnɪə/
flag  n  /flæg/
flight  n  /flaɪt/
gate (in an airport)  n  /geɪt/
give up (= stop)  v  /ˌgɪv ˈʌp/
grandson  n  /ˈgrænˌsʌn/
Greece  n  /griːs/
heart attack  n  /ˈhɑːt əˌtæk/
honeymoon  n  /ˈhʌnimuːn/
horn (on a car)  n  /hɔːn/
Hungary  n  /ˈhʌŋgəri/
jewels  n pl  /ˈdʒuːəlz/
jumbo jet  n  /ˈdʒʌmbəʊ ˈdʒet/
jump  v  /dʒʌmp/
last call  n  /ˌlɑːst ˈkɔːl/
let (sb) down (= disappoint)  v  /ˌlet ˈdaʊn/
lottery  n  /ˈlɒtəri/
loud  adj  /laʊd/
luggage  n  /ˈlʌgɪdʒ/
lung cancer  n  /ˈlʌŋ ˌkænsə/
marmalade  n  /ˈmɑːməleɪd/
millionaire  n  /ˌmɪljəˈneə/
miss  v  /mɪs/
niece  n  /niːs/
now boarding  /ˌnaʊ ˈbɔːdɪŋ/
pack (a bag)  v  /pæk/
passenger  n  /ˈpæsɪndʒə/
passport control  /ˈpɑːspɔːt kənˈtrəʊl/
pipe (to smoke)  n  /paɪp/
pneumonia  n  /njuːˈməʊnɪə/
remind  v  /rɪˈmaɪnd/
rheumatic fever  n  /ruːˈmætɪk ˈfiːvə/
seat  n  /siːt/
secretary  n  /ˈsekrətri/
serious  adj  /ˈsɪərɪəs/
suitcase  n  /ˈsuːtkeɪs/
tractor  n  /ˈtræktə/
trolley  n  /ˈtrɒli/

# Appendix 1

## IRREGULAR VERBS

| Base form | Past Simple | Past Participle |
|---|---|---|
| be | was/were | been |
| become | became | become |
| begin | began | begun |
| break | broke | broken |
| bring | brought | brought |
| build | built | built |
| buy | bought | bought |
| can | could | been able |
| catch | caught | caught |
| choose | chose | chosen |
| come | came | come |
| cost | cost | cost |
| cut | cut | cut |
| do | did | done |
| drink | drank | drunk |
| drive | drove | driven |
| eat | ate | eaten |
| fall | fell | fallen |
| feel | felt | felt |
| fight | fought | fought |
| find | found | found |
| fly | flew | flown |
| forget | forgot | forgotten |
| get | got | got |
| give | gave | given |
| go | went | gone/been |
| grow | grew | grown |
| have | had | had |
| hear | heard | heard |
| hit | hit | hit |
| keep | kept | kept |
| know | knew | known |
| learn | learnt/learned | learnt/learned |
| leave | left | left |
| lose | lost | lost |
| make | made | made |
| meet | met | met |
| pay | paid | paid |
| put | put | put |
| read /ri:d/ | read /red/ | read /red/ |
| ride | rode | ridden |
| run | ran | run |
| say | said | said |
| see | saw | seen |
| sell | sold | sold |
| send | sent | sent |
| shut | shut | shut |
| sing | sang | sung |
| sit | sat | sat |
| sleep | slept | slept |
| speak | spoke | spoken |
| spend | spent | spent |
| stand | stood | stood |
| steal | stole | stolen |
| swim | swam | swum |
| take | took | taken |
| tell | told | told |
| think | thought | thought |
| understand | understood | understood |
| wake | woke | woken |
| wear | wore | worn |
| win | won | won |
| write | wrote | written |

# Appendix 2

## VERB PATTERNS

| Verb + -ing | |
|---|---|
| like | |
| love | swimming |
| enjoy | |
| hate | cooking |
| finish | |
| stop | |

| Verb + *to* + infinitive | |
|---|---|
| choose | |
| decide | |
| forget | |
| promise | to go |
| need | |
| help | |
| hope | |
| try | to work |
| want | |
| would like | |
| would love | |

| Verb + -ing or *to* + infinitive | |
|---|---|
| begin | raining/to rain |
| start | |

| Modal auxiliary verbs | |
|---|---|
| can | |
| could | go |
| shall | |
| will | arrive |
| would | |

# Phonetic symbols

## Consonants

| | | | | |
|---|---|---|---|---|
| 1 | /p/ | as in | **pen** | /pen/ |
| 2 | /b/ | as in | **big** | /bɪg/ |
| 3 | /t/ | as in | **tea** | /tiː/ |
| 4 | /d/ | as in | **do** | /duː/ |
| 5 | /k/ | as in | **cat** | /kæt/ |
| 6 | /g/ | as in | **go** | /gəʊ/ |
| 7 | /f/ | as in | **four** | /fɔː/ |
| 8 | /v/ | as in | **very** | /ˈveri/ |
| 9 | /s/ | as in | **son** | /sʌn/ |
| 10 | /z/ | as in | **zoo** | /zuː/ |
| 11 | /l/ | as in | **live** | /lɪv/ |
| 12 | /m/ | as in | **my** | /maɪ/ |
| 13 | /n/ | as in | **near** | /nɪə/ |
| 14 | /h/ | as in | **happy** | /ˈhæpi/ |
| 15 | /r/ | as in | **red** | /red/ |
| 16 | /j/ | as in | **yes** | /jes/ |
| 17 | /w/ | as in | **want** | /wɒnt/ |
| 18 | /θ/ | as in | **thanks** | /θæŋks/ |
| 19 | /ð/ | as in | **the** | /ðə/ |
| 20 | /ʃ/ | as in | **she** | /ʃiː/ |
| 21 | /ʒ/ | as in | **television** | /ˈtelɪvɪʒn/ |
| 22 | /tʃ/ | as in | **child** | /tʃaɪld/ |
| 23 | /dʒ/ | as in | **German** | /ˈdʒɜːmən/ |
| 24 | /ŋ/ | as in | **English** | /ˈɪŋglɪʃ/ |

## Vowels

| | | | | |
|---|---|---|---|---|
| 25 | /iː/ | as in | **see** | /siː/ |
| 26 | /ɪ/ | as in | **his** | /hɪz/ |
| 27 | /i/ | as in | **twenty** | /ˈtwenti/ |
| 28 | /e/ | as in | **ten** | /ten/ |
| 29 | /æ/ | as in | **stamp** | /stæmp/ |
| 30 | /ɑː/ | as in | **father** | /ˈfɑːðə/ |
| 31 | /ɒ/ | as in | **hot** | /hɒt/ |
| 32 | /ɔː/ | as in | **morning** | /ˈmɔːnɪŋ/ |
| 33 | /ʊ/ | as in | **football** | /ˈfʊtbɔːl/ |
| 34 | /uː/ | as in | **you** | /juː/ |
| 35 | /ʌ/ | as in | **sun** | /sʌn/ |
| 36 | /ɜː/ | as in | **learn** | /lɜːn/ |
| 37 | /ə/ | as in | **letter** | /ˈletə/ |

## Diphthongs (two vowels together)

| | | | | |
|---|---|---|---|---|
| 38 | /eɪ/ | as in | **name** | /neɪm/ |
| 39 | /əʊ/ | as in | **no** | /nəʊ/ |
| 40 | /aɪ/ | as in | **my** | /maɪ/ |
| 41 | /aʊ/ | as in | **how** | /haʊ/ |
| 42 | /ɔɪ/ | as in | **boy** | /bɔɪ/ |
| 43 | /ɪə/ | as in | **hear** | /hɪə/ |
| 44 | /eə/ | as in | **where** | /weə/ |
| 45 | /ʊə/ | as in | **tour** | /tʊə/ |

# OXFORD
UNIVERSITY PRESS

Great Clarendon Street, Oxford OX2 6DP

Oxford University Press is a department of the University of Oxford. It furthers the University's objective of excellence in research, scholarship, and education by publishing worldwide in

Oxford  New York

Auckland  Cape Town  Dar es Salaam
Hong Kong  Karachi  Kuala Lumpur  Madrid
Melbourne  Mexico City  Nairobi  New Delhi
Shanghai  Taipei  Toronto

With offices in

Argentina  Austria  Brazil  Chile  Czech Republic
France  Greece  Guatemala  Hungary  Italy  Japan
Poland  Portugal  Singapore  South Korea
Switzerland  Thailand  Turkey  Ukraine  Vietnam

OXFORD and OXFORD ENGLISH are registered trade marks of Oxford University Press in the UK and in certain other countries

© Oxford University Press 2004

The moral rights of the author have been asserted
Database right Oxford University Press (maker)

First published 2000

**No unauthorized photocopying**

All rights reserved. No part of this publication may be reproduced, stored in a retrieval system, or transmitted, in any form or by any means, without the prior permission in writing of Oxford University Press, or as expressly permitted by law, or under terms agreed with the appropriate reprographics rights organization. Enquiries concerning reproduction outside the scope of the above should be sent to the ELT Rights Department, Oxford University Press, at the address above

You must not circulate this book in any other binding or cover and you must impose this same condition on any acquirer

Any websites referred to in this publication are in the public domain and their addresses are provided by Oxford University Press for information only. Oxford University Press disclaims any responsibility for the content.

ISBN: 978 0 19 436677 9  INTERNATIONAL EDITION
2014  2013  2012  2011
30  29  28  27  26  25  24  23  22

ISBN: 978 0 19 437875 8  GERMAN EDITION
2014  2013  2012  2011
20  19  18  17  16  15

Printed in Spain by Orymu, S.A.

This book is printed on paper from certified and well-managed sources.

ACKNOWLEDGEMENTS

*The authors and publisher are grateful to those who have given permission to reproduce the following extracts and adaptations of copyright material:* p24 'It's a job for nine men, but someone's got to do it' by Rebecca Fowler. *The Mail Night* and *Day Magazine* 3 May 1998. © *The Mail on Sunday*.

p40 'The jet settler' by Andy Lines. *The Mirror, Cover Magazine* March 1999. © Mirror Group Newspapers.

p48 'Refugee's daughter hailed as new Picasso' by Nigel Reynolds. *The Daily Telegraph* 12 March 1996. © Telegraph Group Ltd.

p48 'Shy 10-year-old piano prodigy' by David Ward. *The Guardian* 23 September 1997. © *The Guardian*.

p87 'What a wonderful world'. Words and Music by George David Weiss and George Douglas © 1967 Range Road Music, Inc., Quartet Music, Inc. and Abilene Music, Inc., USA. - Copyright Renewed - All Rights Reserved. 50% Lyric reproduction by kind permission of Carlin Music Corporation, 50% by kind permission of Memory Lane Music Limited.

p102 'The Story-Teller' from Tooth and Claw (Oxford Bookworms Series) by Rosemary Border.

p110 'Discover the secrets of a long life' by Katy Macdonald. *The Daily Mail* 2 November 1993. © *The Daily Mail*.

p112 'Leaving on a jet plane' by John Denver © 1967, Cherry Lane Music Limited, c/o Harmony Music Limited, 11 Uxbridge Street, London W8 7TQ.

Every endeavour has been made to identify the sources of all material used. The publisher apologises for any omissions.

*Illustrations by*: Kathy Baxendale pp17, 96; Rowie Christopher pp45, 86-87, 98-99; Martin Cottam pp103, 104; Neil Gower pp43, 81; Jane Hadfield p66; John Holder pp102-3, 104; Sarah Jones pp11, 65; Ian Kellas pp31, 32, 44, 69, 76, 84-5, 92, 97, 100; Andy Parker p84; Pierre Paul Pariseau pp96-7; Debbie Ryder p80; Colin Salmon p40; Harry Venning pp6, 16, 34, 39, 62, 77, 81, 85, 88, 98, 99, 101

*The publishers would like to thank the following for their kind permission to reproduce photographs*: AKG Photos pp47 (Mozart), 62 (Levi Strauss), 79 (Eric Lessing/Vienna Operahouse); *Associated Press* pp42 (Susan Sterner/beach), 59 (Big Ben), 74; *Barnabys Picture Library* pp20 (doctor), 26 (nurse), 32 (autumn), 108 (Stuart D Hall/Brad & Marilyn); *Bayer* p62 (Hoffman & Aspirin bottle); *John Birdsill Photography* pp12, 51 (black woman on phone), 82 (Nadia & Rudi), 83 (Flora & Toni); *Catherine Blackie* p110 (Tommy young, Joyce young and old); *Anthony Blake Photo Library* pp26 (John Sims/barman), 71 (John Sims/bananas), 72 (Sian Irving/pasta, Andrew Sydenham/chocolate cakes, Gerrit Buntrock/bacon & eggs); *Bridgeman Art Library* pp56 (The Hall of Representatives/The Signing of the Constitution of the United States in 1787, 1940 by Howard Chandler Christy), 57 (Pennsylvania Academy of Fine Arts, Philadelphia/George Washington at Princeton by Charles Willson Peale 1741-1827), 79 (Coram Foundation/Handel's Messiah); *Camera Press* pp55 (Mark Stewart/flowers), 56 (M Thatcher & family, Jon Blau/M Thatcher at conference), 61 (cars); *Collections* pp26 (Brian Shuel/shopkeeper, Nick Oakes/architect), 110 (old Tommy), 111 (Anthea Sieveking/Alice old); *Corbis Images* pp47 (Einstein), 53 (cotton picking), 62 (JL Baird); *Corbis Sygma* pp26 (Mathiew/Journalist), 55 (R Ellis/Clinton & Blair), 57 (M Polak/M Thatcher resignation), 82 (Ruth, Cathy & Jane); *Zoe Dominic* p47 (Nureyev); *European Commission* p26 (interpreter); *Format Photographers* pp11 (Joanne O'Brien/Leo), 83 (Ulrike Preuss/Becca); *Greg Evans International* pp42 (Greg Balfour Evans/Alise), 58 (Greg Balfour Evans/Easter Eggs), 112 (Greg Balfour Evans/plane; *Food Features* p72 (Indian curry); *Getty One Stone* pp7 (John Riley/Max & Lisa), 16-17 (Joseph Pobereskin/Central Park), 25 (David Tomlinson), 32 (Manuela, Chad Ehlers/beach), 33 (Bruce Ayres/Toshi, cherry blossom, Rich Iwasaki/maple trees), 42 (Dennis McColeman/Toronto), 55 (P Crowther & S Carter/Euro Symbol), 58 (Bob Thomas/wedding), 58 (Bruce Ayres/Thanksgiving, James Randklev/Christmas tree), p59 (Andrew Olney/girl & cake), 64 (Phil Schofield/fisherman, Martin Rogers/man & laptop, Walter Hodges/girl on computer, Michelangelo Gratton/girl on beach), 64-5 (Mark Andrew/message in bottle), 71 (Wayne astep/Shammar tribe eating, Yann Lavma/China woman & child, David Baird/strawberry crates), 72 (Martin Barraud/Sally), 73 (Timothy Shonnard), 79 (ferry), 83 (Ian O'Leary/businessman), 86-7 (baby), 93 (Suzanne & Nick Geary/tulips), 93 (safari, Donald Nausbaum/Copacabana Beach, John Lamb/Red Square), 108 (Paul Figura/Ryan); *Sue Glass* p95 (Sue Glass racing & portrait); *The Guardian* pp48-9 (Don McPhee/Lukas Vondracek); *Robert Harding Picture Library* pp8 (P Bouchon/Maria), 26 (pilot, Ken Gilham/postman), 32 (Norma Joseph/Al Wheeler), 42 (J Lightfoot/Lisbon, Int Stock/Ray & Elsie), 51 (teenager on phone), 54 (Bob Jacobson/Simon), 59 (Mark Mawson/pumpkin), 72 (Rex Rouchon/Lucy), 76 (Norma Joseph/Plaza), 83 (Tony Demi/Angela, David Hughes/Juan), 93 (pyramids, Taj Mahal); *Hulton Getty Picture Collection* pp47 (Picasso), 52 (Cotton picking), 56 (G. W. as farmer), 60 (jeans), 61 (phone calls, television); *Image Bank* pp8 (Juan Silva/Lena & Miguel), 11 (Stephen Derr/Mary), 61 (Archive Photos/hamburgers); *Impact Photos* pp21 (Andy Johnstone/barman), 51 (Giles Barnard/female bank worker), 59 (Simon Shepherd/Valentines Day); *Insight* pp24-25; *Katz* p60 (Mansell/planes), 71 (Benoit Decout/restaurants Lyon); *Sally Lack* p111 (Alice); *The Mandarin Hotel* p76; *Network Photographers* pp8 (Pierre), 20 (Peter Jordan/Scientist), 51 (Homer Sykes/man on phone); *Pictures* p72 (Chinese food); *Popperfoto* pp15 (M.C.C./family at dinner table), 55 (Bob Thomas/World Cup), 60 (Coca Cola, records, photograph), 61 (bikes); *Clem Quinn* p95 (Clem Quinn skydiving & portrait); *Quadrant Picture Library* p113; *Redferns* pp78 (David Redfern), 86; *Henry Reichhold* pp108-9; *Rex Features* pp40-1, 48-9 (Di Crollalanza/Alexandra Nechita); *The Savoy Group* p76 (Claridges); *The Stock Market* pp8 (Anna), 75, 93 (K Owaki/canyon and Mt Fuji), 93 (Great Wall, dancer), 94 (skydivers); *Telegraph Colour Library* pp11 (Benelux Press/Flora), 52 (Colorific/woman on verandah); *Topham Picturepoint* pp71 (Japanese restaurant), 79 (Beatles); *Trip Photo Library* pp7 (E James/Rafael, M Fairman/Tomoko), 8 (B North/Yasima, D Morgan/Irina, A Tovy/László & Ilona), 9 (E James), 11 (M Stevenson/Edward), 15 (Japanese family, S Grant/Mixed race family, B Seed/Portugese family), 22, 23, 26 (S Grant/accountant), 39 (P Treanor/Pierre), 42 (D Cole/Samoan house, Mike Clement/Manola, N Menneer/Brad), 45 (H Rogers/Tina), 51 (H Rogers/woman in T shirt), 51 (Grant/man in office), 70 (H Rogers/S. Indian children), 71 (F Good/rice harvest, H Rogers/ship), 72 (Andrews/Gavin. H Rogers/Graham and Lucy)

*Commissioned photography by*: Gareth Boden: pp6, 7 (school), 8 (Richard/Kurt), 11 (Bianca)35, 67 (school dinners), 75; *Haddon Davies*: pp37, 67 (biscuits), 89, 105; *Mark Mason*: pp10, 18, 27, 68; *Maggie Milner*: pp14, 19, 46; *Stephen Ogilvy*: p17

*We would like to thank the following for their assistance*: Bell Language School, British Telecom plc, Gabucci, Leventhorpe School, Photosound

# Wortschatz: chronologisch

Diese Wortschatzliste ist pro Unit chronologisch geordnet. Alles wird so übersetzt, wie es im Text- und Übungszusammenhang erscheint. Die Beispielsätze in der dritten Spalte weisen auf Wörter und Ausdrücke (gekennzeichnet durch ~) hin, die besondere Aufmerksamkeit verdienen, und zeigen, wie diese Wörter angewendet werden.

## UNIT 1

### INTRODUCTIONS

| | | | |
|---|---|---|---|
| hello [hə'ləʊ] | hallo | | |
| what [wɒt] | was, welche(r,s) | W~'s your name? | |
| where [weə] | wo | "W~ are you from?" – | |
| from [frəm] | von, aus | "I'm ~ Munich." | |
| this [ðɪs] | dies, diese/r/s | T~ is David. | |

### PRACTICE

| | | |
|---|---|---|
| teacher ['tiːtʃə] | Lehrer/in | She is a ~. |
| sister ['sɪstə] | Schwester | |
| doctor ['dɒktə] | Arzt, Ärztin | My brother is a ~ and his wife is a ~ too. |
| married ['mærɪd] | verheiratet | Rafael and Carla are ~. |
| to have [həv] | haben | He has a new flat in London. |
| children ['tʃɪldrən] | Kinder | I have three ~. |
| to live [lɪv] | wohnen, leben | |
| house [haʊs] | Haus | I live in a ~ in Berlin. |
| to want [wɒnt] | wollen | I ~ to learn English. |
| to learn [lɜːn] | lernen | |
| job [dʒɒb] | Arbeit, Beruf | "What is your ~?" – "I'm a teacher." |
| brother ['brʌðə] | Bruder | |
| flat [flæt] | Wohnung | I live in a ~, not a house. |
| because [bɪ'kɒz] | weil | I'm at the VHS ~ I want to learn English. |

### VOCABULARY AND PRONUNCIATION

| | | |
|---|---|---|
| word [wɜːd] | Wort | |
| part of speech [ˌpɑːt əv 'spiːtʃ] | Wortart | What ~ is 'orange'? |
| noun [naʊn] | Hauptwort, Substantiv, Nomen | |
| apple ['æpl] | Apfel | |
| pronunciation [prəˌnʌnsi'eɪʃn] | Aussprache | What is the ~ of 'job'? |
| stamp [stæmp] | Briefmarke | |
| bag [bæg] | Tasche, Tüte | |
| key [kiː] | Schlüssel | |
| camera ['kæmərə] | Fotoapparat, Kamera | |
| ticket ['tɪkɪt] | (Fahr-)Karte, Eintrittskarte | |
| postcard ['pəʊstkɑːd] | Postkarte | |
| letter ['letə] | Brief | |
| orange ['ɒrɪndʒ] | Apfelsine, Orange | |
| dictionary ['dɪkʃənri] | Wörterbuch | Here are the dictionaries. |
| newspaper ['njuːspeɪpə] | Zeitung | |
| magazine [ˌmægə'ziːn] | Zeitschrift, Illustrierte | |
| number ['nʌmbə] | (Telefon-)Nummer, Zahl, Ziffer | What ~ is your house? |
| how [haʊ] | wie | |
| to spell [spel] | buchstabieren | How do you ~ 'apple'? |

### EVERYDAY ENGLISH

| | | |
|---|---|---|
| double ['dʌbl] | doppelt, zweimal | |
| phone number ['fəʊn nʌmbə] | Telefonnummer | My ~ is 0-1-2-7-8 7-8-double 9-0-double 2. |
| thank you very much [ˌθæŋk ju ˌveri 'mʌtʃ] | vielen Dank | |
| I'm fine [aɪm 'faɪn] | mir geht es gut | |
| thanks [θæŋks] | danke | |
| How are you? [haʊ ə 'juː] | Wie geht es dir/Ihnen? | "H~?" – "I'm fine, thanks. And you?" – "Not bad, thanks." |
| extension [ɪk'stenʃn] | Apparat | |
| goodbye [ˌgʊd'baɪ] | auf Wiedersehen | |
| nice [naɪs] | schön, nett | Have a ~ day. |
| day [deɪ] | Tag | |
| yes [jes] | ja | |
| cinema ['sɪnəmə] | Kino | |
| to see [siː] | sehen | S~ you at the cinema. |
| evening ['iːvnɪŋ] | Abend | See you this ~. |
| bad [bæd] | schlecht | "How are you" – "Not ~, thanks." |
| very well [veri 'wel] | sehr gut | I'm ~, thank you. |
| hi [haɪ] | hallo | |

## UNIT 2

### WHO IS SHE?

| | | |
|---|---|---|
| surname ['sɜːneɪm] | Nachname | My ~ is Hübner. |
| first name ['fɜːst neɪm] | Vorname | My ~ is Johann. |
| country ['kʌntri] | Land, Staat | |
| address [ə'dres] | Adresse | What's your ~? |
| age [eɪdʒ] | Alter, Zeitalter | |
| how old [haʊ 'əʊld] | wie alt | "H~ are you?" – "I'm 28." |
| no [nəʊ] | nein | |
| policeman [pə'liːsmən] | Polizist | |

### PRACTICE

| | | |
|---|---|---|
| accountant [ə'kaʊntənt] | Buchhalter/in, Steuerberater/in | |

### PATRICK'S FAMILY

| | | |
|---|---|---|
| father ['fɑːðə] | Vater | |
| daughter ['dɔːtə] | Tochter | |
| wife [waɪf] | (Ehe-)Frau | This is my ~, Sarah. |
| aunt [ɑːnt] | Tante | |
| grandmother ['grænmʌðə] | Großmutter, Oma | |
| boyfriend ['bɔɪfrend] | Freund | Have you got a ~? |
| girlfriend ['gɜːlfrend] | Freundin | |
| husband ['hʌzbənd] | (Ehe-)Mann | |
| mother ['mʌðə] | Mutter | |
| son [sʌn] | Sohn | |
| uncle ['ʌŋkl] | Onkel | |
| grandfather ['grænfɑːðə] | Großvater, Opa | |
| photo ['fəʊtəʊ] | Foto | This is a ~ of my younger sister. |
| nurse [nɜːs] | Krankenschwester, Krankenpfleger/in | |
| who [huː] | wer | "W~'s David?" – "He's my husband." |

## PRACTICE

| | | |
|---|---|---|
| **at home** [ət 'həʊm] | zu Hause | *Are you ~ today?* |
| **in class** [ɪn 'klɑːs] | im Unterricht, in der Schule | *We are ~.* |
| **today** [tə'deɪ] | heute | |
| **at work** [ət 'wɜːk] | bei der Arbeit | *My wife is ~.* |
| **year** [jɪə] | Jahr | *I am 45 ~s old.* |
| **coffee bar** ['kɒfi bɑː] | Café | |
| **classroom** ['klɑːsruːm] | Klassenzimmer | |

## VOCABULARY

| | | |
|---|---|---|
| **big** [bɪg] | groß | *opp* small |
| **new** [njuː] | neu | *opp* old |
| **lovely** ['lʌvli] | schön, hübsch, reizend | *opp* horrible |
| **easy** ['iːzi] | einfach, leicht | *opp* difficult |
| **hot** [hɒt] | heiß, warm | *opp* cold |
| **expensive** [ɪk'spensɪv] | teuer | *opp* cheap |
| **fast** [fɑːst] | schnell | *opp* slow |
| **horrible** ['hɒrəbl] | schrecklich, furchtbar | *opp* lovely |
| **young** [jʌŋ] | jung | *opp* old |
| **difficult** ['dɪfɪkəlt] | schwer, schwierig | *opp* easy |
| **cheap** [tʃiːp] | billig | *opp* expensive |
| **cold** [kəʊld] | kalt | *opp* hot |
| **slow** [sləʊ] | langsam | *opp* fast |
| **small** [smɔːl] | klein | *opp* big |

## READING AND LISTENING

| | | |
|---|---|---|
| **dear** [dɪə] | liebe/r | *D~ John, Thank you for your letter ...* |
| **practice** ['præktɪs] | Übung | |
| **college** ['kɒlɪdʒ] | (Berufs-)Fachschule, Fachhochschule | |
| **community** [kə'mjuːnəti] | Gemeinde | |
| **all** [ɔːl] | alle | *The children are ~ at home.* |
| **different** ['dɪfrənt] | anders, verschieden, unterschiedlich | *We go to ~ colleges.* |
| **country** ['kʌntri] | Land, Staat | *All the students are from different countries.* |
| **very** ['veri] | sehr | *The flat is ~ small.* |
| **apartment** [ə'pɑːtmənt] | Wohnung | |
| **girl** [gɜːl] | Mädchen | |
| **dancer** ['dɑːnsə] | Tänzer/in | |
| **friendly** ['frendli] | freundlich | *My teacher is very ~.* |
| **to understand** [ˌʌndə'stænd] | verstehen, begreifen | *English isn't easy to ~.* |
| **to speak** [spiːk] | sprechen, reden | *He ~s very bad English.* |
| **exciting** [ɪk'saɪtɪŋ] | aufregend, spannend | |
| **subway** ['sʌbweɪ] | U-Bahn | |
| **to use** [juːz] | benutzen, verwenden | *Do you ~ the subway?* |
| **now** [naʊ] | nun, jetzt | *I'm at school ~.* |
| **snow** [snəʊ] | Schnee | |
| **happy** ['hæpi] | glücklich, froh | |
| **here** [hɪə] | hier | *It's very cold ~.* |
| **to write** [raɪt] | schreiben | *Please ~ to me soon.* |
| **soon** [suːn] | bald | *See you ~.* |
| **love** [lʌv] | Liebe (Grüße) | *L~ Paola* |
| **holiday** ['hɒlədeɪ] | Urlaub | *We are on ~.* |
| **both** [bəʊθ] | beide | *B~ John and I are teachers. We are ~ on holiday now.* |

## EVERYDAY ENGLISH

| | | |
|---|---|---|
| **pound** [paʊnd] | Pfund (Sterling) | |
| **p** [piː] | Pence | *This is one pound fifty ~.* |
| **snack bar** ['snæk bɑː] | Imbissstube | |
| **chips** [tʃɪps] | Pommes frites | |
| **chicken** ['tʃɪkɪn] | Huhn, Hähnchen | |
| **tuna** ['tjuːnə] | Thunfisch | |
| **egg** [eg] | Ei | |
| **salad** ['sæləd] | Salat | |
| **ice cream** [ˌaɪs 'kriːm] | Speiseeis | |
| **chocolate cake** ['tʃɒklət keɪk] | Schokoladenkuchen | |
| **coffee** ['kɒfi] | Kaffee | |
| **tea** [tiː] | Tee | |
| **orange juice** ['ɒrɪndʒ dʒuːs] | Orangensaft | |
| **mineral water** ['mɪnərəl wɔːtə] | Mineralwasser | |
| **how much** [haʊ 'mʌtʃ] | wie viel | *H~ is the chocolate cake?* |
| **(good) morning** [ˌgʊd 'mɔːnɪŋ] | guten Morgen | |
| **can** [kæn] | können, dürfen | *C~ I help you?* |
| **please** [pliːz] | bitte | |
| **here you are** [hɪə ju 'ɑː] | hier, bitte | *"An orange juice, please." – "H~."* |
| **anything** ['eniθɪŋ] | etwas | |
| **else** [els] | andere(r,s) | *"Anything ~?" – "No, thanks."* |
| **to help** [help] | helfen | |
| **to drink** [drɪŋk] | trinken | *Anything else to ~?* |

# UNIT 3

## THREE JOBS

| | | |
|---|---|---|
| **scientist** ['saɪəntɪst] | (Natur-)Wissenschaftler/in | |
| **to come** [kʌm] | kommen | *Where do you ~ from?* |
| **to work** [wɜːk] | arbeiten | |
| **week** [wiːk] | Woche | |
| **language** ['læŋgwɪdʒ] | Sprache | |
| **to like** [laɪk] | mögen, gern haben | *Paul ~s his job.* |
| **skiing** ['skiːɪŋ] | Skilaufen | |
| **winter** ['wɪntə] | Winter | *I like skiing in the ~.* |
| **to go for a walk** [gəʊ fər ə 'wɔːk] | spazieren gehen | *I like going for a walk.* |
| **summer** ['sʌmə] | Sommer | |
| **town** [taʊn] | Stadt | |
| **ordinary** ['ɔːdnri] | gewöhnlich, normal | |
| **flying doctor** [ˌflaɪɪŋ 'dɒktə] | fliegender Arzt | |
| **every** ['evri] | jede/r/s | *I work here ~ day.* |
| **people** ['piːpl] | Leute, Menschen | |
| **to fly** [flaɪ] | fliegen | |
| **non-stop** [ˌnɒn'stɒp] | durchgehend, ununterbrochen | |
| **to love** [lʌv] | sehr gern mögen, lieben | |
| **free time** [ˌfriː 'taɪm] | Freizeit, freie Zeit | *I learn English in my ~.* |
| **city** ['sɪti] | Stadt, (Groß-)Stadt | |
| **sick** [sɪk] | krank | *David's very ~ today.* |
| **never** ['nevə] | nie(mals) | *I ~ use the subway.* |

## PRACTICE

| | | |
|---|---|---|
| **barman** ['bɑːmən] | Barkeeper | |

| | | | |
|---|---|---|---|
| **place of work** [ˌpleɪs əv 'wɜːk] | Arbeitsstelle | | |
| **centre** ['sentə] | Mitte, Zentrum | | |
| **little** ['lɪtl] | klein, wenig | | |
| **dog** [dɒg] | Hund | | |
| **to walk** [wɔːk] | ausführen, (zu Fuß) gehen | *I ~ to work.* | |
| **to play** [pleɪ] | spielen | *He ~s football on Saturday.* | |
| **football** ['fʊtbɔːl] | Fußball | | |
| **interpreter** [ɪn'tɜːprɪtə] | Dolmetscher/in | | |
| **United Nations** [juːˌnaɪtɪd 'neɪʃnz] | Vereinte Nationen | | |
| **office** ['ɒfɪs] | Büro | *I work in an ~.* | |
| **to listen** ['lɪsn tə] | anhören, zuhören | *L~ to this music! It's nice.* | |
| **music** ['mjuːzɪk] | Musik | | |
| **how many** [haʊ 'meni] | wie viele | *H~ languages do you speak?* | |

## READING AND LISTENING

| | | | |
|---|---|---|---|
| **shop** [ʃɒp] | Laden, Geschäft | | |
| **to make** [meɪk] | machen, zubereiten | | |
| **breakfast** ['brekfəst] | Frühstück | | |
| **guest** [gest] | Gast | | |
| **petrol** ['petrəl] | Benzin | | |
| **to deliver** [dɪ'lɪvə] | austragen, zustellen | | |
| **beer** [bɪə] | Bier | | |
| **to collect** [kə'lekt] | abholen, einsammeln | *Can you ~ the children from school, please?* | |
| **boat** [bəʊt] | Boot, Schiff | | |
| **to drive** [draɪv] | (mit dem Auto) fahren | *David ~s to work.* | |
| **school** [skuːl] | Schule | | |
| **glass** [glɑːs] | Glas | | |
| **wine** [waɪn] | Wein | | |
| **as** [əz] | als | *He works ~ a doctor.* | |
| **undertaker** ['ʌndəteɪkə] | Leichenbestatter | | |
| **busy** ['bɪzi] | beschäftigt | *I'm very ~ today.* | |
| **man** [mæn] | Mann | | |
| **fireman** ['faɪəmən] | Feuerwehrmann | | |
| **taxi driver** ['tæksi draɪvə] | Taxifahrer/in | | |
| **school-bus driver** [ˌskuːlbʌs 'draɪvə] | Schulbusfahrer/in | | |
| **boatman** ['bəʊtmən] | Bootsmann | | |
| **ambulance man** ['æmbjələns mən] | Krankenwagenfahrer | | |
| **petrol attendant** [ˌpetrəl ə'tendənt] | Tankwart/in | | |
| **also** ['ɔːlsəʊ] | auch, außerdem | *The firemen here are ~ ambulance men.* | |
| **north** [nɔːθ] | Norden | *We live in the ~ of England.* | |
| **only** ['əʊnli] | nur | *There is ~ one hotel here.* | |
| **but** [bʌt] | aber | | |
| **by** [baɪ] | mit | *We all come to work ~ bus.* | |
| **weekday** ['wiːkdeɪ] | Wochentag, Werktag | | |
| **to get up** [ˌget 'ʌp] | aufstehen | | |
| **island** ['aɪlənd] | Insel | | |
| **only** ['əʊnli] | einzig | *This is the ~ hotel here.* | |
| **too** [tuː] | auch | *The firemen here are ambulance men, ~.* | |
| **to watch television** [ˌwɒtʃ 'telɪvɪʒn] | fernsehen | | |
| **supper** ['sʌpə] | (das) Abendessen | | |
| **to do the accounts** [duː ðiː ə'kaʊnts] | abrechnen | | |
| **to go to bed** [gəʊ tə 'bed] | ins Bett gehen | *It's time ~.* | |
| **perhaps** [pə'hæps] | vielleicht | *"I'm very cold." – "P~ you're sick."* | |
| **chocolate** ['tʃɒklət] | Schokolade | | |
| **vanilla** [və'nɪlə] | Vanille | | |
| **my dear** [maɪ 'dɪə] | meine Liebe, mein Lieber | | |
| **boy** [bɔɪ] | Junge | | |
| **to hurry up** [ˌhʌri 'ʌp] | sich beeilen | *H~! We're late.* | |
| **late** [leɪt] | spät | *Sorry, I'm ~.* | |
| **to sit** [sɪt] | sitzen, sich setzen | *You can ~ down now.* | |
| **quiet** ['kwaɪət] | still, ruhig, leise | *Please be ~.* | |

## VOCABULARY AND PRONUNCIATION

| | | | |
|---|---|---|---|
| **pilot** ['paɪlət] | Pilot/in, Flugzeugführer/in | | |
| **postman** ['pəʊstmən] | Briefträger | | |
| **architect** ['ɑːkɪtekt] | Architekt/in | | |
| **shopkeeper** ['ʃɒp kiːpə] | Ladeninhaber/in | | |
| **to design** [dɪ'zaɪn] | entwerfen, konstruieren, bauen | | |
| **house** [haʊs] | Haus | | |
| **to look after** [lʊk 'ɑːftə] | betreuen, sich kümmern um | *A nurse looks after sick people.* | |
| **hospital** ['hɒspɪtl] | Krankenhaus | | |
| **money** ['mʌni] | Geld | *How much ~ do you have?* | |
| **to translate** [træns'leɪt] | übersetzen | | |
| **thing** [θɪŋ] | Sache, Ding | | |
| **to sell** [sel] | verkaufen | *This shop ~s books.* | |
| **plane** [pleɪn] | Flugzeug | | |
| **to serve** [sɜːv] | servieren | | |

## EVERYDAY ENGLISH

| | | | |
|---|---|---|---|
| **o'clock** [ə'klɒk] | volle Stunde, um ... Uhr | *It's ten ~.* | |
| **half** [hɑːf] | halb | *It's ~ past seven.* | |
| **past** [pɑːst] | nach | | |
| **quarter** ['kwɔːtə] | Viertel | *It's ~ to eight.* | |
| **to** [tə, tʊ] | vor, (bis) zu | | |
| **about** [ə'baʊt] | etwa, ungefähr, zirka | *It's ~ six o'clock.* | |
| **excuse me** [ɪk'skjuːz mi] | Entschuldigung, entschuldige(n Sie) | *E~. Where is the bank, please?* | |
| **to tell** [tel] | sagen | *Excuse me, can you ~ me the time, please?* | |
| **time** [taɪm] | Zeit | *What ~ is it, please?* | |
| **of course** [əf 'kɔːs] | natürlich, selbstverständlich | | |
| **I'm sorry** [aɪm 'sɒri] | es tut mir Leid | | |
| **to know** [nəʊ] | kennen, wissen | *I'm sorry, I don't ~ what time it is.* | |
| **watch** [wɒtʃ] | (Armband-)Uhr | | |
| **never mind** [ˌnevə 'maɪnd] | Schon gut., Macht nichts. | *"I don't know." – "N~."* | |

# UNIT 4

## WEEKDAYS AND WEEKENDS

| | | | |
|---|---|---|---|
| **to interview** ['ɪntəvjuː] | interviewen, befragen | | |

| | | | |
|---|---|---|---|
| to start [stɑːt] | beginnen, anfangen | She ~s work at 9.00. | |
| weekend [ˌwiːkˈend] | Wochenende | He doesn't work at ~s. | |
| famous [ˈfeɪməs] | berühmt | | |
| early [ˈɜːli] | früh, frühzeitig | I get up very ~. | |
| news [njuːz] | Nachricht(en) | The ~ is at eight o'clock. | |
| programme [ˈprəʊɡræm] | Sendung, Programm | This is an interesting ~. | |
| (to be) called [bɪ ˈkɔːld] | heißen, nennen | This news programme is ~ 'Newsnight'. | |
| domestic [dəˈmestɪk] | häuslich | | |
| morning [ˈmɔːnɪŋ] | Morgen | | |
| before [bɪˈfɔː] | vor, bevor | I go jogging ~ I go to work. | |
| gym [dʒɪm] | Turnhalle, Sportstudio | | |
| food [fuːd] | Essen, Lebensmittel | | |
| dinner [ˈdɪnə] | Abendessen | | |
| most [məʊst] | der/die/das meiste, die meisten | John walks to work ~ mornings. | |
| fortunately [ˈfɔːtʃənətli] | glücklicherweise | | |
| cooking [ˈkʊkɪŋ] | Kochen, Essen | | |
| block [blɒk] | (Wohn-)Block | | |
| afternoon [ˌɑːftəˈnuːn] | Nachmittag | Sue doesn't work in the ~. | |
| kids [kɪdz] | Kinder | | |
| sometimes [ˈsʌmtaɪmz] | manchmal | I ~ eat out on Saturday evenings. | |
| friend [frend] | Freund/in | | |
| to relax [rɪˈlæks] | (sich) entspannen, ausruhen | I ~ in the evenings. | |
| to visit [ˈvɪzɪt] | besichtigen, besuchen | At weekends he ~s his parents. | |
| to go out [ˌɡəʊ ˈaʊt] | ausgehen | | |
| to take [teɪk] | nehmen, bringen | I always ~ the kids to school. | |
| to buy [baɪ] | kaufen | | |
| to cook [kʊk] | kochen | | |
| work [wɜːk] | Arbeit | I start ~ early. | |
| why [waɪ] | warum | W~ do you want to learn English? | |
| life [laɪf] | Leben | | |

PRACTICE

| | | | |
|---|---|---|---|
| to travel [ˈtrævl] | fahren, reisen | | |
| when [wen] | wenn, wann | W~ do you want to leave? | |
| homework [ˈhəʊmwɜːk] | Hausaufgaben | My ~ is difficult. | |
| always [ˈɔːlweɪz] | immer | I ~ drive to work. | |
| to leave [liːv] | abfahren, verlassen | | |
| to read [riːd] | lesen | | |
| a lot [ə ˈlɒt] | viel, sehr | Anna cooks ~. | |
| to smoke [sməʊk] | rauchen | I don't ~. | |
| tired [ˈtaɪəd] | müde | You look ~. | |

READING AND LISTENING

| | | | |
|---|---|---|---|
| long [lɒŋ] | lang | | |
| short [ʃɔːt] | kurz, klein | | |
| near [nɪə] | nahe, in der Nähe von | We live ~ a bank. | |
| lake [leɪk] | (Binnen-)See | | |
| to go sailing [ˌɡəʊ ˈseɪlɪŋ] | segeln | | |
| baseball [ˈbeɪsbɔːl] | Baseball | | |
| ice hockey [ˈaɪs hɒki] | Eishockey | | |
| ice-skating [ˈaɪs skeɪtɪŋ] | Schlittschuhlaufen | | |
| favourite [ˈfeɪvərɪt] | liebste(r,s), Lieblings- | What is your ~ season? | |
| season [ˈsiːzn] | Jahreszeit | | |
| autumn [ˈɔːtəm] | Herbst | | |
| fall [fɔːl] | Herbst | In Great Britain we say 'autumn'. In the USA people say '~'. | |
| colour [ˈkʌlə] | Farbe | | |
| tree [triː] | Baum | | |
| red [red] | rot | | |
| gold [ɡəʊld] | golden | | |
| orange [ˈɒrɪndʒ] | orange | | |
| yellow [ˈjeləʊ] | gelb | | |
| brown [braʊn] | braun | | |
| sunny [ˈsʌni] | sonnig | | |
| often [ˈɒfn] | oft, häufig | I ~ go to the cinema at weekends. | |
| wet [wet] | nass, feucht | | |
| grey [ɡreɪ] | grau | | |
| to meet [miːt] | treffen, sich treffen (mit) | Paul usually ~s his friends in the pub. | |
| to chat [tʃæt] | sich unterhalten, plaudern | | |
| then [ðen] | dann | Let's cook dinner, ~ go to the cinema. | |
| suddenly [ˈsʌdnli] | plötzlich | | |
| beach [biːtʃ] | Strand | | |
| to sunbathe [ˈsʌnbeɪð] | sonnenbaden | | |
| export department [ˈekspɔːt dɪpɑːtmənt] | Exportabteilung | | |
| special [ˈspeʃl] | besondere(r,s) | Maria uses a ~ camera. | |
| to take photographs [teɪk ˈfəʊtəɡrɑːfs] | fotografieren | I always take a lot of photographs on holiday. | |
| flower [ˈflaʊə] | Blume | | |
| especially [ɪˈspeʃəli] | besonders | I like reading, ~ on holiday. | |
| spring [sprɪŋ] | Frühling, Frühjahr | | |
| to sing [sɪŋ] | singen | | |
| too [tuː] | zu | I don't want to go out. I'm ~ tired. | |
| shy [ʃaɪ] | schüchtern, scheu | I'm too ~ to sing. | |

VOCABULARY AND SPEAKING

| | | | |
|---|---|---|---|
| much [mʌtʃ] | viel | I don't like Karl ~. | |
| Really? [ˈrɪəli] | Wirklich? | "I want to visit Bavaria." – "R~? Why?" | |
| boring [ˈbɔːrɪŋ] | langweilig | | |

EVERYDAY ENGLISH

| | | | |
|---|---|---|---|
| traffic [ˈtræfɪk] | (Straßen-)Verkehr | | |
| to worry [ˈwʌri] | sich Sorgen machen | Don't ~! Be happy! | |
| quite [kwaɪt] | ziemlich, ganz | It's ~ cold here in winter. | |
| to open [ˈəʊpən] | öffnen, aufmachen | Can I ~ the window, please? | |
| window [ˈwɪndəʊ] | Fenster | | |
| to matter [ˈmætə] | etw ausmachen, darauf ankommen | "I'm sorry, I don't know." – "OK, it doesn't really ~." | |
| Pardon? [ˈpɑːdn] | Wie bitte?, Verzeihung | | |
| exposure [ɪkˈspəʊʒə] | Belichtung | | |
| to mean [miːn] | bedeuten, meinen | What does 'exposure' ~? | |
| picture [ˈpɪktʃə] | Bild | This is a ~ of my children on holiday. | |

# UNIT 5

| | | | |
|---|---|---|---|
| **living room** ['lɪvɪŋ ruːm] | Wohnzimmer | | |
| **kitchen** ['kɪtʃɪn] | Küche | | |
| **armchair** ['ɑːmtʃeə] | Sessel, Lehnstuhl | | |
| **fridge** [frɪdʒ] | Kühlschrank | | |
| **television** ['telɪvɪʒn] | Fernsehen, Fernseher | | |
| **coffee table** ['kɒfi teɪbl] | Couchtisch | | |
| **table** ['teɪbl] | Tisch | | |
| **shelf** [ʃelf] | Regal(brett) | *The plural of '~' is 'shelves'.* | |
| **plant** [plɑːnt] | Pflanze | | |
| **lamp** [læmp] | Lampe, Leuchte | | |
| **cooker** ['kʊkə] | Herd | | |
| **washing machine** ['wɒʃɪŋ məʃiːn] | Waschmaschine | | |
| **telephone** ['telɪfəʊn] | Telefon | | |
| **cupboard** ['kʌbəd] | Schrank | | |
| **cup** [kʌp] | Tasse | | |

## WHAT'S IN THE LIVING ROOM?

| | | |
|---|---|---|
| **cat** [kæt] | Katze | |
| **mirror** ['mɪrə] | Spiegel | |
| **fire** ['faɪə] | Feuer, Kamin, Heizung(sgerät) | |
| **rug** [rʌg] | Läufer, Brücke, Vorleger | |
| **bookshelves** ['bʊkʃelvz] | (Bücher-)Regal | |
| **on** [ɒn] | auf | *The plant is ~ the table.* |
| **under** ['ʌndə] | unter | *The cat is ~ the table.* |
| **next to** ['nekst tə] | (direkt) neben | *The phone is ~ the stereo.* |
| **in front of** [ɪn 'frʌnt əv] | vor | *The cat is ~ the fire.* |
| **wall** [wɔːl] | Wand, Mauer | *There is a photo on the ~.* |

## PRACTICE

| | | |
|---|---|---|
| **exactly** [ɪg'zæktli] | exakt, genau | *Where are the cups ~?* |

## WHAT'S IN THE KITCHEN?

| | | |
|---|---|---|
| **well** [wel] | nun | *W~, the cups are there.* |
| **plate** [pleɪt] | Teller | |
| **knife** [naɪf] | Messer | *The plural of '~' is 'knives'.* |
| **fork** [fɔːk] | Gabel | |
| **spoon** [spuːn] | Löffel | |
| **champagne** [ʃæm'peɪn] | Champagner | |
| **Cheers!** [tʃɪəz] | Prost! | |
| **to give** [gɪv] | geben | *Can you ~ me a plate, please?* |

## PRACTICE

| | |
|---|---|
| **floor** [flɔː] | (Fuß-)Boden |
| **pen** [pen] | Füller, Kugelschreiber, (Filz-)Stift |
| **dirty** ['dɜːti] | schmutzig, dreckig |
| **briefcase** ['briːfkeɪs] | Aktentasche |
| **notebook** ['nəʊtbʊk] | Notizbuch |
| **bus ticket** ['bʌs tɪkɪt] | Busfahrschein |
| **mobile phone** [ˌməʊbaɪl 'fəʊn] | Mobiltelefon, Handy |
| **address book** [ə'dres bʊk] | Adressbuch |
| **to look at** ['lʊk ət] | ansehen | *L~ this photo.* |
| **over there** [ˌəʊvə 'ðeə] | da drüben, dort (drüben) | *The phone is ~, on the coffee table.* |

## READING AND SPEAKING

| | | |
|---|---|---|
| **steps** [steps] | Treppe, Leiter | *The ~ are here.* |
| **flight attendant** [ˌflaɪt ə'tendənt] | Flugbegleiter/in | |
| **first class section** [ˌfɜːst klɑːs 'sekʃn] | Erster-Klasse-Abteil | |
| **emergency exit** [ɪ'mɜːdʒənsi eksɪt] | Notausgang | |
| **door** [dɔː] | Tür | |
| **toilet** ['tɔɪlət] | Toilette | |
| **grandson** ['grænsʌn] | Enkel | |
| **bedroom** ['bedruːm] | Schlafzimmer | |
| **lady** ['leɪdi] | Dame | |
| **visit** ['vɪzɪt] | Besuch | |
| **front door** [ˌfrʌnt 'dɔː] | Haustür | |
| **at the top** [ət ðə 'tɒp] | oben | |
| **passport** ['pɑːspɔːt] | (Reise-)Pass | |
| **luxury** ['lʌkʃəri] | Luxus, Luxus- | *L~ hotels are very expensive.* |
| **bath** [bɑːθ] | Badewanne | *There's a ~ in the bathroom.* |
| **No Smoking** [ˌnəʊ 'sməʊkɪŋ] | Rauchen verboten | |
| **sign** [saɪn] | Zeichen, Schild | *The ~ says 'No Smoking'.* |
| **world** [wɜːld] | Welt | |
| **air conditioning** ['eə kəndɪʃnɪŋ] | Klimaanlage | |
| **even** ['iːvn] | sogar, selbst | *This house doesn't ~ have a telephone.* |
| **dishwasher** ['dɪʃwɒʃə] | Geschirrspülmaschine | |
| **time** [taɪm] | Zeit, Mal | *Chicago is boring, I want to go to Florida this ~.* |
| **upstairs** [ˌʌp'steəz] | die Treppe hinauf/herauf, Obergeschoss | |
| **downstairs** [ˌdaʊn'steəz] | die Treppe hinunter, Untergeschoss | |
| **to need** [niːd] | benötigen, brauchen | |

## LISTENING AND SPEAKING

| | | |
|---|---|---|
| **extra information** [ˌekstrə ɪnfə'meɪʃn] | Zusatzinformation(en) | *This ~ is very interesting.* |
| **garden** ['gɑːdn] | Garten | |

## EVERYDAY ENGLISH

| | |
|---|---|
| **aspirin** ['æsprɪn] | Aspirin |
| **bank** [bæŋk] | Bank |
| **bus stop** ['bʌs stɒp] | Bushaltestelle |
| **bookshop** ['bʊkʃɒp] | Buchhandlung |
| **supermarket** ['suːpəmɑːkɪt] | Supermarkt |
| **post office** ['pəʊst ɒfɪs] | Postamt |
| **public toilet** [ˌpʌblɪk 'tɔɪlət] | öffentliche Toilette |
| **chemist** ['kemɪst] | Apotheke(r) |
| **music (CD) shop** ['mjuːzɪk ʃɒp] | Musikladen |
| **phone box** ['fəʊnbɒks] | Telefonzelle |

| | | |
|---|---|---|
| **travel agent** ['trævl eɪdʒənt] | Reisebüro | |
| **post box** ['pəʊst bɒks] | Briefkasten | |
| **newsagent** ['nju:zeɪdʒənt] | Zeitungshändler | |
| **swimming pool** ['swɪmɪŋ pu:l] | Schwimmbad | |
| **first** [fɜ:st] | erste(r,s) | |
| **right** [raɪt] | rechts, rechte(r,s), rechte Seite | |
| **straight ahead** [ˌstreɪt ə'hed] | geradeaus | *Take the first right, then go ~.* |
| **left** [left] | linke(r,s), links, linke Seite | |

## UNIT 6

| | | |
|---|---|---|
| **a little** [ə 'lɪtl] | ein wenig, ein bisschen | |

### WHAT CAN YOU DO?

| | | |
|---|---|---|
| **well** [wel] | gut | *Maria can sing very ~.* |
| **to swim** [swɪm] | schwimmen | |
| **question** ['kwestʃən] | Frage | |

### PRACTICE

| | | |
|---|---|---|
| **piano** [pi'ænəʊ] | Klavier | |
| **poetry** ['pəʊətri] | Dichtung, Gedichte | *Karl writes very bad ~.* |
| **to laugh** [lɑ:f] | lachen | |
| **chess** [tʃes] | Schach | |
| **to hear** [hɪə] | hören | *I can ~ the traffic.* |
| **to check spellings** [tʃek 'spelɪŋz] | Rechtschreibung überprüfen | |
| **to feel** [fi:l] | (sich) fühlen, empfinden | *I ~ tired.* |
| **to think** [θɪŋk] | denken | |
| **conversation** [ˌkɒnvə'seɪʃn] | Gespräch, Unterhaltung | |
| **to fall in love** [ˌfɔ:l ɪn 'lʌv] | sich verlieben | *He fell in love with a girl from Spain.* |
| **yesterday** ['jestədeɪ] | gestern | *Y~ was Monday.* |
| **month** [mʌnθ] | Monat | |
| **last** [lɑ:st] | letzte(r,s) | *John was sick ~ week.* |

### PRACTICE

| | | |
|---|---|---|
| **night** [naɪt] | Nacht, Abend | *We were at home last ~.* |
| **there** [ðeə] | da, dort(hin) | |
| **brilliant** ['brɪliənt] | großartig, toll | |
| **genius** ['dʒi:niəs] | Genie | |
| **(to be) born** [bi 'bɔ:n] | geboren werden/ sein | *I was ~ in London in 1973.* |
| **not ... until** [nɒt ən'tɪl] | erst als | *I couldn't talk until I was five.* |
| **to paint** [peɪnt] | malen | |
| **to dance** [dɑ:ns] | tanzen | |
| **to talk** [tɔ:k] | sprechen, reden | |
| **to ride a bike** [ˌraɪd ə 'baɪk] | Rad fahren | |

### READING AND SPEAKING

| | | |
|---|---|---|
| **super** ['su:pə] | großartig | |
| **to meet** [mi:t] | treffen, begegnen, kennen lernen | *Come and ~ my wife, she's just over there.* |
| **lots of** ['lɒts əv] | viel, viele | *He has ~ friends.* |
| **concert** ['kɒnsət] | Konzert | |
| **to practise** ['præktɪs] | üben | |
| **not ... at all** [nɒt ət 'ɔ:l] | überhaupt nicht | *Paul can't cook at all.* |
| **large** [lɑ:dʒ] | groß | |
| **picture** ['pɪktʃə] | Bild | |
| **cubist style** ['kju:bɪst staɪl] | kubistischer Stil | |
| **between** [bɪ'twi:n] | zwischen | *The post office is ~ the bank and the pub.* |
| **parents** ['peərənts] | Eltern | |
| **sad** [sæd] | traurig | *Karl is a very ~ man.* |
| **to stop** [stɒp] | aufhören (mit) | |
| **after** ['ɑ:ftə] | nach | *I often go shopping ~ work.* |
| **hour** ['aʊə] | Stunde | |
| **until** [ən'tɪl] | bis | *I sometimes work ~ 7.00.* |
| **bedtime** ['bedtaɪm] | Schlafenszeit | |
| **to spend** [spend] | ausgeben | *I always ~ a lot of money on CDs.* |
| **to save** [seɪv] | sparen, aufheben | |
| **poor** [pʊə] | arm | |
| **fantastic** [fæn'tæstɪk] | fantastisch | |
| **first of all** [fɜ:st əv 'ɔ:l] | zu(aller)erst | *F~ we need a drink.* |

### VOCABULARY AND PRONUNCIATION

| | | |
|---|---|---|
| **black eye** [blæk 'aɪ] | blaues Auge | |
| **answer** ['ɑ:nsə] | Antwort, Lösung | |
| **to wear** [weə] | tragen, anhaben | |
| **right** [raɪt] | richtig | *Is this the ~ house?* |
| **sun** [sʌn] | Sonne | |
| **hat** [hæt] | Hut, Mütze | |

### EVERYDAY ENGLISH

| | | |
|---|---|---|
| **Directory Enquiries** [dəˌrektəri ɪn'kwaɪəriz] | (Telefon-) Auskunft | *If you need a phone number, you can phone ~.* |
| **operator** ['ɒpəreɪtə] | Telefonist/in, (Telefon-)Vermittlung | |
| **initial** e[ɪ'nɪʃl] | Initiale(n), Anfangsbuchstabe(n) | *My ~s are TRP.* |
| **recorded message** [rɪˌkɔ:dɪd 'mesɪdʒ] | aufgezeichnete Nachricht | |
| **to require** [rɪ'kwaɪə] | brauchen, benötigen | |
| **to take a message** [ˌteɪk ə 'mesɪdʒ] | etw ausrichten | *Can I ~?* |
| **great** [greɪt] | groß(artig), toll, prima | |
| **bye** [baɪ] | tschüs | |
| **next time** [nekst 'taɪm] | nächstes Mal | *See you ~!* |
| **just** [dʒʌst] | einfach, mal | *I must ~ finish my homework and then we can go out.* |
| **to ring back** [ˌrɪŋ 'bæk] | zurückrufen | |
| **manager** ['mænɪdʒə] | Geschäftsführer/in | |
| **still** [stɪl] | (immer) noch | *Is Sunday ~ OK for dinner?* |
| **wedding** ['wedɪŋ] | Hochzeit, Trauung | |
| **I'm afraid** [aɪm ə'freɪd] | leider | *I~ I don't know.* |
| **all right** [ɔ:l 'raɪt] | in Ordnung, okay | |

# UNIT 7

## WHEN I WAS YOUNG

| | | | |
|---|---|---|---|
| alone [ə'ləʊn] | allein(e) | | My sister lives ~. |
| next [nekst] | nächste/r/s, danach | | I'm on holiday ~ week. |
| outside [ˌaʊt'saɪd] | draußen | | It's sunny, we can eat ~. |
| verandah [və'rændə] | Veranda | | |
| past [pɑːst] | vergangen | | Her ~ life was difficult. |
| poem ['pəʊɪm] | Gedicht | | |
| cotton field ['kɒtn fiːld] | Baumwollfeld | | |
| to create [kri'eɪt] | (er)schaffen | | |
| head [hed] | Kopf | | |
| to earn [ɜːn] | verdienen | | Maria ~s £35,000 a year. |
| to marry ['mæri] | heiraten | | They married in 1960. |
| to die [daɪ] | sterben | | |
| to hate [heɪt] | hassen, gar nicht mögen | | |
| sure [ʃʊə] | sicher(lich) | | I'm ~ this is the right address. |
| ago [ə'gəʊ] | vor | | He died four years ~. |
| so [səʊ] | also | | I live near the office, ~ I walk to work. |
| important [ɪm'pɔːtnt] | wichtig | | |

## PRACTICE

| | | |
|---|---|---|
| subject ['sʌbdʒɪkt] | (Schul-)Fach | |

## THE END OF THE 20TH CENTURY

| | | |
|---|---|---|
| to begin [bɪ'gɪn] | anfangen, beginnen | |
| to get [get] | bekommen, erhalten | I always ~ a lot of Christmas cards. |
| to study ['stʌdi] | studieren | Many students ~ languages at this university. |
| to become [bɪ'kʌm] | werden | She became a grandmother at the age of forty-five. |
| to win [wɪn] | gewinnen | |
| to lose [luːz] | verlieren | I lost my keys yesterday. |
| university [ˌjuːnɪ'vɜːsəti] | Universität | Sue goes to ~ in Oxford. |
| graphic design [ˌgræfɪk dɪ'zaɪn] | technisches Zeichnen | |
| advertising agency ['ædvətaɪzɪŋ eɪdʒənsi] | Werbeagentur | |
| together [tə'geðə] | zusammen | John and Anna live ~. |
| World Cup [ˌwɜːld 'kʌp] | Weltmeisterschaft | |
| politics ['pɒlətɪks] | (die) Politik | |
| Prime Minister [ˌpraɪm 'mɪnɪstə] | Premierminister | |
| president ['prezɪdənt] | Präsident/in | |
| car crash ['kɑː kræʃ] | Autounfall | |
| funeral ['fjuːnərəl] | Beerdigung, Begräbnis | |

## PRACTICE

| | | |
|---|---|---|
| to happen ['hæpən] | passieren, geschehen | How did the car crash ~? |
| to end [end] | (be)enden | How did the evening ~? |
| moon [muːn] | Mond | |
| to go shopping [gəʊ 'ʃɒpɪŋ] | einkaufen gehen | We always ~ on Friday. |
| someone ['sʌmwʌn] | jemand | Can ~ help me, please? |
| kiss [kɪs] | Kuss | |
| something ['sʌmθɪŋ] | etwas | Do you want ~ to eat? |
| present ['preznt] | Geschenk | He gave her a lovely ~. |
| shoe [ʃuː] | Schuh | |

## READING AND SPEAKING

| | | |
|---|---|---|
| grocer ['grəʊsə] | Lebensmittelhändler/in, Kaufmann | |
| slave [sleɪv] | Sklave, Sklavin | |
| politician [ˌpɒlə'tɪʃn] | Politiker/in | |
| twin [twɪn] | Zwilling, Zwillings- | David is my ~ brother. We're ~s. |
| widow ['wɪdəʊ] | Witwe | |
| (in) tears [ɪn 'tɪəz] | unter Tränen | John was in ~ when he lost his job. |
| to agree [ə'griː] | zustimmen | I ~d with him about the wine – it was horrible. |
| to bomb [bɒm] | bombardieren | |
| to grow [grəʊ] | wachsen, anbauen | |
| to fight [faɪt] | kämpfen | |
| to own [əʊn] | besitzen | Do you ~ a television? |
| to resign [rɪ'zaɪn] | zurücktreten (von) | The politician ~ed last week. |
| to survive [sə'vaɪv] | überleben | |
| War of Independence [ˌwɔːr əv ˌɪndɪ'pendəns] | Unabhängigkeitskrieg | |
| farm [fɑːm] | Bauernhof, Farm | |
| education [ˌedʒu'keɪʃn] | Erziehung, (Schul-)Bildung | |
| during ['djʊərɪŋ] | während | He was a soldier ~ the war. |
| farmer ['fɑːmə] | Bauer, Bäuerin | |
| soldier ['səʊldʒə] | Soldat/in | |
| tobacco [tə'bækəʊ] | Tabak | |
| horse [hɔːs] | Pferd | |
| hard [hɑːd] | schwer, hart | I work ~ during the week. |
| theatre ['θɪətə] | Theater | Let's go to the ~. |
| Commander-in-Chief [kə'mɑːndər ɪn 'tʃiːf] | Oberbefehlshaber | |
| army ['ɑːmi] | Armee, Heer | |
| finally ['faɪnəli] | schließlich, zum Schluss | Great, it's ~ Friday! |
| capital city [ˌkæpɪtl 'sɪti] | Hauptstadt | |
| to build [bɪld] | bauen | |
| by [baɪ] | um | B~ 1790 he was president. |
| tired of ['taɪəd əv] | überdrüssig | We are all ~ work by 5.00. |
| woman ['wʊmən] | Frau | |
| above [ə'bʌv] | über | The flat is ~ the shop. |
| chemistry ['kemɪstri] | Chemie | |
| rich [rɪtʃ] | reich, wohlhabend | |
| businessman ['bɪznəsmən] | Geschäftsmann | |
| interest ['ɪntrəst] | Interesse | Do you have any special ~s? |
| sleep [sliːp] | Schlaf | I always go to bed early. I need my ~. |
| leader ['liːdə] | Führer/in | |
| strong [strɒŋ] | stark | |
| personality [ˌpɜːsə'næləti] | Persönlichkeit | |
| afraid: to be afraid of [bi ə'freɪd əv] | Angst haben vor, sich fürchten vor | Karl is ~ of cats. |
| Iron Lady [ˌaɪən 'leɪdi] | Eiserne Lady | |
| terrorist ['terərɪst] | Terrorist/in | |
| in office [ɪn 'ɒfɪs] | im Amt | John loved politics, but he was never ~. |

## EVERYDAY ENGLISH

| | | | |
|---|---|---|---|
| occasion [əˈkeɪʒn] | Ereignis, Anlass | This is an important ~ for all of us. |
| birthday [ˈbɜːθdeɪ] | Geburtstag | It's my ~ today. Yesterday it was my husband's ~. |
| wedding day [ˈwedɪŋ deɪ] | Hochzeitstag | |
| Christmas Day [ˌkrɪsməs ˈdeɪ] | 1. Weihnachtsfeiertag | |
| New Year's Eve [ˌnjuː jɪəz ˈiːv] | Silvester | |
| Easter Day [ˌiːstə ˈdeɪ] | Ostersonntag | |
| tomorrow [təˈmɒrəʊ] | morgen | T~ is Christmas Day. |
| Mother's Day [ˈmʌðəz deɪ] | Muttertag | She always sees her family on ~. |
| Thanksgiving [ˈθæŋksgɪvɪŋ] | Erntedankfest | |
| Valentine's Day [ˈvæləntaɪnz deɪ] | Valentinstag | |
| again [əˈgen] | wieder | Are you going home for Thanksgiving ~? |
| card [kɑːd] | Karte | |
| rose [rəʊz] | Rose | |
| violet [ˈvaɪələt] | Veilchen | V~s are my favourite flowers. |
| blue [bluː] | blau | |
| no idea [ˌnəʊ aɪˈdɪə] | keine Ahnung | "Where's John?" – "~." |
| Congratulations! [kənˌgrætʃuˈleɪʃnz] | Herzlichen Glückwunsch! | C~! When's the big day? |
| midnight [ˈmɪdnaɪt] | Mitternacht | |
| everybody [ˈevrɪbɒdi] | jede/r | E~ laughs at Karl. |
| thank goodness [ˌθæŋk ˈgʊdnəs] | Gott sei Dank | Well, ~ she's not here. I really don't like her at all. |
| same to you [ˌseɪm tə ˈjuː] | gleichfalls | "Merry Christmas!" – "Thanks, and the ~!" |

## UNIT 8

| | | | |
|---|---|---|---|
| to eat [iːt] | essen | |

### FAMOUS INVENTIONS

| | | | |
|---|---|---|---|
| record [ˈrekɔːd] | (Schall-)Platte | |
| car [kɑː] | Auto | I go to work by ~. |
| phone call [ˈfəʊn kɔːl] | Anruf | |
| bike [baɪk] | Fahrrad, Rad | Sometimes I go by ~. |
| to invent [ɪnˈvent] | erfinden | |

### PRACTICE

| | | | |
|---|---|---|---|
| inventor [ɪnˈventə] | Erfinder/in | |
| cloth [klɒθ] | Stoff, Tuch | |
| way [weɪ] | Weg, Methode | What's the best ~ to make tea? |
| trousers [ˈtraʊzəz] | Hose | These ~ are too expensive. |
| workman [ˈwɜːkmən] | Arbeiter | |
| fashionable [ˈfæʃnəbl] | modisch, modern | |
| to transmit [trænsˈmɪt] | übertragen | |
| workroom [ˈwɜːkrʊm] | Arbeitszimmer | |
| to send [send] | senden, schicken | I sent you the money this morning. |
| to produce [prəˈdjuːs] | produzieren, herstellen | |
| company [ˈkʌmpəni] | Unternehmen, Firma | |
| drug [drʌg] | Medikament, Arzneimittel | |
| arthritis [ɑːˈθraɪtɪs] | Arthritis, Gelenkentzündung | |
| best-selling [ˌbestˈselɪŋ] | meistgekauft | He bought a book by ~ author Rosamunde Pilcher. |
| painkiller [ˈpeɪnkɪlə] | Schmerzmittel | |
| astronaut [ˈæstrənɔːt] | Astronaut/in | |
| philosopher [fəˈlɒsəfə] | Philosoph/in | |
| to call [kɔːl] | nennen | I ~ed you last night, but you weren't there. |
| century [ˈsentʃəri] | Jahrhundert | |
| to bring back [ˈbrɪŋ bæk] | mitbringen | |
| incredible [ɪnˈkredəbl] | unglaublich | |
| true [truː] | richtig, wahr | |
| to believe [bɪˈliːv] | glauben | That can't be true. I don't ~ you. |
| term [tɜːm] | Semester, Trimester | |
| to arrive [əˈraɪv] | ankommen | I finally ~d home at midnight. |
| last [lɑːst] | zuletzt | When did you ~ see her? |
| to get married [get ˈmærɪd] | heiraten | They got married last week. |
| coffee break [ˈkɒfi breɪk] | Kaffeepause | We always have a ~ at 11 o'clock. |

### VOCABULARY AND PRONUNCIATION

| | | | |
|---|---|---|---|
| banana [bəˈnɑːnə] | Banane | |
| fruit [fruːt] | Frucht, Obst | I buy a lot of ~, but in the winter it is very expensive. |
| recipe [ˈresəpi] | (Koch-)Rezept | |
| vacuum cleaner [ˈvækjuəm kliːnə] | Staubsauger | |
| to kiss [kɪs] | küssen | |
| to throw [θrəʊ] | werfen | The boy threw a ball. |
| to find [faɪnd] | finden, suchen | I can't ~ my keys. |
| green [griːn] | grün | |
| delicious [dɪˈlɪʃəs] | köstlich, lecker | |
| face [feɪs] | Gesicht | |
| eye [aɪ] | Auge | |
| mouth [maʊθ] | Mund | |
| leg [leg] | Bein | |
| clock [klɒk] | Uhr | The ~ on the wall is very old. |
| funny [ˈfʌni] | komisch, lustig | The film was very ~. |
| nervous [ˈnɜːvəs] | nervös | She was very ~ before her exam. |
| worried [ˈwʌrid] | besorgt, beunruhigt | |
| to get engaged [get ɪnˈgeɪdʒd] | sich verloben | They got engaged six months ago. |
| joke [dʒəʊk] | Witz, Scherz | |
| hurry: to be in a hurry [bi ɪn ə ˈhʌri] | es eilig haben | Don't talk to me, I'm in a ~. |
| good luck [ˌgʊd ˈlʌk] | viel Glück | G~ in your exams! |
| exam [ɪgˈzæm] | Prüfung, Examen | |

### LISTENING AND SPEAKING

| | | | |
|---|---|---|---|
| to invite [ɪnˈvaɪt] | einladen | Maria ~d all her friends to dinner. |
| nowadays [ˈnaʊədeɪz] | heutzutage | Children ~ are so polite! |
| business [ˈbɪznəs] | Geschäft | |
| to look for [ˈlʊk fə] | suchen nach | |
| fisherman [ˈfɪʃəmən] | Fischer | |

| | | | |
|---|---|---|---|
| to put [pʊt] | setzen, stellen, legen | Please ~ the plates on the table. |
| bottle ['bɒtl] | Flasche | |
| sea [siː] | Meer, (die) See | |
| mile [maɪl] | Meile | |
| away [ə'weɪ] | weg, entfernt | I want to go to the beach, but it's miles ~. |
| couple ['kʌpl] | Paar, Ehepaar | |
| sentence ['sentəns] | Satz | |
| face to face [ˌfeɪs tə 'feɪs] | von Angesicht zu Angesicht | |
| to stand [stænd] | stehen | |
| grandparents ['grænpeərənts] | Großeltern | |

### EVERYDAY ENGLISH
| | | | |
|---|---|---|---|
| date [deɪt] | Datum | What ~ is it today? |
| Independence Day [ˌɪndɪ'pendəns deɪ] | Unabhängigkeitstag | |
| public holiday [ˌpʌblɪk 'hɒlədeɪ] | gesetzlicher Feiertag | Today is a ~. |

## UNIT 9

| | | | |
|---|---|---|---|
| vegetable ['vedʒtəbl] | Gemüse | My children like ~s. |

### FOOD AND DRINK
| | | | |
|---|---|---|---|
| apple juice ['æpl dʒuːs] | Apfelsaft | |
| yoghurt ['jɒgət] | Joghurt | |
| cheese [tʃiːz] | Käse | |
| strawberry ['strɔːbəri] | Erdbeere | |
| pea [piː] | Erbse | |
| carrot ['kærət] | Karotte, Möhre | |
| tomato [tə'mɑːtəʊ] | Tomate | |
| biscuit ['bɪskɪt] | Keks | |
| to count [kaʊnt] | zählen | Can you ~ to one hundred? |
| some [sʌm] | einige, etwas | Would you like ~ tea? Or ~ biscuits, perhaps? |

### PRACTICE
| | | | |
|---|---|---|---|
| mushroom ['mʌʃrʊm] | Pilz | |
| bread [bred] | Brot | "Do we need any ~?" – "Yes, please buy one loaf of ~." |
| milk [mɪlk] | Milch | |
| meat [miːt] | Fleisch | |
| rice [raɪs] | Reis | |
| cigarette [ˌsɪgə'ret] | Zigarette | |
| coke [kəʊk] | Cola | |
| ready ['redi] | fertig, bereit | Are you ~ to order? |
| to order ['ɔːdə] | bestellen | |
| sort [sɔːt] | Art, Sorte | What ~ of vegetables do you like? |

### GOING SHOPPING
| | | | |
|---|---|---|---|
| any ['eni] | irgendetwas, irgendwelche(r/s) | Have you got ~ good red wine? |
| chewing gum ['tʃuːɪŋ gʌm] | Kaugummi | |

### PRACTICE
| | | | |
|---|---|---|---|
| room [ruːm] | Zimmer, Raum | |
| pocket ['pɒkɪt] | Tasche | |
| pence [pens] | Pence | |
| full [fʊl] | voll | The room was ~ of cigarette smoke. |
| to be hungry [bi 'hʌŋgri] | Hunger haben | The little boy was very hungry. |

### READING AND SPEAKING
| | | | |
|---|---|---|---|
| around [ə'raʊnd] | rund um, herum | John walked ~ the block to look for the dog. |
| human ['hjuːmən] | menschlich | |
| history ['hɪstri] | Geschichte | |
| to move on [ˌmuːv 'ɒn] | weiterziehen | After ten years, I thought it was time to ~. |
| to farm [fɑːm] | bebauen, bearbeiten | |
| to control [kən'trəʊl] | beherrschen, kontrollieren | |
| environment [ɪn'vaɪrənmənt] | Umwelt, Lebensraum | |
| kind [kaɪnd] | Art, Sorte | What ~ of bread do you like? |
| to depend on [dɪ'pend ɒn] | abhängig sein von, abhängen von | Karl ~s on his parents for everything. |
| which [wɪtʃ] | welche(r,s) | |
| part [pɑːt] | Teil | Which ~ of the letter don't you understand? |
| for example [fər ɪg'zɑːmpl] | zum Beispiel | Sue likes fruit, ~ apples, bananas, etc. |
| south [saʊθ] | Süden | |
| noodles ['nuːdlz] | Nudeln | |
| herring ['herɪŋ] | Hering | |
| sardine [ˌsɑː'diːn] | Sardine | |
| central ['sentrəl] | Mittel-, Zentral- | |
| sausage ['sɒsɪdʒ] | Wurst | |
| course [kɔːs] | (Essens-)Gang | The second ~ was chicken with broccoli.. |
| meal [miːl] | Essen, Mahlzeit | |
| chopstick ['tʃɒpstɪk] | (Ess-)Stäbchen | |
| finger ['fɪŋgə] | Finger | |
| to pick up [ˌpɪk 'ʌp] | aufnehmen, einnehmen | |
| possible ['pɒsəbl] | möglich | Is it ~ to order tickets on the Internet? |
| to transport [træn'spɔːt] | transportieren, befördern | |
| other ['ʌðə] | andere(r,s) | OK, you have that part, I'll have the ~. |
| typical ['tɪpɪkl] | typisch | John's late again? ~. |
| family ['fæməli] | Familie | |
| main [meɪn] | Haupt-, hauptsächlich | |

### EVERYDAY ENGLISH
| | | | |
|---|---|---|---|
| polite [pə'laɪt] | höflich | |
| request [rɪ'kwest] | Bitte | |
| to pass [pɑːs] | reichen, geben | Could you ~ the salt, please? |
| salt [sɔːlt] | Salz | |
| dessert [dɪ'zɜːt] | Nachspeise, Dessert | |
| help [help] | Hilfe | Would you like some ~? |
| washing-up [ˌwɒʃɪŋ'ʌp] | Abwasch | |
| glad [glæd] | froh | I'm ~ you could come. |
| fizzy ['fɪzi] | sprudelnd, mit Kohlensäure | |
| still [stɪl] | still, ohne Kohlensäure | Would you like fizzy or ~ mineral water? |
| menu ['menjuː] | Speisekarte | I'm afraid chicken is not on the ~ today. |
| to lend [lend] | leihen, borgen | Never ~ Karl money! |

| | | | |
|---|---|---|---|
| to borrow ['bɒrəʊ] | (sich etw) borgen, leihen | He ~ed £100 from me and spent it all on CDs. | |

## UNIT 10

| | | | |
|---|---|---|---|
| tall [tɔːl] | groß (gewachsen) | | |
| than [ðən] | als | She's taller ~ me. | |

### CITY LIFE
| | | | |
|---|---|---|---|
| dangerous ['deɪndʒərəs] | gefährlich | | |
| noisy ['nɔɪzi] | laut, geräuschvoll | | |
| unfriendly [ʌn'frendli] | unfreundlich | | |
| clean [kliːn] | sauber, rein | | |
| safe [seɪf] | sicher | | |

### PRACTICE
| | | |
|---|---|---|
| building ['bɪldɪŋ] | Gebäude | Paul works in an old ~. |
| underground ['ʌndəɡraʊnd] | U-Bahn | In London the subway is called the ~. |

### COUNTRY LIFE
| | | |
|---|---|---|
| everything ['evriθɪŋ] | alles | E~ is very expensive here. |
| air [eə] | Luft | |
| street [striːt] | Straße | I live in a busy ~. |

### PRACTICE
| | | |
|---|---|---|
| tonight [tə'naɪt] | heute Abend/Nacht | Do you want to go out ~? |
| library ['laɪbrəri] | Bücherei, Bibliothek | |
| exercise ['eksəsaɪz] | Übung | |
| millionaire [ˌmɪljə'neə] | Millionär/in | |
| castle ['kɑːsl] | Burg, Schloss | |
| nothing ['nʌθɪŋ] | nichts | |

### THE WORLD'S BEST HOTELS
| | | |
|---|---|---|
| mins ['mɪnɪts] | Minuten | |
| airport ['eəpɔːt] | Flughafen | |
| far [fɑː] | weit, weit (entfernt) | How ~ away does Anna live? Further than you? |

### PRACTICE
| | | |
|---|---|---|
| village ['vɪlɪdʒ] | Dorf | |
| pretty ['prɪti] | hübsch, nett | |
| cosmopolitan [ˌkɒzmə'pɒlɪtən] | kosmopolitisch, international | London and New York are both very ~ cities. |
| popular ['pɒpjələ] | beliebt, populär | He is a very ~ person. |

### READING AND SPEAKING
| | | |
|---|---|---|
| travel ['trævl] | Reisen | |
| cousin ['kʌzn] | Cousin/e | |
| to found [faʊnd] | gründen, begründen | The university was ~ed by a famous teacher. |
| trade [treɪd] | Handel | |
| sugar ['ʃʊɡə] | Zucker | |
| spice [spaɪs] | Gewürz | |
| immigrant ['ɪmɪɡrənt] | Einwanderer, Einwanderin | |
| population [ˌpɒpju'leɪʃn] | Bevölkerung(szahl) | The UK has a ~ of over 60 million. |
| carnival ['kɑːnɪvl] | Karneval | |
| to name [neɪm] | (be)nennen | We ~d the children after their grandparents. |

| | | | |
|---|---|---|---|
| quarter ['kwɔːtə] | Viertel | Many immigrants live in this cosmopolitan ~. |
| excellent ['eksələnt] | ausgezeichnet, hervorragend | |
| mixture ['mɪkstʃə] | Mischung | |
| song [sɒŋ] | Lied | |
| hymn [hɪm] | Hymne | |
| black [blæk] | schwarz | |
| musician [mjuː'zɪʃn] | Musiker/in | |
| philharmonic [ˌfɪlɑː'mɒnɪk] | Philharmonie- | |
| orchestra ['ɔːkɪstrə] | Orchester | |
| bank [bæŋk] | Bank, Ufer | |
| gateway ['ɡeɪtweɪ] | Tor | |
| east [iːst] | Osten | |
| west [west] | Westen | |
| empire ['empaɪə] | (Welt-)Reich | |
| cultural ['kʌltʃərəl] | kulturell, Kultur- | |
| art [ɑːt] | Kunst | |
| learning ['lɜːnɪŋ] | Unterricht | A university is a centre for study and ~. |
| psychiatrist [saɪ'kaɪətrɪst] | Psychiater/in | |
| passenger ['pæsɪndʒə] | Passagier, Personen- | |
| group [ɡruːp] | Gruppe | |
| top ten [ˌtɒp 'ten] | die zehn besten (Schlager) | And now, this week's ~ CDs. |

### VOCABULARY AND PRONUNCIATION
| | | |
|---|---|---|
| wood [wʊd] | (kleinerer) Wald | I like walking in the ~s. |
| church [tʃɜːtʃ] | Kirche | |
| cathedral [kə'θiːdrəl] | Dom, Kathedrale | |
| bridge [brɪdʒ] | Brücke | |
| car park ['kɑː pɑːk] | Parkplatz, -haus | |
| port [pɔːt] | Hafen(stadt) | |
| factory ['fæktəri] | Fabrik | |
| field [fiːld] | Feld, Acker | |
| night club ['naɪt klʌb] | Nachtklub | |
| hill [hɪl] | Hügel, Berg | |
| mountain ['maʊntən] | (größerer) Berg | |
| cottage ['kɒtɪdʒ] | kleines (Land-)Haus, Ferienhaus | I want to buy a ~ in the mountains. |
| river ['rɪvə] | Fluss | |
| high [haɪ] | hoch | How ~ is that mountain? |
| ship [ʃɪp] | Schiff | |
| cow [kaʊ] | Kuh | |

### EVERYDAY ENGLISH
| | | |
|---|---|---|
| to turn [tɜːn] | abbiegen | T~ right at the church. |
| to take [teɪk] | dauern | It ~s me 20 minutes to get to work. |
| along [ə'lɒŋ] | entlang, weiter, vorwärts | Go ~ the main road until you see the cinema. |
| down [daʊn] | (nach) unten, hin-, herunter | |
| into ['ɪntə] | in … hinein | |
| out of ['aʊt əv] | aus (heraus/hinaus) | |
| over ['əʊvə] | über, vorüber, vorbei | Go ~ the hill and turn left. |
| through [θruː] | durch (… hindurch) | I never walk ~ the park at night. |
| up [ʌp] | (nach) oben, hinauf | |
| garage ['ɡærɑːʒ] | (Auto-)Werkstatt, Tankstelle, Garage | |

| road [rəʊd] | (Land-)Straße | There is always a lot of traffic on this ~. |
| hedge [hedʒ] | Hecke | |

## UNIT 11

| coat [kəʊt] | Mantel, Jacke | |
| jumper ['dʒʌmpə] | Pullover | 'Pullover' is another word for '~'. |
| shirt [ʃɜːt] | Hemd | |
| dress [dres] | Kleid | Why is Jonathan wearing a ~? |
| skirt [skɜːt] | Rock | |
| jacket ['dʒækɪt] | Jacke, Jackett | |
| suit [suːt] | Anzug, Kostüm | |
| trainers ['treɪnəz] | Turnschuhe | |
| boot [buːt] | Stiefel | I need a pair of ~s. |
| white [waɪt] | weiß | |

### DESCRIBING PEOPLE
| fair [feə] | blond, hell | |
| hair [heə] | Haar/e | She has fair ~. Her ~ is very long. |
| dark [dɑːk] | dunkel | |
| to smile [smaɪl] | lächeln | |
| to stand up [ˌstænd 'ʌp] | aufstehen | Please ~ for the hymn. |
| to run [rʌn] | laufen, rennen | |

### PRACTICE
| to rain [reɪn] | regnen | You can't go outside, it's raining. |
| to chew [tʃuː] | kauen | |
| gum [gʌm] | (Kau-)Gummi | |

### A DAY IN THE PARK
| baseball cap ['beɪsbɔːl kæp] | Baseballmütze | |
| sunglasses ['sʌnglɑːsɪz] | Sonnenbrille | Where are my ~? |
| skateboard ['skeɪtbɔːd] | Skateboard | |
| umbrella [ʌm'brelə] | (Regen-)Schirm | |
| whose [huːz] | wessen | W~ sunglasses are these? |

### PRACTICE
| racket ['rækɪt] | Schläger | |
| ballet ['bæleɪ] | Ballett | |
| suitcase ['suːtkeɪs] | Koffer | |

### LISTENING AND SPEAKING
| to shake [ʃeɪk] | schütteln | S~ hands and say sorry. |
| starry ['stɑːri] | Sternen- | |
| cloud [klaʊd] | Wolke, Bewölkung | |
| to cry [kraɪ] | weinen, schreien, rufen | The baby cried all night. |
| to bloom [bluːm] | blühen | |
| rainbow ['reɪnbəʊ] | Regenbogen | |
| sky [skaɪ] | Himmel | |
| wonderful ['wʌndəfl] | wunderbar, wundervoll | |
| bright [braɪt] | leuchtend, hell, heiter | |

### VOCABULARY AND PRONUNCIATION
| to rhyme [raɪm] | sich reimen | 'Egg' ~s with 'leg'. They ~. |

| list [lɪst] | Liste | |
| to pay [peɪ] | (be)zahlen | "How would you like to ~?" – "By credit card, please." |
| fresh [freʃ] | frisch | |
| silly ['sɪli] | töricht, albern | |
| shiny ['ʃaɪni] | glänzend | |
| to choose [tʃuːz] | wählen, aussuchen | |

### EVERYDAY ENGLISH
| to try on [ˌtraɪ 'ɒn] | anprobieren | Try the suit on before you buy it. |
| to go with ['gəʊ wɪð] | passen zu | Does this colour ~ my skirt? |
| changing room ['tʃeɪndʒɪŋ ruːm] | Umkleideraum | Where are the ~s, please? |
| credit card ['kredɪt kɑːd] | Kreditkarte | You can pay by cash, cheque or ~. |
| size [saɪz] | Größe | What ~ are you? |

## UNIT 12

| to retire [rɪ'taɪə] | in den Ruhestand treten, in Rente/Pension gehen | Life begins when you ~. |

### FUTURE PLANS
| blouse [blaʊz] | Bluse | |

### PRACTICE
| to catch [kætʃ] | bekommen, erwischen | I normally ~ the bus at 8 o'clock. |
| to wash [wɒʃ] | (sich) waschen | |
| to sneeze [sniːz] | niesen | |
| to jump [dʒʌmp] | springen | He ~ed over the hedge. |
| to fall [fɔːl] | fallen | |
| meeting ['miːtɪŋ] | Sitzung, Besprechung, Treffen | He's in a ~. Can I take a message? |
| due [djuː] | fällig | The money is ~ next week. |
| oh dear [əʊ 'dɪə] | Ach du liebe Zeit! | |
| bless you ['bles ju] | Gesundheit | Oh, ~! That was a big sneeze. |

### I WANT TO TRAVEL THE WORLD
| pyramid ['pɪrəmɪd] | Pyramide | |
| tulip ['tjuːlɪp] | Tulpe | |
| lion ['laɪən] | Löwe | |

### READING AND SPEAKING
| to float [fləʊt] | (im Wasser) treiben | |
| accident ['æksɪdənt] | Zufall, Unfall | I saw an ~ on the road. |
| water ['wɔːtə] | Wasser | |
| mark [mɑːk] | Note, Zensur | How many ~s did you get in the exam? |
| race [reɪs] | (Wett-)Rennen, (Wett-)Lauf | |
| windsurfing ['wɪndsɜːfɪŋ] | Windsurfen | |
| motor racing ['məʊtə reɪsɪŋ] | Autorennen | |
| sky-diving ['skaɪdaɪvɪŋ] | Fallschirmspringen | |
| interested in ['ɪntrəstɪd ɪn] | interessiert an | Sue is ~ fast cars. |
| to teach [tiːtʃ] | unterrichten | |

| | | | |
|---|---|---|---|
| future | ['fju:tʃə] | (zu)künftig | |
| text | [tekst] | Text | |
| to refer to | [rɪ'fɜ: tə] | sich beziehen auf | *What does this ~?* |
| sky-diver | ['skaɪdaɪvə] | Fallschirmspringer | |
| racing driver | ['reɪsɪŋ draɪvə] | Rennfahrer/in | |
| off | [ɒf] | von ... (herunter) | *We all jumped ~ the train together.* |
| shed | [ʃed] | Schuppen | |
| to grow up | [ˌgrəʊ 'ʌp] | aufwachsen | *I grew up in Scotland.* |
| parachute | ['pærəʃu:t] | Fallschirm | |
| jump | [dʒʌmp] | Sprung | |
| to decide | [dɪ'saɪd] | beschließen, sich entschließen | *I can't ~ what to give John for his birthday.* |
| to move | [mu:v] | (um)ziehen | *Sue decided to ~ to London.* |
| full-time | [ˌfʊl 'taɪm] | ganztägig, Ganztags- | *I need a ~ job.* |
| forever | [fə'revə] | für immer, unendlich (weit) | |
| coast | [kəʊst] | Küste | |
| view | [vju:] | Sicht, Ausblick | |
| to forget | [fə'get] | vergessen | *Don't ~ about dinner.* |
| worry | ['wʌri] | Sorge | *Sue has a lot of worries.* |
| skydive | ['skaɪdaɪv] | Fallschirmsprung | |
| record | ['rekɔ:d] | Rekord | |
| circuit | ['sɜ:kɪt] | Rennstrecke, Rennbahn | |
| corner | ['kɔ:nə] | Ecke | *There is a small shop on the ~.* |
| mph | [ˌem pi: 'eɪtʃ] | Meilen pro Stunde | |
| course | [kɔ:s] | Kurs, Lehrgang | *I'm doing a ~ in English.* |
| amazed | [ə'meɪzd] | erstaunt | |
| championship | ['tʃæmpiənʃɪp] | Meisterschaft | |
| to beat | [bi:t] | schlagen, besser sein als | *I can ~ anyone at tennis.* |
| excitement | [ɪk'saɪtmənt] | Aufregung | |
| frightened | ['fraɪtnd] | verängstigt | |
| to race | [reɪs] | Rennen fahren | *R~ you to the cinema!* |

### VOCABULARY AND SPEAKING

| | | | |
|---|---|---|---|
| windy | ['wɪndi] | windig | |
| to snow | [snəʊ] | schneien | |
| cloudy | ['klaʊdi] | wolkig, bewölkt | |
| foggy | ['fɒgi] | neblig | |
| cool | [ku:l] | kühl | |
| dry | [draɪ] | trocken | |
| weather | ['weðə] | Wetter | |
| like: What ... like? | [wɒt 'laɪk] | Wie? | *"What's the hotel like?" – "It's fine." – "And what are the people like?"* |
| degree | [dɪ'gri:] | Grad | *10 ~s C is quite cool.* |
| noon | [nu:n] | Mittag | |

### EVERYDAY ENGLISH

| | | | |
|---|---|---|---|
| suggestion | [sə'dʒestʃən] | Vorschlag | *She made a good ~.* |
| swimming costume | ['swɪmɪŋ kɒstju:m] | Badeanzug | |

## UNIT 13

### A QUIZ

| | | | |
|---|---|---|---|
| general knowledge | [ˌdʒenrəl 'nɒlɪdʒ] | Allgemeinwissen | |
| state | [steɪt] | Staat | |
| elephant | ['elɪfənt] | Elefant | |
| to weigh | [weɪ] | wiegen | *How much do you ~?* |
| end | [end] | Ende, Schluss | *At the ~ of the film he dies.* |
| bird | [bɜ:d] | Vogel | |
| to migrate | [maɪ'greɪt] | wegziehen, wegfliegen | |

### PRACTICE

| | | | |
|---|---|---|---|
| clothes | [kləʊðz] | Kleidung, Kleider | *All my ~ are old.* |
| leather | ['leðə] | Leder, aus Leder | |
| to stay | [steɪ] | wohnen, übernachten | *We ~ed in a nice hotel last year.* |
| guitar | [gɪ'tɑ:] | Gitarre | |
| team | [ti:m] | Mannschaft | |
| to support | [sə'pɔ:t] | befürworten, unterstützen | |
| usually | ['ju:ʒuəli] | normalerweise, gewöhnlich, meistens | *I ~ walk to work, but today I drove.* |

### DO IT CAREFULLY!

| | | | |
|---|---|---|---|
| habit | ['hæbɪt] | Gewohnheit, Angewohnheit | |
| match | [mætʃ] | Spiel, Wettkampf | *Our team won the ~.* |
| carefully | ['keəfəli] | sorgfältig | *She drives ~.* |
| game | [geɪm] | Spiel | |
| cook | [kʊk] | Koch, Köchin | |
| fluently | ['flu:əntli] | fließend | *He speaks English ~.* |
| quickly | ['kwɪkli] | schnell, rasch | |

### PRACTICE

| | | | |
|---|---|---|---|
| unfortunately | [ʌn'fɔ:tʃənətli] | unglücklicherweise, leider | *U~ I can't come to the party.* |
| terrible | ['terəbl] | schrecklich, furchtbar | |
| police | [pə'li:s] | Polizei | *The ~ are here. They came immediately.* |
| immediate | [ɪ'mi:diət] | sofort, umgehend | *She needs ~ help.* |
| test | [test] | Prüfung, Klassenarbeit | |
| to pass | [pɑ:s] | bestehen | *He ~ed the exam.* |
| fast asleep | [fɑ:st ə'sli:p] | fest eingeschlafen | *The little girl is ~.* |
| gun | [gʌn] | (Schuss-)Waffe, Pistole | |
| immediately | [ɪ'mi:diətli] | sofort, umgehend | *We called the police ~.* |
| to whistle | ['wɪsl] | pfeifen, Pfeife | |

### VOCABULARY

| | | | |
|---|---|---|---|
| bored | [bɔ:d] | gelangweilt | *My teacher is very boring. I'm always ~ in class.* |
| excited | [ɪk'saɪtɪd] | (freudig) aufgeregt, erregt | *Our children are always very ~ before Christmas.* |
| annoyed | [ə'nɔɪd] | verärgert | *Sandra was ~ because I was very late.* |
| interesting | ['ɪntrəstɪŋ] | interessant | *This is an ~ book. I'm very interested in it.* |

| | | | |
|---|---|---|---|
| **tiring** ['taɪərɪŋ] | anstrengend, ermüdend | *Running can be very ~.* |
| **runner** ['rʌnə] | Läufer/in | |
| **annoying** [ə'nɔɪɪŋ] | ärgerlich, lästig | *His behaviour is very ~.* |
| **behaviour** [bɪ'heɪvjə] | Verhalten, Benehmen | |
| **nobody** ['nəʊbədi] | niemand | |
| **worrying** ['wʌriɪŋ] | beunruhigend, quälend | *I find Karl's behaviour ~.* |

### READING AND LISTENING

| | | | |
|---|---|---|---|
| **train** [treɪn] | Bahn, Zug | *Tom goes to work by ~.* |
| **journey** ['dʒɜːni] | Reise, Fahrt | |
| **loudly** ['laʊdli] | laut | |
| **countryside** ['kʌntrisaɪd] | Landschaft, Gegend | |
| **sheep** [ʃiːp] | Schaf(e) | *There are a lot of ~ in this field.* |
| **to ask** [ɑːsk] | fragen | *Can I ~ you a question?* |
| **another** [ə'nʌðə] | ein/e andere/r/s | |
| **grass** [grɑːs] | Gras | |
| **story** ['stɔːri] | Erzählung, Geschichte | |
| **indeed** [ɪn'diːd] | in der Tat, tatsächlich, allerdings | *The journey was very long ~.* |
| **beautiful** ['bjuːtɪfl] | schön | |
| **to behave** [bɪ'heɪv] | sich verhalten, sich benehmen | *The children ~ed badly.* |
| **to save** [seɪv] | retten | *Help! S~ me from this horrible man!* |
| **stupid** ['stjuːpɪd] | dumm, blöde | |
| **ridiculous** [rɪ'dɪkjələs] | lächerlich | *It's ~ how stupid Karl can be.* |
| **to describe** [dɪ'skraɪb] | beschreiben | *Can you ~ the man?* |
| **badly-behaved** [ˌbædli bɪ'heɪvd] | ungezogen | |
| **once upon a time** [ˌwʌns əpɒn ə 'taɪm] | es war einmal | *O~ there was a little girl ... and she lived happily ever after.* |
| **well-behaved** [ˌwel bɪ'heɪvd] | gut erzogen | |
| **to please** [pliːz] | gefallen, Freude machen | *He went to the opera to ~ me.* |
| **untidy** [ʌn'taɪdi] | unordentlich | |
| **rude** [ruːd] | unhöflich | |
| **lie** [laɪ] | Lüge | *Never tell your parents ~s.* |
| **medal** ['medl] | Medaille | |
| **anyway** ['eniweɪ] | jedenfalls | *Who are you, ~?* |
| **king** [kɪŋ] | König | |
| **palace** ['pæləs] | Palast | |
| **to put on** [ˌpʊt 'ɒn] | anziehen | *Put your coat on before you go out.* |
| **to pin** [pɪn] | heften, festmachen | |
| **front** [frʌnt] | Vorderseite, -teil | |
| **wolf** [wʊlf] | Wolf | |
| **to clink** [klɪŋk] | klimpern | |
| **towards** [tə'wɔːdz] | auf ... zu, in Richtung auf | *He was walking ~ the bank.* |
| **to answer** ['ɑːnsə] | antworten | |
| **to try** [traɪ] | versuchen | *Maria tried to call Tom.* |
| **heavy** ['hevi] | schwer | *It is difficult to carry this bag. It is so ~.* |
| **bit** [bɪt] | Stück | *Can I have a ~ of that cake, please?* |
| **except** [ɪk'sept] | außer | *You can take everything ~ the TV.* |
| **station** ['steɪʃn] | Bahnhof | |

### EVERYDAY ENGLISH

| | | | |
|---|---|---|---|
| **timetable** ['taɪmteɪbl] | Fahrplan | |
| **departure** [dɪ'pɑːtʃə] | Abfahrt, Abreise | |
| **arrival** [ə'raɪvl] | Ankunft | |
| **look: to have a look** [hæv ə 'lʊk] | ansehen | *I must ~ at the train timetable.* |
| **to get in** [ˌget 'ɪn] | einsteigen | |
| **return** [rɪ'tɜːn] | Rückfahrkarte | *Two day ~s to Bristol.* |
| **change** [tʃeɪndʒ] | Wechsel-, Klein-, Restgeld | |
| **platform** ['plætfɔːm] | Bahnsteig, Gleis | |
| **note** [nəʊt] | Geldschein, Note | |
| **period return** [ˌpɪəriəd rɪ'tɜːn] | zeitlich begrenzte Rückfahrkarte | |
| **cash** [kæʃ] | Bargeld, Barzahlung | *Could you lend me some ~, please?* |

## UNIT 14

| | | | |
|---|---|---|---|
| **flag** [flæg] | Flagge, Fahne | |

### IN MY LIFE

| | | | |
|---|---|---|---|
| **ever** ['evə] | je(mals), schon (ein)mal | *Have you ~ seen that film?* |

### PRACTICE

| | | | |
|---|---|---|---|
| **foreign** ['fɒrən] | Auslands-, ausländisch | *Many ~ business people stay in this hotel.* |
| **play** [pleɪ] | (Theater-)Stück, Schauspiel | *We saw a good ~ yesterday.* |
| **tractor** ['træktə] | Traktor | |
| **competition** [ˌkɒmpə'tɪʃn] | Wettkampf, Wettbewerb | |

### A HONEYMOON IN LONDON

| | | | |
|---|---|---|---|
| **honeymoon** ['hʌnimuːn] | Flitterwochen, Hochzeitsreise | |
| **ride** [raɪd] | Fahrt | |
| **double-decker** [ˌdʌbl'dekə] | Doppeldeckerbus | |

### READING AND SPEAKING

| | | | |
|---|---|---|---|
| **pneumonia** [njuː'məʊniə] | Lungenentzündung | |
| **ambulance** ['æmbjələns] | Krankenwagen | |
| **engineer** [ˌendʒɪ'nɪə] | Ingenieur/in, Techniker/in | |
| **heart attack** ['hɑːt ətæk] | Herzinfarkt, Herzanfall | *My father had a ~ last year.* |
| **lung cancer** [lʌŋ 'kænsə] | Lungenkrebs | |
| **rheumatic fever** [ruːˌmætɪk 'fiːvə] | (akutes) Gelenkrheuma | |
| **secretary** ['sekrətri] | Sekretär/in | |
| **dressmaker** ['dresmeɪkə] | Damenschneiderin | |
| **illness** ['ɪlnəs] | Krankheit | |
| **centenarian** [ˌsentɪ'neəriən] | Hundertjährige/r | |
| **to give up** [ˌgɪv 'ʌp] | aufgeben | *I drink too much. My doctor told me to ~.* |
| **serious** ['sɪəriəs] | ernst, schwer | |
| **to return** [rɪ'tɜːn] | zurückkehren, zurückkommen | *Please ~ to your car.* |
| **niece** [niːs] | Nichte | |
| **aged** [eɪdʒd] | im Alter von | *She died of a heart attack ~ 98.* |

| | | | |
|---|---|---|---|
| **exercise** ['eksəsaɪz] | Sport treiben, trainieren | | |
| **pipe** [paɪp] | Pfeife | | |
| **ill** [ɪl] | krank | *He became ~ on holiday.* | |
| **certificate** [sə'tɪfɪkət] | Zeugnis, Urkunde, Zertifikat | | |
| **bacon** ['beɪkən] | Schinkenspeck | | |
| **marmalade** ['mɑːməleɪd] | (Orangen-)Marmelade | | |
| **abroad** [ə'brɔːd] | im Ausland | *A lot of things are much cheaper ~.* | |
| **grandchild** ['græntʃaɪld] | Enkel/in | | |
| **great-grandchild** [ˌgreɪt 'græntʃaɪld] | Urenkel | | |
| **long-lived** [ˌlɒŋ 'lɪvd] | langlebig | | |

LISTENING

| | | | |
|---|---|---|---|
| **jet plane** ['dʒet pleɪn] | Düsenflugzeug | | |
| **to pack** [pæk] | packen | | |
| **to wake (up)** [ˌweɪk 'ʌp] | aufwecken | *"Sorry, did I wake you?" – "No, I woke up hours ago."* | |
| **dawn** [dɔːn] | (Morgen-)Dämmerung, Sonnenaufgang | | |
| **to break** [breɪk] | anbrechen | | |
| **morn'** [mɔːn] | Morgen | | |
| **to blow the horn** [bləʊ ðə 'hɔːn] | hupen | | |
| **already** [ɔːl'redi] | schon, bereits | *I have ~ done my homework.* | |
| **lonesome** ['ləʊnsəm] | einsam | | |
| **to let go** [ˌlet 'gəʊ] | gehen lassen | *L~ of my arm!* | |
| **'cos** [kɒz] | weil | | |
| **to let down** [ˌlet 'daʊn] | im Stich lassen, enttäuschen | *You let me down when I depended on you most.* | |
| **horn** [hɔːn] | Hupe | | |
| **trumpet** ['trʌmpɪt] | Trompete | | |
| **to hold** [həʊld] | (fest)halten | *Can you ~ this for me?* | |

EVERYDAY ENGLISH

| | | | |
|---|---|---|---|
| **lounge** [laʊndʒ] | Warteraum | | |
| **to board** [bɔːd] | an Bord gehen, besteigen | | |
| **trolley** ['trɒli] | (Gepäck-)Wagen | | |
| **luggage** ['lʌgɪdʒ] | Gepäck | | |
| **duty-free** [ˌdjuːti'friː] | zollfrei | | |
| **to check in** [ˌtʃek 'ɪn] | (sich) einchecken, abgeben | *Please ~ one hour before departure.* | |
| **boarding pass** ['bɔːdɪŋ pɑːs] | Bordkarte | | |
| **passport control** ['pɑːspɔːt kənˌtrəʊl] | Passkontrolle | | |
| **to check** [tʃek] | kontrollieren, (über)prüfen | | |
| **board** [bɔːd] | (Anzeige-)Tafel | *Let's look at the departure ~.* | |
| **gate** [geɪt] | Flugsteig | | |
| **flight** [flaɪt] | Flug | *Have a good ~!* | |
| **destination** [ˌdestɪ'neɪʃn] | (Reise-)Ziel, Bestimmungsort | | |
| **remark** [rɪ'mɑːk] | Bemerkung | | |
| **delayed** [dɪ'leɪd] | verspätet | *The flight was ~ for two hours.* | |
| **hall** [hɔːl] | Halle | | |
| **check-in desk** ['tʃekɪn desk] | Abfertigungsschalter | | |
| **each other** [iːtʃ 'ʌðə] | einander | *Do you all know ~?* | |
| **announcement** [ə'naʊnsmənt] | Durchsage, Ankündigung | *Did you understand the ~?* | |
| **seat** [siːt] | (Sitz-)Platz | *I'd like a window ~, please.* | |
| **terrific** [tə'rɪfɪk] | großartig, phantastisch | | |
| **to miss** [mɪs] | verpassen | *You ~ed an exciting race.* | |

# Wortschatz: alphabetisch

Hier finden Sie die wichtigsten Wörter und Ausdrücke des Buches in alphabetischer Reihenfolge. Die Ziffer am Ende jeden Eintrages zeigt, in welcher Unit das Wort zuerst vorkommt.

**a little** ein wenig, ein bisschen *6*
**a lot** viel, sehr *4*
**about** etwa, ungefähr, zirka *3*
**above** über *7*
**abroad** im Ausland *14*
**accident** Zufall, Unfall *12*
**accountant** Buchhalter/in, Steuerberater/in *2*
**address** Adresse *2*
**address book** Adressbuch *5*
**advertising agency** Werbeagentur *7*
**afraid: to be afraid of** Angst haben vor *7*
**after** nach *6*
**afternoon** Nachmittag *4*
**again** wieder *7*
**age** Alter, Zeitalter *2*
**aged** im Alter von *14*
**ago** vor *7*
**to agree** zustimmen *7*
**air** Luft *10*
**air conditioning** Klimaanlage *5*
**airport** Flughafen *10*
**all** alle *2*
**all right** in Ordnung, okay *6*
**alone** allein(e) *7*
**along** entlang, weiter, vorwärts *10*
**already** schon, bereits *14*
**also** auch, außerdem *3*
**always** immer *4*
**amazed** erstaunt *12*
**ambulance** Krankenwagen *14*
**ambulance man** Krankenwagenfahrer *3*
**announcement** Durchsage, Ankündigung *14*
**annoyed** verärgert *13*
**annoying** ärgerlich, lästig *13*
**another** ein/e andere/r/s *13*
**answer** Antwort, Lösung *6*
**to answer** antworten *13*
**any** irgendetwas, irgendwelche(r/s) *9*
**anything** etwas *2*
**anyway** jedenfalls *13*
**apartment** Wohnung *2*
**apple** Apfel *1*
**architect** Architekt/in *3*
**armchair** Sessel, Lehnstuhl *5*
**army** Armee, Heer *7*
**around** rund um, herum *9*
**arrival** Ankunft *13*
**to arrive** ankommen *8*
**art** Kunst *10*
**arthritis** Arthritis, Gelenkentzündung *8*
**as** als *3*
**to ask** fragen *13*
**aspirin** Aspirin *5*
**astronaut** Astronaut/in *8*
**at home** zu Hause *2*
**at the top** oben *5*
**at work** bei der Arbeit *2*
**aunt** Tante *2*

**autumn** Herbst *4*
**away** weg, entfernt *8*

**bacon** Schinkenspeck *14*
**bad** schlecht *1*
**badly** schlecht *13*
**badly-behaved** ungezogen *13*
**bag** Tasche, Tüte *1*
**ballet** Ballett *11*
**banana** Banane *8*
**bank** Bank, Ufer *5, 10*
**barman** Barkeeper *3*
**baseball** Baseball *4*
**baseball cap** Baseballmütze *11*
**bath** Badewanne *5*
**beach** Strand *4*
**to beat** schlagen, besser sein als *12*
**beautiful** schön *13*
**because** weil *1*
**to become** werden *7*
**bedroom** Schlafzimmer *5*
**bedtime** Schlafenszeit *6*
**beer** Bier *3*
**before** vor, bevor *4*
**to begin** anfangen, beginnen *7*
**to behave** sich verhalten, sich benehmen *13*
**behaviour** Verhalten, Benehmen *13*
**to believe** glauben *8*
**best-selling** meistgekauft *8*
**between** zwischen *6*
**big** groß *2*
**bike** Fahrrad, Rad *8*
**bird** Vogel *13*
**birthday** Geburtstag *7*
**biscuit** Keks *9*
**bit** Stück *13*
**black** schwarz *10*
**black eye** blaues Auge *6*
**bless you** Gesundheit *12*
**block** (Wohn-)Block *4*
**to bloom** blühen *11*
**blouse** Bluse *12*
**to blow the horn** hupen *14*
**blue** blau *7*
**board** (Anzeige-)Tafel *14*
**to board** an Bord gehen, besteigen *14*
**boarding pass** Bordkarte *14*
**boat** Boot, Schiff *3*
**boatman** Bootsmann *3*
**to bomb** bombardieren *7*
**bookshelves** (Bücher-)Regal *5*
**bookshop** Buchhandlung *5*
**boot** Stiefel *11*
**bored** gelangweilt *13*
**boring** langweilig *4*
**(to be) born** geboren werden/sein *6*
**to borrow** (sich etw) borgen, leihen *9*
**both** beide *2*
**bottle** Flasche *8*
**boy** Junge *3*
**boyfriend** Freund *2*
**bread** Brot *9*
**break** Pause *8*
**to break** anbrechen *14*
**breakfast** Frühstück *3*
**bridge** Brücke *10*
**briefcase** Aktentasche *5*
**bright** leuchtend, hell, heiter *11*

**brilliant** großartig, toll *6*
**to bring back** mitbringen *8*
**brother** Bruder *1*
**brown** braun *4*
**to build** bauen *7*
**building** Gebäude *10*
**bus stop** Bushaltestelle *5*
**bus ticket** Busfahrschein *5*
**business** Geschäft *8*
**businessman** Geschäftsmann *7*
**busy** beschäftigt *3*
**but** aber *3*
**to buy** kaufen *4*
**by** mit, um *3, 7*
**bye** tschüs *6*

**call** Anruf *8*
**to call** nennen *8*
**(to be) called** heißen, nennen *4*
**camera** Fotoapparat, Kamera *1*
**can** können, dürfen *2*
**capital city** Hauptstadt *7*
**car** Auto *8*
**car crash** Autounfall *7*
**car park** Parkplatz, -haus *10*
**card** Karte *7*
**carefully** sorgfältig *13*
**carnival** Karneval *10*
**carrot** Karotte, Möhre *9*
**cash** Bargeld, Barzahlung *13*
**castle** Burg, Schloss *10*
**cat** Katze *5*
**to catch** bekommen, erwischen *12*
**cathedral** Dom, Kathedrale *10*
**centenarian** Hundertjährige/r *14*
**central** Mittel-, Zentral- *9*
**centre** Mitte, Zentrum *3*
**century** Jahrhundert *8*
**certificate** Zeugnis, Urkunde, Zertifikat *14*
**champagne** Champagner *5*
**championship** Meisterschaft *12*
**change** Wechsel-, Klein-, Restgeld *13*
**changing room** Umkleideraum *11*
**to chat** sich unterhalten, plaudern *4*
**cheap** billig *2*
**to check** kontrollieren, (über)prüfen *14*
**to check in** (sich) einchecken, abgeben *14*
**check-in desk** Abfertigungsschalter *14*
**to check spellings** Rechtschreibung überprüfen *6*
**Cheers!** Prost! *5*
**cheese** Käse *9*
**chemist** Apotheke(r) *5*
**chemistry** Chemie *7*
**chess** Schach *6*
**to chew** kauen *11*
**chewing gum** Kaugummi *9*
**chicken** Huhn, Hähnchen *2*
**children** Kinder *1*
**chips** Pommes frites *2*
**chocolate** Schokolade *3*
**chocolate cake** Schokoladenkuchen *2*
**to choose** wählen, aussuchen *11*
**chopstick** (Ess-)Stäbchen *9*
**Christmas Day** 1. Weihnachtsfeiertag *7*
**church** Kirche *10*
**cigarette** Zigarette *9*
**cinema** Kino *1*

**city** Stadt, (Groß-)Stadt *3*
**classroom** Klassenzimmer *2*
**clean** sauber, rein *10*
**to clink** klimpern *13*
**clock** Uhr *8*
**cloth** Stoff, Tuch *8*
**clothes** Kleidung, Kleider *13*
**cloud** Wolke, Bewölkung *11*
**cloudy** wolkig, bewölkt *12*
**coast** Küste *12*
**coat** Mantel, Jacke *11*
**coffee** Kaffee *2*
**coffee bar** Café *2*
**coffee table** Couchtisch *5*
**coke** Cola *9*
**cold** kalt *2*
**to collect** abholen, einsammeln *3*
**college** (Berufs-)Fachschule, Fachhochschule *2*
**colour** Farbe *4*
**to come** kommen *3*
**Commander-in-Chief** Oberbefehlshaber *7*
**community** Gemeinde *2*
**company** Unternehmen, Firma *8*
**competition** Wettkampf, Wettbewerb *14*
**concert** Konzert *6*
**Congratulations!** Herzlichen Glückwunsch! *7*
**to control** beherrschen, kontrollieren *9*
**conversation** Gespräch, Unterhaltung *6*
**cook** Koch, Köchin *13*
**to cook** kochen *4*
**cooker** Herd *5*
**cooking** Kochen, Essen *4*
**cool** kühl *12*
**corner** Ecke *12*
**'cos** weil *14*
**cosmopolitan** kosmopolitisch, international *10*
**cottage** kleines (Land-)Haus, Ferienhaus *10*
**cotton field** Baumwollfeld *7*
**to count** zählen *9*
**country** Land, Staat *2*
**countryside** Landschaft, Gegend *13*
**couple** Paar, Ehepaar *8*
**course** (Essens-)Gang, Kurs, Lehrgang *9, 12*
**cousin** Cousin/e *10*
**cow** Kuh *10*
**to create** (er)schaffen *7*
**credit card** Kreditkarte *11*
**to cry** weinen, schreien, rufen *11*
**cubist style** kubistischer Stil *6*
**cultural** kulturell, Kultur- *10*
**cup** Tasse *5*
**cupboard** Schrank *5*

**to dance** tanzen *6*
**dancer** Tänzer/in *2*
**dangerous** gefährlich *10*
**dark** dunkel *11*
**date** Datum *8*
**daughter** Tochter *2*
**dawn** (Morgen-)Dämmerung, Sonnenaufgang *14*
**day** Tag *1*
**dear** liebe/r *2*
**to decide** beschließen, sich entschließen *12*

**degree** Grad *12*
**delayed** verspätet *14*
**delicious** köstlich, lecker *8*
**to deliver** austragen, zustellen *3*
**departure** Abfahrt, Abreise *13*
**to depend on** abhängig sein von, abhängen von *9*
**to describe** beschreiben *13*
**to design** entwerfen, konstruieren, bauen *3*
**dessert** Nachspeise, Dessert *9*
**destination** (Reise-)Ziel, Bestimmungsort *14*
**dictionary** Wörterbuch *1*
**to die** sterben *7*
**different** anders, verschieden, unterschiedlich *2*
**difficult** schwer, schwierig *2*
**dinner** Abendessen *4*
**Directory Enquiries** (Telefon-)Auskunft *6*
**dirty** schmutzig, dreckig *5*
**dishwasher** Geschirrspülmaschine *5*
**to do the accounts** abrechnen *3*
**doctor** Arzt, Ärztin *1*
**dog** Hund *3*
**domestic** häuslich *4*
**door** Tür *5*
**double** doppelt, zweimal *1*
**double-decker** Doppeldeckerbus *14*
**down** (nach) unten, hin-, herunter *10*
**downstairs** die Treppe hinunter, Untergeschoss *5*
**dress** Kleid *11*
**dressmaker** Damenschneiderin *14*
**to drink** trinken *2*
**to drive** (mit dem Auto) fahren *3*
**drug** Medikament, Arzneimittel *8*
**dry** trocken *12*
**due** fällig *12*
**during** während *7*
**duty-free** zollfrei *14*

**each other** einander *14*
**early** früh, frühzeitig *4*
**to earn** verdienen *7*
**east** Osten *10*
**Easter Day** Ostersonntag *7*
**easy** einfach, leicht *2*
**to eat** essen *8*
**education** Erziehung, (Schul-)Bildung *7*
**egg** Ei *2*
**elephant** Elefant *13*
**else** andere(r,s) *2*
**emergency exit** Notausgang *5*
**empire** (Welt-)Reich *10*
**end** Ende, Schluss *13*
**to end** (be)enden *7*
**engineer** Ingenieur/in, Techniker/in *14*
**environment** Umwelt, Lebensraum *9*
**especially** besonders *4*
**even** sogar, selbst *5*
**evening** Abend *1*
**ever** je(mals), schon (ein)mal *14*
**every** jede/r/s *3*
**everybody** jede/r *7*
**everything** alles *10*
**exactly** exakt, genau *5*
**exam** Prüfung, Examen *8*
**excellent** ausgezeichnet, hervorragend *10*

**except** außer *13*
**excited** (freudig) aufgeregt, erregt *13*
**excitement** Aufregung *12*
**exciting** aufregend, spannend *2*
**excuse me** Entschuldigung, entschuldige(n Sie) *3*
**exercise** Übung *10*
**to exercise** Sport treiben, trainieren *14*
**expensive** teuer *2*
**export department** Exportabteilung *4*
**exposure** Belichtung *4*
**extension** Apparat *1*
**extra information** Zusatzinformation(en) *5*
**eye** Auge *8*

**face** Gesicht *8*
**face to face** von Angesicht zu Angesicht *8*
**factory** Fabrik *10*
**fair** blond, hell *11*
**fall** Herbst *4*
**to fall** fallen *12*
**to fall in love** sich verlieben *6*
**family** Familie *9*
**famous** berühmt *4*
**fantastic** fantastisch *6*
**far** weit, weit (entfernt) *10*
**farm** Bauernhof, Farm *7*
**to farm** bebauen, bearbeiten *9*
**farmer** Bauer, Bäuerin *7*
**fashionable** modisch, modern *8*
**fast** schnell *2*
**fast asleep** fest eingeschlafen *13*
**father** Vater *2*
**favourite** liebste(r,s), Lieblings- *4*
**to feel** (sich) fühlen, empfinden *6*
**field** Feld, Acker *10*
**to fight** kämpfen *7*
**finally** schließlich, zum Schluss *7*
**to find** finden, suchen *8*
**fine: I'm fine** mir geht es gut *1*
**finger** Finger *9*
**fire** Feuer, Kamin, Heizung(sgerät) *5*
**fireman** Feuerwehrmann *3*
**first** erste(r,s) *5*
**first class section** Erster-Klasse-Abteil *5*
**first name** Vorname *2*
**first of all** zu(aller)erst *6*
**fisherman** Fischer *8*
**fizzy** sprudelnd, mit Kohlensäure *9*
**flag** Flagge, Fahne *14*
**flat** Wohnung *1*
**flight** Flug *14*
**flight attendant** Flugbegleiter/in *5*
**to float** (im Wasser) treiben *12*
**floor** (Fuß-)Boden *5*
**flower** Blume *4*
**fluently** fließend *13*
**to fly** fliegen *3*
**flying doctor** fliegender Arzt *3*
**foggy** neblig *12*
**food** Essen, Lebensmittel *4*
**football** Fußball *3*
**for example** zum Beispiel *9*
**foreign** Auslands-, ausländisch *14*
**forever** für immer, unendlich (weit) *12*
**to forget** vergessen *12*
**fork** Gabel *5*
**fortunately** glücklicherweise *4*

**to found** gründen, begründen *10*
**free time** Freizeit, freie Zeit *3*
**fresh** frisch *11*
**fridge** Kühlschrank *5*
**friend** Freund/in *4*
**friendly** freundlich *2*
**frightened** verängstigt *12*
**from** von, aus *1*
**front** Vorderseite, -teil *13*
**front door** Haustür *5*
**fruit** Frucht, Obst *8*
**full** voll *9*
**full-time** ganztägig, Ganztags- *12*
**funeral** Beerdigung, Begräbnis *7*
**funny** komisch, lustig *8*
**future** (zu)künftig *12*

**game** Spiel *13*
**garage** (Auto-)Werkstatt, Tankstelle, Garage *10*
**garden** Garten *5*
**gate** Flugsteig *14*
**gateway** Tor *10*
**general knowledge** Allgemeinwissen *13*
**genius** Genie *6*
**to get** bekommen, erhalten *7*
**to get engaged** sich verloben *8*
**to get in** einsteigen *13*
**to get married** heiraten *8*
**to get up** aufstehen *3*
**girl** Mädchen *2*
**girlfriend** Freundin *2*
**to give** geben *5*
**to give up** aufgeben *14*
**glad** froh *9*
**glass** Glas *3*
**to go for a walk** spazieren gehen *3*
**to go out** ausgehen *4*
**to go to bed** ins Bett gehen *3*
**to go with** passen zu *11*
**gold** golden *4*
**good luck** viel Glück *8*
**goodbye** auf Wiedersehen *1*
**grandchild** Enkel/in *14*
**grandfather** Großvater, Opa *2*
**grandmother** Großmutter, Oma *2*
**grandparents** Großeltern *8*
**grandson** Enkel *5*
**graphic design** technisches Zeichnen *7*
**grass** Gras *13*
**great** groß(artig), toll, prima *6*
**great-grandchild** Urenkel *14*
**green** grün *8*
**grey** grau *4*
**grocer** Lebensmittelhändler/in, Kaufmann *7*
**group** Gruppe *10*
**to grow** wachsen, anbauen *7*
**to grow up** aufwachsen *12*
**guest** Gast *3*
**guitar** Gitarre *13*
**gum** (Kau-)Gummi *11*
**gun** (Schuss-)Waffe, Pistole *13*
**gym** Turnhalle, Sportstudio *4*

**habit** Gewohnheit, Angewohnheit *13*
**hair** Haar/e *11*
**half** halb *3*
**hall** Halle *14*

**to happen** passieren, geschehen *7*
**happy** glücklich, froh *2*
**hard** schwer, hart *7*
**hat** Hut, Mütze *6*
**to hate** hassen, gar nicht mögen *7*
**to have** haben *1*
**head** Kopf *7*
**to hear** hören *6*
**heart attack** Herzinfarkt, Herzanfall *14*
**heavy** schwer *13*
**hedge** Hecke *10*
**hello** Hallo *1*
**help** Hilfe *9*
**to help** helfen *2*
**here** hier *2*
**here you are** hier, bitte *2*
**herring** Hering *9*
**hi** hallo *1*
**high** hoch *10*
**hill** Hügel, Berg *10*
**history** Geschichte *9*
**to hold** (fest)halten *14*
**holiday** Ferien, Urlaub *2*
**homework** Hausaufgaben *4*
**honeymoon** Flitterwochen, Hochzeitsreise *14*
**horn** Hupe *14*
**horrible** schrecklich, furchtbar *2*
**horse** Pferd *7*
**hospital** Krankenhaus *3*
**hot** heiß, warm *2*
**hour** Stunde *6*
**house** Haus *1*
**how** wie *1*
**how are you?** Wie geht es dir/Ihnen? *1*
**how many** wie viele *3*
**how much** wie viel *2*
**how old** wie alt *2*
**human** menschlich *9*
**hungry: to be hungry** Hunger haben *9*
**to hurry** es eilig haben *8*
**hurry up** sich beeilen *3*
**husband** (Ehe-)Mann *2*
**hymn** Hymne *10*

**I'm afraid** leider *6*
**ice cream** Speiseeis *2*
**ice hockey** Eishockey *4*
**ice-skating** Schlittschuhlaufen *4*
**ill** krank *14*
**illness** Krankheit *14*
**immediate** sofort, umgehend *13*
**immediately** sofort, umgehend *13*
**immigrant** Einwanderer, Einwanderin *10*
**important** wichtig *7*
**in class** im Unterricht, in der Schule *2*
**in front of** vor *5*
**in office** im Amt *7*
**incredible** unglaublich *8*
**indeed** in der Tat, tatsächlich, allerdings *13*
**Independence Day** Unabhängigkeitstag *8*
**initial** Initiale(n), Anfangsbuchstabe(n) *6*
**interest** Interesse *7*
**interested in** interessiert an *12*
**interesting** interessant *13*
**interpreter** Dolmetscher/in *3*
**to interview** interviewen, befragen *4*
**into** in … hinein *10*

**to invent** erfinden *8*
**inventor** Erfinder/in *8*
**to invite** einladen *8*
**Iron Lady** Eiserne Lady *7*
**island** Insel *3*

**jacket** Jacke, Jackett *11*
**jet plane** Düsenflugzeug *14*
**job** Arbeit, Beruf *1*
**joke** Witz, Scherz *8*
**journey** Reise, Fahrt *13*
**jump** Sprung *12*
**to jump** springen *12*
**jumper** Pullover *11*
**just** einfach, mal *6*

**key** Schlüssel *1*
**kids** Kinder *4*
**kind** Art, Sorte *9*
**king** König *13*
**kiss** Kuss *7*
**to kiss** küssen *8*
**kitchen** Küche *5*
**knife** Messer *5*
**to know** kennen, wissen *3*

**lady** Dame *5*
**lake** (Binnen-)See *4*
**lamp** Lampe, Leuchte *5*
**language** Sprache *3*
**large** groß *6*
**last** letzte(r,s), zuletzt *6, 8*
**late** spät *3*
**to laugh** lachen *6*
**leader** Führer/in *7*
**to learn** lernen *1*
**learning** Unterricht *10*
**leather** Leder, aus Leder *13*
**to leave** abfahren, verlassen *4*
**left** linke(r,s), links, linke Seite *5*
**leg** Bein *8*
**to lend** leihen, borgen *9*
**to let down** im Stich lassen, enttäuschen *14*
**to let go** gehen lassen *14*
**letter** Brief *1*
**library** Bücherei, Bibliothek *10*
**lie** Lüge *13*
**life** Leben *4*
**like: What … like?** Wie …? *12*
**to like** mögen, gern haben *3*
**lion** Löwe *12*
**list** Liste *11*
**to listen to** anhören, zuhören *3*
**little** klein, wenig *3*
**to live** wohnen, leben *1*
**living room** Wohnzimmer *5*
**lonesome** einsam *14*
**long** lang *4*
**long-lived** langlebig *14*
**look: to have a look** ansehen *13*
**to look after** betreuen, sich kümmern um *3*
**to look at** ansehen *5*
**to look for** suchen nach *8*
**to lose** verlieren *7*
**lots of** viel, viele *6*
**loudly** laut *13*
**lounge** Warteraum *14*
**love** Liebe (Grüße) *2*

**to love** sehr gern mögen, lieben *3*
**lovely** schön, hübsch, reizend *2*
**luggage** Gepäck *14*
**lung cancer** Lungenkrebs *14*
**luxury** Luxus, Luxus- *5*

**magazine** Zeitschrift, Illustrierte *1*
**main** Haupt-, hauptsächlich *9*
**to make** machen, zubereiten *3*
**man** Mann *3*
**manager** Geschäftsführer/in *6*
**mark** Note, Zensur *12*
**marmalade** (Orangen-)Marmelade *14*
**married** verheiratet *1*
**to marry** heiraten *7*
**match** Spiel, Wettkampf *13*
**to matter** etw ausmachen, darauf ankommen *4*
**meal** Essen, Mahlzeit *9*
**to mean** bedeuten, meinen *4*
**meat** Fleisch *9*
**medal** Medaille *13*
**to meet** treffen, begegnen, kennen lernen, sich treffen (mit) *4, 6*
**meeting** Sitzung, Besprechung, Treffen *12*
**menu** Speisekarte *9*
**midnight** Mitternacht *7*
**to migrate** wegziehen, wegfliegen *13*
**mile** Meile *8*
**milk** Milch *9*
**millionaire** Millionär/in *10*
**mineral water** Mineralwasser *2*
**mins** Minuten *10*
**mirror** Spiegel *5*
**to miss** verpassen *14*
**mixture** Mischung *10*
**mobile phone** Mobiltelefon, Handy *5*
**money** Geld *3*
**month** Monat *6*
**moon** Mond *7*
**morn'** Morgen *14*
**morning** Morgen *4*
**(good) morning** guten Morgen *2*
**most** der/die/das meiste, die meisten *4*
**mother** Mutter *2*
**Mother's Day** Muttertag *7*
**motor racing** Autorennen *12*
**mountain** (größerer) Berg *10*
**mouth** Mund *8*
**to move** (um)ziehen *12*
**to move on** weiterziehen *9*
**mph** Meilen pro Stunde *12*
**much** viel *4*
**mushroom** Pilz *9*
**music** Musik *3*
**music (CD) shop** Musikladen *5*
**musician** Musiker/in *10*
**my dear** meine Liebe, mein Lieber *3*

**to name** (be)nennen *10*
**near** nahe, in der Nähe von *4*
**to need** benötigen, brauchen *5*
**nervous** nervös *8*
**never** nie(mals) *3*
**never mind** Schon gut., Macht nichts. *3*
**New Year's Eve** Silvester *7*
**new** neu *2*
**news** Nachricht(en) *4*

**newsagent** Zeitungshändler *1*
**newspaper** Zeitung *5*
**next** nächste/r/s, danach *7*
**next time** nächstes Mal *6*
**next to** (direkt) neben *5*
**nice** schön, nett *1*
**niece** Nichte *14*
**night** Nacht, Abend *6*
**night club** Nachtklub *10*
**no** nein *2*
**no idea** keine Ahnung *7*
**No Smoking** Rauchen verboten *5*
**nobody** niemand *13*
**noisy** laut, geräuschvoll *10*
**non-stop** durchgehend, ununterbrochen *3*
**noodles** Nudeln *9*
**noon** Mittag *12*
**north** Norden *3*
**not ... at all** überhaupt nicht *6*
**not ... until** erst als *6*
**note** Geldschein, Note *13*
**notebook** Notizbuch *5*
**nothing** nichts *10*
**noun** Hauptwort, Substantiv, Nomen *1*
**now** nun, jetzt *2*
**nowadays** heutzutage *8*
**number** (Telefon-)Nummer, Zahl, Ziffer *1*
**nurse** Krankenschwester, Krankenpfleger/in *2*

**o'clock** volle Stunde, um ... Uhr *3*
**occasion** Ereignis, Anlass *7*
**of course** natürlich, selbstverständlich *3*
**off** von ... (herunter) *12*
**office** Büro *3*
**often** oft, häufig *4*
**oh dear** ach du liebe Zeit! *12*
**on** auf *5*
**once upon a time** es war einmal *13*
**only** nur, einzig *3*
**to open** öffnen, aufmachen *4*
**operator** Telefonist/in, (Telefon-)Vermittlung *6*
**orange** Apfelsine, Orange, orange *1, 4*
**orange juice** Orangensaft *2*
**orchestra** Orchester *10*
**to order** bestellen *9*
**ordinary** gewöhnlich, normal *3*
**other** andere(r,s) *9*
**out of** aus (heraus/hinaus) *10*
**outside** draußen *7*
**over** über, vorüber, vorbei *10*
**over there** da drüben, dort (drüben) *5*
**to own** besitzen *7*

**p** Pence *2*
**to pack** packen *14*
**painkiller** Schmerzmittel *8*
**to paint** malen *6*
**palace** Palast *13*
**parachute** Fallschirm *12*
**Pardon?** Wie bitte?, Verzeihung *4*
**parents** Eltern *6*
**part** Teil *9*
**part of speech** Wortart *1*
**to pass** bestehen, reichen, geben *9, 13*
**passenger** Passagier, Personen- *10*
**passport** (Reise-)Pass *5*

**passport control** Passkontrolle *14*
**past** nach, vergangen *3, 7*
**to pay** be)zahlen *11*
**pea** Erbse *9*
**pen** Füller, Kugelschreiber, (Filz-)Stift *5*
**people** Leute, Menschen *3*
**perhaps** vielleicht *3*
**period return** zeitlich begrenzte Rückfahrkarte *13*
**personality** Persönlichkeit *7*
**petrol** Benzin *3*
**petrol attendant** Tankwart/in *3*
**philharmonic** Philharmonie- *10*
**philosopher** Philosoph/in *8*
**phone box** Telefonzelle *5*
**phone call** Anruf *8*
**phone number** Telefonnummer *1*
**photo** Foto *2*
**piano** Klavier *6*
**to pick up** aufnehmen, einnehmen *9*
**picture** Bild *4*
**pilot** Pilot/in, Flugzeugführer/in *3*
**to pin** heften, festmachen *13*
**pipe** Pfeife *14*
**place of work** Arbeitsstelle *3*
**plane** Flugzeug *3*
**plant** Pflanze *5*
**plate** Teller *5*
**platform** Bahnsteig, Gleis *13*
**play** (Theater-)Stück, Schauspiel *14*
**to play** spielen *3*
**please** bitte *2*
**to please** gefallen, Freude machen *13*
**pneumonia** Lungenentzündung *14*
**pocket** Tasche *9*
**poem** Gedicht *7*
**poetry** Dichtung, Gedichte *6*
**police** Polizei *13*
**policeman** Polizist *2*
**polite** höflich *9*
**politician** Politiker/in *7*
**politics** (die) Politik *7*
**poor** arm *6*
**popular** beliebt, populär *10*
**population** Bevölkerung(szahl) *10*
**port** Hafen(stadt) *10*
**possible** möglich *9*
**post box** Briefkasten *5*
**post office** Postamt *5*
**postcard** Postkarte *1*
**postman** Briefträger *3*
**pound** Pfund (Sterling) *2*
**practice** Praxis, Übung *2*
**to practise** üben *6*
**present** Geschenk *7*
**president** Präsident/in *7*
**pretty** hübsch, nett *7*
**Prime Minister** Premierminister *7*
**to produce** produzieren, herstellen *8*
**programme** Sendung, Programm *4*
**pronunciation** Aussprache *1*
**psychiatrist** Psychiater/in *10*
**public holiday** gesetzlicher Feiertag *8*
**public toilet** öffentliche Toilette *5*
**to put** setzen, stellen, legen *8*
**to put on** anziehen *13*
**pyramid** Pyramide *12*

**quarter** Viertel 3, 10
**question** Frage 6
**quickly** schnell, rasch 13
**quiet** still, ruhig, leise 3
**quite** ziemlich, ganz 4

**race** (Wett-)Rennen, (Wett-)Lauf 12
**to race** Rennen fahren 12
**racing circuit** Rennstrecke, Rennbahn 12
**racing driver** Rennfahrer/in 12
**racket** Schläger 11
**to rain** regnen 11
**rainbow** Regenbogen 11
**ready** fertig, bereit 9
**Really?** Wirklich? 4
**recipe** (Koch-)Rezept 8
**record** (Schall-)Platte, Rekord 8, 12
**recorded message** aufgezeichnete Nachricht 6
**red** rot 4
**to refer to** sich beziehen auf 12
**to relax** (sich) entspannen, ausruhen 4
**remark** Bemerkung 14
**request** Bitte 9
**to require** brauchen, benötigen 6
**to resign** zurücktreten (von) 7
**to retire** in den Ruhestand treten, in Rente/Pension gehen 12
**return** Rückfahrkarte 13
**to return** zurückkehren, zurückkommen 14
**rheumatic fever** (akutes) Gelenkrheuma 14
**to rhyme** sich reimen 11
**rice** Reis 9
**rich** reich, wohlhabend 7
**ride** Fahrt 14
**to ride a bike** Rad fahren 6
**ridiculous** lächerlich 13
**right** rechts, rechte Seite, richtig 5, 6
**to ring back** zurückrufen 6
**river** Fluss 10
**road** (Land-)Straße 10
**room** Zimmer, Raum 9
**rose** Rose 7
**rude** unhöflich 13
**rug** Läufer, Brücke, Vorleger 5
**to run** laufen, rennen 11
**runner** Läufer/in 13

**sad** traurig 6
**safe** sicher 10
**(to go) sailing** segeln (gehen) 4
**salad** Salat 2
**salt** Salz 9
**same to you** gleichfalls 7
**sardine** Sardine 9
**sausage** Wurst 9
**to save** retten, sparen, aufheben 6, 13
**school** Schule 3
**school-bus driver** Schulbusfahrer/in 3
**scientist** (Natur-)Wissenschaftler/in 3
**sea** Meer, (die) See 8
**season** Jahreszeit 4
**seat** (Sitz-)Platz 14
**secretary** Sekretär/in 14
**to see** sehen 1
**to sell** verkaufen 3
**to send** senden, schicken 8

**sentence** Satz 8
**serious** ernst, schwer 14
**to serve** servieren 3
**to shake** schütteln 11
**shed** Schuppen 12
**sheep** Schaf(e) 13
**shelf** Regal(brett) 5
**shiny** glänzend 11
**ship** Schiff 10
**shirt** Hemd 11
**shoe** Schuh 7
**shop** Laden, Geschäft 3
**shopkeeper** Ladeninhaber/in 3
**(to go) shopping** einkaufen (gehen) 7
**short** kurz, klein 4
**shy** schüchtern, scheu 4
**sick** krank 3
**sign** Zeichen, Schild 5
**silly** töricht, albern 11
**to sing** singen 4
**sister** Schwester 1
**to sit** sitzen, sich setzen 3
**size** Größe 11
**skateboard** Skateboard 11
**skiing** Skilaufen 3
**skirt** Rock 11
**sky** Himmel 11
**sky-diver** Fallschirmspringer 12
**sky-diving** Fallschirmspringen 12
**skydive** Fallschirmsprung 12
**slave** Sklave, Sklavin 7
**sleep** Schlaf 7
**slow** langsam 2
**small** klein 2
**to smile** lächeln 11
**to smoke** rauchen 4
**snack bar** Imbissstube 2
**to sneeze** niesen 12
**snow** Schnee 2
**to snow** schneien 12
**so** also 7
**soldier** Soldat/in 7
**some** einige, etwas 9
**someone** jemand 7
**something** etwas 7
**sometimes** manchmal 4
**son** Sohn 2
**song** Lied 10
**soon** bald 2
**sorry: I'm sorry** es tut mir Leid 3
**sort** Art, Sorte 9
**south** Süden 9
**to speak** sprechen, reden 2
**special** besondere(r,s) 4
**to spell** buchstabieren, schreiben 1
**to spend** ausgeben 6
**spice** Gewürz 10
**spoon** Löffel 5
**spring** Frühling, Frühjahr 4
**stamp** Briefmarke 1
**to stand** stehen 8
**to stand up** aufstehen 11
**starry** Sternen- 11
**to start** beginnen, anfangen 4
**state** Staat 13
**station** Bahnhof 13
**to stay** wohnen, übernachten 13
**steps** Treppe, Leiter 5

**still** (immer) noch, still, ohne Kohlensäure 6, 9
**to stop** aufhören (mit) 6
**story** Erzählung, Geschichte 13
**straight ahead** geradeaus 5
**strawberry** Erdbeere 9
**street** Straße 10
**strong** stark 7
**to study** studieren 7
**stupid** dumm, blöde 13
**subject** (Schul-)Fach 7
**subway** U-Bahn 2
**suddenly** plötzlich 4
**sugar** Zucker 10
**suggestion** Vorschlag 12
**suit** Anzug, Kostüm 11
**suitcase** Koffer 11
**summer** Sommer 3
**sun** Sonne 6
**to sunbathe** sonnenbaden 4
**sunglasses** Sonnenbrille 11
**sunny** sonnig 4
**super** großartig 6
**supermarket** Supermarkt 5
**supper** (das) Abendessen 3
**to support** befürworten, unterstützen 13
**sure** sicher(lich) 7
**surname** Nachname 2
**to survive** überleben 7
**to swim** schwimmen 6
**swimming costume** Badeanzug 12
**swimming pool** Schwimmbad 5

**table** Tisch 5
**to take** nehmen, bringen, dauern 4, 10
**to take a message** etw ausrichten 6
**to take photographs** fotografieren 4
**to talk** sprechen, reden 6
**tall** groß (gewachsen) 10
**taxi driver** Taxifahrer/in 3
**tea** Tee 2
**to teach** unterrichten 12
**teacher** Lehrer/in 1
**team** Mannschaft 13
**(in) tears** unter Tränen 7
**telephone** Telefon 5
**television** Fernsehen, Fernseher 5
**to tell** sagen 3
**term** Semester, Trimester 8
**terrible** schrecklich, furchtbar 13
**terrific** großartig, phantastisch 14
**test** Prüfung, Klassenarbeit 13
**than** als 10
**thank goodness** Gott sei Dank 7
**thank you very much** vielen Dank 1
**thanks** danke 1
**Thanksgiving** Erntedankfest 7
**theatre** Theater 7
**then** dann 4
**there** da, dort(hin) 6
**thing** Sache, Ding 3
**to think** denken 6
**this** dies, diese/r/s 1
**through** durch (... hindurch) 10
**to throw** werfen 8
**ticket** (Fahr-)Karte, Eintrittskarte 1
**time** Zeit, Mal 3, 5
**timetable** Fahrplan 13

Wortschatz 19

**tired** müde *4*
**tired of** überdrüssig *7*
**tiring** anstrengend, ermüdend *13*
**to** vor, (bis) zu *3*
**tobacco** Tabak *7*
**today** heute *2*
**together** zusammen *7*
**toilet** Toilette *5*
**tomato** Tomate *9*
**tomorrow** morgen *7*
**tonight** heute Abend/Nacht *10*
**too** auch, zu *3, 4*
**top: at the top** oben *5*
**top ten** die zehn besten (Schlager) *10*
**towards** auf ... zu, in Richtung auf *13*
**town** Stadt *3*
**tractor** Traktor *14*
**trade** Handel *10*
**traffic** (Straßen-)Verkehr *4*
**train** Bahn, Zug *13*
**trainers** Turnschuhe *11*
**to translate** übersetzen *3*
**to transmit** übertragen *8*
**to transport** transportieren, befördern *9*
**travel** Reisen *10*
**to travel** fahren, reisen *4*
**travel agent** Reisebüro *5*
**tree** Baum *4*
**trolley** (Gepäck-)Wagen *14*
**trousers** Hose *8*
**true** richtig, wahr *8*
**trumpet** Trompete *14*
**to try** versuchen *13*
**to try on** anprobieren *11*
**tulip** Tulpe *12*
**tuna** Thunfisch *2*
**to turn** abbiegen *10*
**twin** Zwilling, Zwillings- *7*
**typical** typisch *9*

**umbrella** (Regen-)Schirm *11*
**uncle** Onkel *2*
**under** unter *5*
**underground** U-Bahn *10*
**to understand** verstehen, begreifen *2*

**undertaker** Leichenbestatter *3*
**unfortunately** unglücklicherweise, leider *13*
**unfriendly** unfreundlich *10*
**United Nations** Vereinte Nationen *3*
**university** Universität *7*
**untidy** unordentlich *13*
**until** bis *6*
**up** (nach) oben, hinauf *10*
**upstairs** die Treppe hinauf/herauf, Obergeschoss *5*
**to use** benutzen, verwenden *2*
**usually** normalerweise, gewöhnlich, meistens *13*

**vacuum cleaner** Staubsauger *8*
**Valentine's Day** Valentinstag *7*
**vanilla** Vanille *3*
**vegetable** Gemüse *9*
**verandah** Veranda *7*
**very** sehr *2*
**very well** sehr gut *1*
**view** Sicht, Ausblick *12*
**village** Dorf *10*
**violet** Veilchen *7*
**visit** Besuch *5*
**to visit** besichtigen, besuchen *4*

**to wake (up)** aufwecken *14*
**to walk** ausführen, (zu Fuß) gehen *3*
**wall** Wand, Mauer *5*
**to want** wollen *1*
**War of Independence** Unabhängigkeitskrieg *7*
**to wash** (sich) waschen *12*
**washing machine** Waschmaschine *5*
**washing-up** Abwasch *9*
**watch** (Armband-)Uhr *3*
**to watch television** fernsehen *3*
**water** Wasser *12*
**way** Weg, Methode *8*
**to wear** tragen, anhaben *6*
**weather** Wetter *12*
**wedding** Hochzeit, Trauung *6*
**wedding day** Hochzeitstag *7*
**week** Woche *3*
**weekday** Wochentag, Werktag *3*

**weekend** Wochenende *4*
**to weigh** wiegen *13*
**well** gut, nun *5, 6*
**well-behaved** gut erzogen *13*
**west** Westen *10*
**wet** nass, feucht *4*
**what** was, welche(r,s) *1*
**when** wenn, wann *4*
**where** wo *1*
**which** welche(r,s) *9*
**to whistle** pfeifen, Pfeife *13*
**white** weiß *11*
**who** wer *2*
**whose** wessen *11*
**why** warum *4*
**widow** Witwe *7*
**wife** (Ehe-)Frau *2*
**to win** gewinnen *7*
**window** Fenster *4*
**windsurfing** Windsurfen *12*
**windy** windig *12*
**wine** Wein *3*
**winter** Winter *3*
**wolf** Wolf *13*
**woman** Frau *7*
**wonderful** wunderbar, wundervoll *11*
**wood** (kleinerer) Wald *10*
**word** Wort *1*
**work** Arbeit *4*
**to work** arbeiten *3*
**workman** Arbeiter *8*
**workroom** Arbeitszimmer *8*
**world** Welt *5*
**World Cup** Weltmeisterschaft *7*
**worried** besorgt, beunruhigt *8*
**worry** Sorge *12*
**to worry** sich Sorgen machen *4*
**worrying** beunruhigend, quälend *13*
**to write** schreiben *2*

**year** Jahr *2*
**yellow** gelb *4*
**yes** ja *1*
**yesterday** gestern *6*
**yoghurt** Joghurt *9*
**young** jung *2*